Dear reader,

I wanted to write this to say thankyou for being right here – in reading this you are taking a step for yourself and your healing. And its a brave step. So, WELCOME! This is a safe space for you to explore within.
When you do this work, you learn to raise your frequency. And when you do this, just watch what happens to your life...

HOW EXCITING!

sending you so much love,

Hayley xxx

The Guiding Star System

HAYLEY GABRIELLA MILLER

Contents

Are you ready?

This book will help you reach a greater understanding of your true Self, and to live life in an authentic way. In this unique process, your connection with Self is explored and likely strengthened. In doing this work, it is likely to create change within you, which will create change in your outside world. This includes everything, including relationships with those who are currently in your life. This process can improve your sense of balance and wholeness within, but it may upset the equilibrium in yourSelf and your life, generating change. It may lead to changes in life perspectives and decisions. Change of any kind can be challenging and potentially a cause of temporary distress, particularly whilst moving through it. This is all a part of the process of your own healing, evolution, and ascension, and a process that you learn to trust in. In doing so, you are reaching greater states of wholeness, purpose, and meaning, as your authentic true Self.

Introduction

What is a successful life? Measuring and assessing *life* itself can be complex and challenging. It is easy to get caught up in the everyday and lose sight of the bigger picture. True presence and consciousness require awareness, and this is gently brought to your focus throughout this book. On the surface, you might appear to have it all, only to discover that you remain unfulfilled and unhappy within. We are taught from a young age to search for happiness and success in all the wrong places. When we finally reach the point that we believe will bring us satisfaction, we often find ourselves unfulfilled. These promised feelings of satisfaction, fulfilment, and happiness are either absent or extremely fleeting. It is then that feelings of unfulfillment, resentment, and unhappiness rise to the surface, often compounded by guilt—the feeling that we *should* be happy now. I know; it's a harsh truth! Yet, it also serves as a guide to help you realise that there is more. Sometimes you need to acknowledge that you are off course in order to find your way back onto your path. We are all on our own journeys, and we all learn at our own pace, all in perfect timing.

To provide some background, I was a very driven and disciplined "Type A" personality. My achievements were largely defined by ego-driven rewards: grades, money, status, material possessions, and societal expectations. I pursued these wholeheartedly, believing they were essential to happiness. This left me profoundly confused when life did not deliver the happiness I expected, especially considering my dedication. I then went on a journey of rabbit holes, all believing that one single path would hold the answers to what I was seeking. It wasn't until I realised that I was focused only on isolated aspects of a larger whole picture that it all clicked into place. This led to the creation of The Guiding Star System.

This book began as a scrapbook over 20 years ago, in the search for something – even though I had no idea what that was. This book offers a guiding map to help you discover your own *something*, whatever that may be. It draws upon numerous sources of information and personal experiences, all compiled into a single, accessible resource that illustrates how they energetically integrate. I'm sharing this guidance in the way I wish had been available for me; through the toughest times, to the most beautiful. As with everything in life, take this with your own personal interpretation; use what feels right for you, and leave what does not.

This book also serves as a practical guide, designed to be worked through along your own journey. It offers the space and support to put the information into action. It is easy to skip to the quick answers, assuming you can address the rest later, only to never get back to those other elements. I've certainly been guilty of that! That's why this book aims to provide everything you need in one place.

I'll begin by explaining the sections of The Guiding Star System, giving you a solid overview before diving into more depth. This is a journey of Self-discovery. The depth of your exploration is entirely up to you; it is a personal choice guided by your current position and needs.

The Guiding Star System (TGSS) uses five categories to illustrate its teachings: Fuel, Movement, Rest, Out, and In. These are common words that each hold deep meaning, far beyond their literal definitions. In each chapter, we will explore these concepts in both foundational and highly insightful ways, to increase your awareness and understanding of each area, and how they interact. These are then linked with our different energy systems, which I introduce in the energy chapter.

This is all formed and measured together in The Guiding Star...

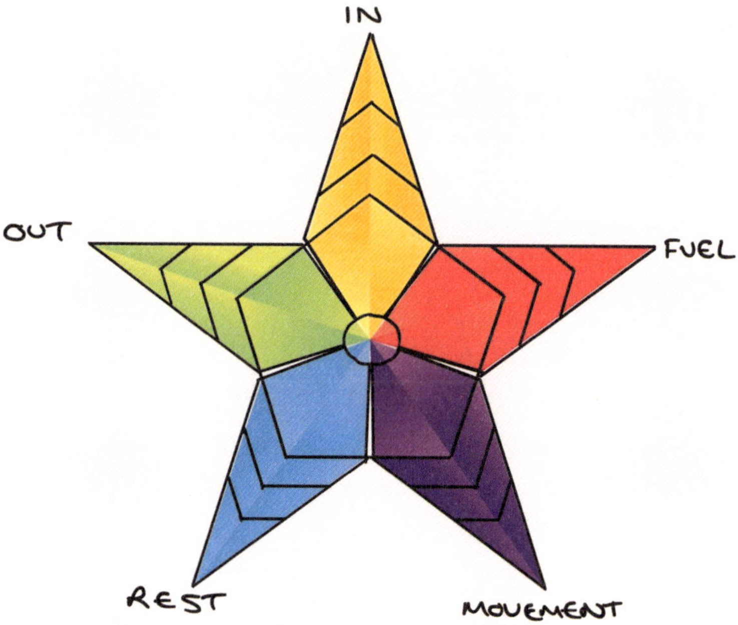

1 – Fuel

The concept of **fuel** refers to everything that nourishes your body. Initially, this encompasses food and drink. Your diet significantly impacts your overall well-being, happiness, and physical health. The food you consume literally becomes the building blocks of your physical body, shaping who you are. We will explore how to optimise this to maximise energy levels.

Beyond food and drink, however, there are other ways to fuel your body and enhance energy. When I first embarked on this research, I would have scoffed at the idea; it seemed nonsensical. Yet, there are numerous, often overlooked, ways to replenish our energy, much like charging a battery. We are electrical beings; every cell within us contributes to our overall energetic frequency and charge. While our current understanding of the human body and universal energy systems is limited, historically, we've had a much deeper intuitive understanding of how to fuel our bodies and how to exist within the energetic landscape of life. Our bodies and Mother Nature share a life force, intricate and complex systems we can use to enhance our well-being. Many ancient civilisations and traditions possessed a far deeper understanding of these systems than we have today. Examples include breathing and breathwork, cold water therapy, forest bathing, Sungazing, sound healing, and the use of positive energy and visualisation. Some things simply *are*; we may not always be able to fully explain them, but their effects are undeniable.

2 – Movement

Life is **movement**. Even when unconscious, our bodies are continually in motion. Our hearts beat, our cells regenerate, and our minds continue to process information. When we think of movement, we often focus only on physical movement, but this represents only a small facet of the whole. Physical movement—the amount and type of movement we engage in—is a beautiful and powerful tool to improve your energy frequency. Movement includes exercise, but is not exclusive to the term. Being active instructs the cells and all associated systems of the body to operate in certain ways, influencing our energy levels throughout the day and even during sleep. Regular physical activity enhances metabolism, even while resting. If you challenge your physical capabilities, your body works to repair and recover, leading to improved fitness and energy utilisation.

Beyond the physical, however, movement also encompasses the flow of energy within your being and throughout your life. This includes mental, emotional, and Spiritual movement. Your progress along your life path is directly correlated with the momentum of this energy. We all experience times when we feel we have strayed from our path; at such times, there is often a clear sign or signal to help us rediscover our way. We'll explore those signs in more depth later in the book.

Human progress is essential. We are all engaged in this process, learning our lessons and moving toward what is meant for us. The pace of this process is unique for each individual, sometimes comfortable, sometimes challenging. Recognising and embracing our forward momentum allows us to gain direction, focus, and motivation to achieve our goals.

Our physical location can also profoundly influence our energy levels. Have you ever travelled, moved to a new home, or even gone on holiday, only to experience a dramatic shift in your energy? This effect is often subtle yet powerful. We'll delve more deeply into this concept, particularly examining the feeling of being *trapped*, helping you gain new perspectives and clarity on challenging situations.

3 – Rest

The word **rest** is inherently linked with sleep—a necessary function for sustaining life. Sleep is vital for our physical and mental well-being, providing time for our bodies to restore and repair. The quality of our sleep has a profound effect on our overall health and happiness. We cycle through different sleep stages, and understanding how to optimise these cycles enhances the restorative process. Getting the recommended amount of sleep is beneficial, but it is equally crucial to ensure the *quality* of that sleep. Poor quality sleep can dramatically impact our mood, behaviour, and functioning. The right amount of high-quality sleep can feel amazing!

While extensive research has been conducted on sleep, there remains no single definitive theory explaining its imperativeness, and why it has escaped evolution. We know it involves distinct states of consciousness, but the potential implications of this knowledge remain to be fully explored. This book will explore the connection between altered states of consciousness and Spirituality, along with the often-unexplained phenomena of amnesia and physical paralysis experienced during sleep.

Rest encompasses more than just sleep. It includes periods of relaxation and downtime—moments of physical and mental respite. This can be as simple as sitting on the sofa, lying on a beach, or just taking a pause.

Even with physical and mental rest, feelings of tiredness and dissatisfaction may linger. In these instances, the concept of *Spiritual rest* emerges, emphasising the need to replenish one's Spiritual energy. Individuals may discover that they require rest and sleep for their physical bodies and their minds, but remain disconnected from their Spirits. It is a personal decision whether to acknowledge and address this need, or not. Upon reading this, many may recognise times when they actively attempted to block this need out.

4 – Out

In the context of The Guiding Star System, **out** refers to your outer world—the physical world, the concept of time, and everything associated with it. This includes all the tangible things you see: buildings, cars, trees, oceans, and your physical body—cells, tissues, muscles, and bones. It also encompasses your physical brain, your memory, and certain thoughts shaped by external conditioning and teachings. Information is physically stored within the body—in memory, in cells, and in DNA. We will explore this in greater depth later.

Your outer world is a mirror of your internal world, which leads us to the next section. Your habitual thoughts reflect your outward reality. On an energetic level, your thoughts determine your frequency, and this frequency directly influences and is reflected back in your physical reality. Scientific principles, such as quantum physics, epigenetics, and the placebo effect, demonstrate this connection.

The *out*er aspect of our existence represents our uniquely human experiences in both our physical bodies and the physical world. This includes our personal lessons—essential aspects of learning and growth in this life. The *out* is the aspect of our lives that ends with death. It includes your personality, Sun sign, emotions, persona, conditioning, and life experiences—all facets of your presence in the physical world.

5 – In

The **in** section of the Guiding Star System focuses on the non-physical aspects of our being—our internal, essential selves. This represents your inner Self, your Spirit, your true essence, your feelings, and your awareness. It is your inner observer, your capacity for introspection, and your deepest connection to yourSelf. This is where your intuition, your authentic Self, and your truest guidance reside. It is the essence of your heart and Soul.

Many people feel uncertain about their beliefs surrounding fundamental questions of life, and in today's fast-paced world, these questions are often overlooked. Many religions offer varying perspectives on the nature of God or Gods. However, the specifics of any single belief system are less critical than the shared understanding that we are all connected by something greater—a higher energy, a profound power, or a fundamental sense of goodness. This unifying essence is Spirit—the purest and most divine form of energy, life, and love. It resides within each of us and every living thing, creating an innate connection to something beyond our physical selves. This is something we access inwardly. This is why this section is called *in*, as it represents the central connection between all other aspects of the system.

These are brief introductions to the areas and concepts that make up The Guiding Star System. What we go on to discover is the invisible link between all of these sections, that is the key to walking the path to all that you know you can be…

A little thought... ★

You will find little sections like these throughout the book. They are intended as my little thoughts, directly to you, the reader, to guide you to get the most out of this book and the process that you are about to embark upon. And they may question you. If you are able to bring your best emotional maturity and Self-awareness, you will remain open to the concepts in this book and will be able to step back to honestly assess yourSelf and your life. The challenges and obstacles that arise may not be what you initially expect them to be. Be open, be kind to yourSelf, and be ready for the life that you desire. It is my sincere hope that the information in this book resonates with you and guides you on your personal journey. Now, let's take the next steps...

Foundational Concepts

Body, Mind, and Soul

The human experience exists in three primary forms of energy: the physical body, the mind, and the Soul. It takes conscious awareness to recognise that we are more than just body and mind. Here are a few of my favourite ways to illustrate this:

The first example involves meditation. When you meditate, you first calm the body and then quiet the mind, to create space for connection with your Soul. Meditators will know; it can be a challenge! Often, the mind wanders—to the shopping list, an urgent task, or whatever else the ego mind uses to distract. It is in those moments that something becomes aware of the mind wandering, and it calls you back to stillness. This *something* is not the mind; it is the observer—the Soul, the Self.

The second example invites you to reflect on your life so far, and how much you have changed. Change is one of the few certainties of the human experience, so transformation is inevitable. As you consider your journey, you begin to see how the mind shifts perspective and grows. But something observes this evolution; that is the Self, the Soul. The Souls energy is a constant, stable presence. You may drift closer to or further from it, but it remains there. By reflecting on this, you may begin to sense the difference between the mind thinking and the Soul being. Some might feel that the Soul evolves through human lessons, but in truth, it is our own alignment and frequency that shifts closer to its vibration.

There is far more to the human body and the world we live in than just the physical. While we might perceive a clear separation between body, mind, and Soul, this division is becoming less relevant.

It is not ideal for us to prioritise any one of these three forms of being over the other, as they are all equally important to our existence. The aim is this; the body to be governed by the mind, and the mind to be governed by the Soul. When this balance is in place, there is a harmonisation between all three, and harmonisation is then our lived experience.

The Difference Between Soul and Spirit

Simply put, Spirit represents the highest form of energy—the purest essence of love, light, and life. It is the ultimate power, transcending our individual selves. The Soul is your unique expression of Spirit. It is the distinct version of Spirit residing within you; it encompasses your energy and everything you are when connected to it. While Spirit and Soul are inextricably linked and often used interchangeably, they are different; they are connected but separate.

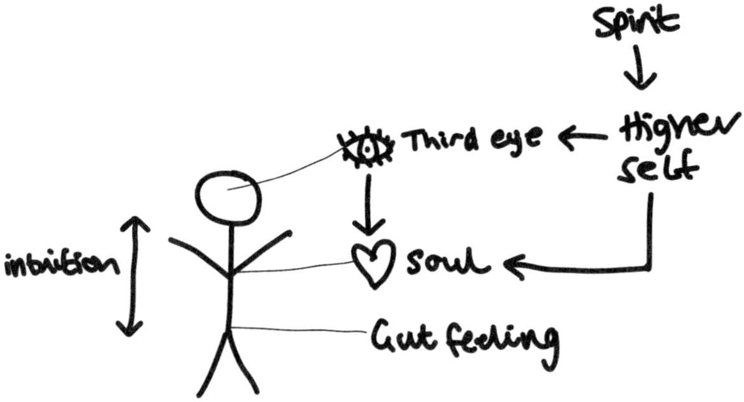

Soul: Your Soul is your inner essence—your purpose, your journey, and the lessons you are here to learn. It's not a physical entity, but it exists within you. It is eternal, incapable of dying or ceasing to exist. The Soul is your unique embodiment of the universal Spirit. While Spirit is singular, the Soul is individual, explaining why each person is unique, with individual purpose and unique potential for growth.

Spirit: Spirit is the universal energy that unites all life. It can be viewed as a collective consciousness shared by all living beings. It is the energy from which we originated and to which we will ultimately return. Spirit represents the highest frequency—pure love, authenticity, and life itself. It is divine. While Spirit itself cannot die, your connection to it can feel lost or diminished. This is often temporary, however, as you always have the power to reconnect with that energy, regardless of how disconnected you may feel. Such disconnection frequently occurs when the connection to your Higher Self and Soul is blocked.

Your Higher Self: Your Higher Self is the interaction between your Soul and your Spirit. It guides and leads you, possessing universal knowledge and being free from ego. By connecting with your Higher Self, you gain access to your innate wisdom. It is unique to you, and you choose your life path and the lessons essential to your Soul's growth. Your Higher Self is not your only access to your Soul; your Soul is within you, always present, waiting to be discovered. The stronger your connection to your Higher Self, the easier it becomes to access your Soul's knowledge and align with your true path.

Self: This is the actual you that exists in this life - navigating the polarities of the human existence and establishing its own balance. It is the Self that is always evolving, and under the main guidance of the Higher Self and Soul. It is the Self that navigates the balance between ego and Soul, and is the observer of the experiences, altering the balance one way or another, as it develops.

Intuition: Intuition is a deep feeling arising from your inner Self and Soul. It is sometimes described as a voice, but it is not a spoken voice. It is a feeling and an intuitive understanding. When your intuition arises, you simply *know*. This doesn't always mean that it will be pleasant or easy. In fact, intuitive guidance may frequently present challenges, as it rarely provides an easy escape from difficult situations or unmet desires. Your intuition emerges from the depths of your Soul and is guided by your Higher Self. It will only come to you when you are present, calm, and receptive. These are often your quietest and most reflective moments.

Differentiating intuition from the anxious promptings of your ego can be challenging. The ego will frequently try to disguise its fears as intuitive warnings, making you believe that something *doesn't feel right*. While this can sometimes be accurate, it is important to distinguish between true intuition and the ego's anxieties. This ability grows with practice but can initially be challenging, as the ego is very skilled at deception and has had many years to perfect this skill.

Intuition differs from *gut instinct*, which is a more immediate and urgent response to potential threats or survival needs. Gut instinct can override other actions and thoughts but stems from the subconscious safety programmes of the brain and ego, often linked to our gut, which is sometimes called the *second brain*. These are usually responses to wounds or trauma, whether we care aware of them or not. Intuition requires a different state of being—presence and receptivity—to be accessed.

The Third Eye: The concept of the *third eye* refers to the awakening of our sixth sense, often symbolised by an eye located in the centre of the forehead. It's considered the *Seat of the Soul*, the point of connection and communication with your Soul. In Ancient Egyptian culture, the *Eye of Horus* represented this all-seeing eye. The symbol closely resembles the pineal gland in the human brain, a gland composed of the same material as the human eye. The pineal gland acts as a frequency receptor, an energy antenna covered in tiny crystals, that most people have not yet learned to utilise. By awakening and tuning into this energy, the crystals become charged, forming a direct connection to your Higher Self, Soul, innate wisdom, and Spiritual gifts.

The Learning Journey

We are all here to learn. Throughout my journey, I have discovered that the lessons I need to learn reveal themselves at precisely the right moment. It is impossible to learn everything in a single lifetime. The specific information we require is uniquely tailored to our individual paths. The information and guidance in this book will also be unique to you, as it will be perceived in your own unique way.

The term *esoteric* originates from ancient Greek mysteries, with *eso* meaning *within*. Traditionally, it referred to secret Spiritual teachings that were shared only within select groups, and were never fully known to the masses. However, in our current age of abundant information, it is easy to become overwhelmed and struggle to locate the essential truths within the plethora of material that is so readily available. While the information you seek may be available, the volume of information and sources means that you must actively seek it out. It's as if you need to navigate a dense jungle. This is why this system is here; to guide you through.

Learning is a beautiful process. Further your curiosity and your desire for truth; absorb as much knowledge as you can. Truth will resonate; you will recognise it. And don't stop with this book; continue to expand your learning and awareness through a variety of sources. There are countless excellent resources available, and taking in information that is presented from different perspectives can help consolidate your understanding.

Don't ever stop learning... something. anything you are drawn to. Expand and challenge yourself always.

Your life's path is made up of the lessons that you learn. Those lessons were pre-determined by your Higher Self before you embarked on this Earthly journey, all designed to nurture and develop your Soul. Whilst you retain an element of free will, your life choices will ultimately lead you to your pre-ordained lessons in some form. The path you choose is the path you were meant to experience, in order for you to learn *your* lessons. This is why we each have such vastly different lives, bodies, circumstances, and lessons. We each also possess unique gifts, talents, attributes, and loves. Your journey is embarked upon at your own pace—sometimes rapidly, sometimes slowly, but one step at a time.

Your Soul, intuition, and Higher Self offer guidance; subtle whispers that direct you to your next step. This guidance steers you toward your path. The degree to which you stray from your path may be pre-determined—exactly what you needed to learn a lesson and return to your path. It is not necessary to wait for an interruption to redirect you back on your path, so know that you can decide to make a change at any point.

The closer you are to your intended path, the more connected and aware of yourSelf you will become, resulting in a higher energetic frequency. Your Soul acts as an elastic band, gently and continually guiding you. The more you resist, the stronger this pull becomes, making life feel harder. When you surrender and follow this guidance, you will find that life supports your journey rather than opposing it.

The elastic band of the soul path

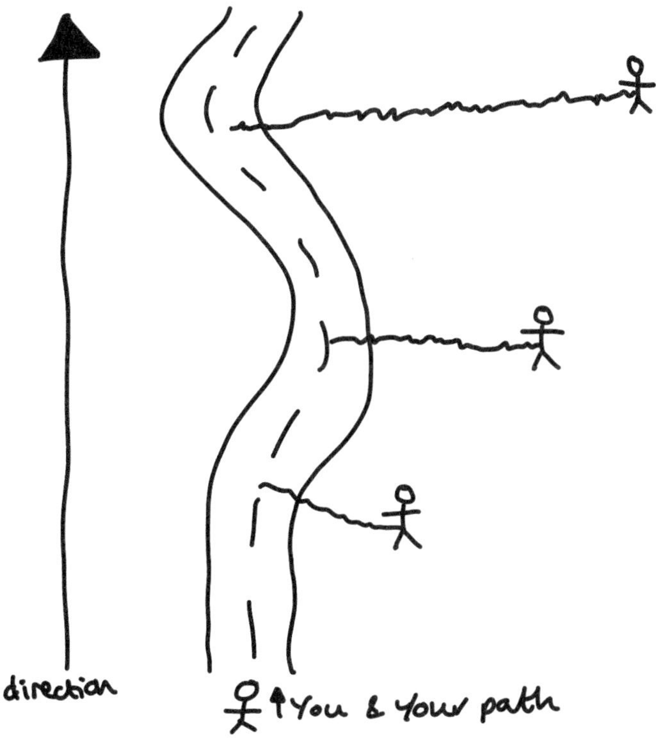

A little thought... ★

There's a fascinating Spiritual concept, introduced to me by Dolores Cannon, a well-respected Spiritual hypnotherapist and past life regressionist. She suggests that whenever we face a major decision or significant life event, the unchosen path is also experienced, albeit in a different realm. A part of our consciousness and Soul lives out the unrealised alternative. This is why we may revisit those "what if" scenarios and why we sometimes dream of those unchosen possibilities. It may even explain the sensation of living a "totally different life" if we had made a different choice. (This concept was utterly mind-blowing for me when I first heard it!)

Have you ever thought of this for yourSelf? When you read this, did any of your life experiences come into your awareness?

The Mind Continuum

The mind operates along a spectrum that ranges from ego to Soul. This is not a linear progression but a continuum, encompassing all points between these two extremes. The ego end is rooted in fear, representing old, stagnant, fixed beliefs and behaviours. The Soul end is rooted in Spirit, representing newness, freedom, growth, evolution, and a capacity for change. Both ego and Soul influence the mind, and we each possess aspects of both. Ultimately, we hold the power to choose which influence predominates in our lives, ensuring we remain firmly in the driver's seat of our own minds.

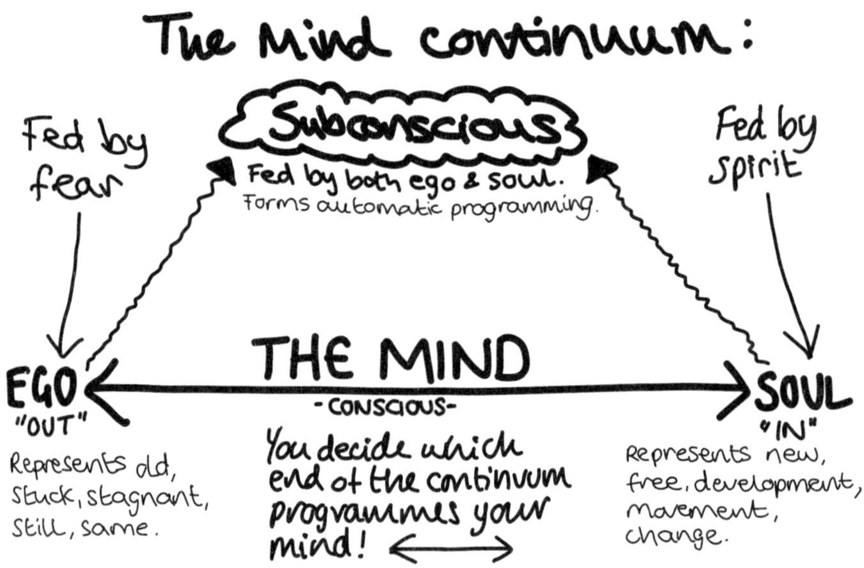

The thoughts that arise in our minds, whether rooted in ego or Soul, feed the subconscious. This subconscious acts as a storage bank, retaining information to streamline our daily cognitive processing, forming automatic behaviours essential for survival.

The Unlearning Spiral

When we are born, we are born as pure Spirit within our unique Soul. This represents the inner circle of the unlearning spiral. As life progresses, we learn necessary lessons that help us survive. Survival is the most basic and dominant of all our human needs, and we adapt to whatever environments we're born into. These adaptations create deeply rooted lessons, beliefs, and often, traumas. Each of these is marked along the unlearning spiral as a point on our individual journey.

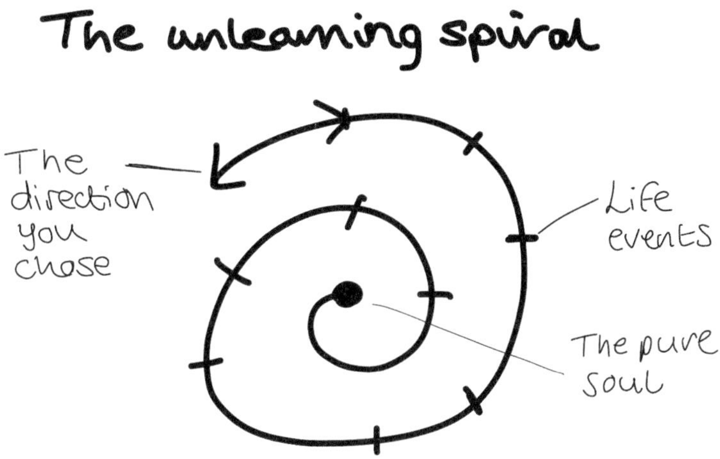

Once we reach a point of awareness—often initiated by challenge, awakening, or desire for change—we can begin to consciously reflect on the beliefs and programming we've acquired. We assess whether these serve us in creating the life we truly want. When life becomes about more than just surviving, when it becomes about *living*, we begin to shift from fear to love. This is a monumental movement in frequency and awareness. In this process, we begin to return to the essence of who we are—the pure Soul at the centre of the spiral. Not all the lessons we've learned are useless. Some are beautiful and vital. But others are heavy, false, or limiting. These are to be released. Each trauma or limiting belief that we release brings us closer to that essence. I don't believe we are meant to reach full purity again in this lifetime—but we *will* return to it when we pass. And the closer we move toward it while alive, the more joy, abundance, and alignment we will experience.

There comes a time in life when we are *ready* to begin this process. We spend our early years learning, and often our adult years unlearning. The spiral is a map of this process. Unlike the layers of an onion analogy, where you peel layers away linearly, the spiral is multi-directional. You can move forward and backwards on the spiral. But the aim is always the same: the centre—your Soul and true Self.

Knowledge vs. Knowing

We live in an age of readily available information, with a seemingly endless supply of knowledge at our fingertips. While this abundance is a significant benefit, acquiring knowledge is just the beginning. For true healing and Self-discovery, it's essential to integrate that knowledge into your being—to truly *know* it. When you *know* it, you believe it, and it becomes a part of you and the systems that govern your existence. For example, you may have heard something from another person or learned something from a book, only to find that the concept only truly becomes meaningful once you experience a similar situation personally. This is the moment of realisation—"Ah! That's what that meant!" While someone can repeat the words of a philosopher, passing along knowledge, that does not mean that knowledge becomes integrated into another person's life and belief system.

The difference between knowledge and knowing is the difference between theoretical understanding and tangible, lived experience. When something truly becomes a part of you, it transforms into part of your belief system and becomes a part of your truth. It's learning at the deepest level. This distinction is crucial to understanding the difference between *knowledge* and *knowing*.

Now that we've explored these foundational concepts, lets dive deeper into The Guiding Star System, with the exploration of an overarching principle: Energy.

Energy

Previously, science has viewed two distinct realms: one of matter and one of immaterial energy. But quantum physics now suggests there is only one: that of energy. What we perceive as matter is an illusion. Everything is composed of atoms, and atoms are energy. At their core is an energy vortex—a powerful field. Energy is measured in vibrational frequency, and every form of energy has its own unique vibration. This aligns with what many ancient traditions have always known: the universe is governed by Spirit energy, an invisible force.

Since we are made of atoms, and atoms are energy, understanding how to maximise this energy is crucial. The vibrational frequency of our atoms—and what they tune into—determines our energy state. The atoms forming our body contain countless receptors or antennae. You are a vibrational being in a vibrational universe. You are an antenna, constantly sending and receiving energy. Your thoughts are not confined to your mind or body; they are broadcast into the collective field of Spirit and consciousness.

You are a vibrational being in a vibrational universe. You are an antennae - both emitting and receiving energy.

So, what happens when the antenna is no longer receiving—when the body dies? The frequency still exists; it simply no longer connected through your unique receptors. Energy cannot die. It can only be transferred or transformed. Your essence returns to the field, to Source. This means that you are Spirit energy and your body is merely its temporary physical representation of that energy in the form of matter.

This means that you are not your human body, or the receptors or your energy; you are the individual frequency that the receptors tune into. Your biology is a manifestation of energy, shaped by the field, which exists with or without your human form. Einstein concluded that *"the field is the sole governing agency of the particle"*, meaning that we are energy before we are cells. When Einstein said, *"everything in life is vibration"*, and Tesla urged us to think in terms of "*energy, frequency, and vibration*", they were revealing universal truths.

Energy is the currency of our life. We each possess a certain amount of energy that allows us to live in our bodies, and how we choose to use it determines our experience. Our energy follows our awareness and focus. Controlling the focus of our energy shapes our lives.

Energy is the true currency of life.

Important and Agreed Principles

Ancient traditions have long taught that the body is made of energy. Science is now beginning to confirm and embrace this truth. We are rediscovering the complexity of what we are: matter is energy. This energy-based system is completely interlinked. When treating the body, you cannot isolate one symptom or part; the whole must be considered. Body, mind, and Soul must function in harmony. They are not separate, so they cannot be treated in isolation. Influencing one part of the energy system impacts the others, and understanding this multi-dimensional system remains at the heart of The Guiding Star System.

Both science and ancient traditions agree: energy cannot be created or destroyed; it can only be transferred or transformed. These concepts are foundational throughout this book. Energy **transference** means moving energy from one source to another in the same form. Energy **transformation** means converting energy into a new form. And to raise our energetic frequency, we must use both principles wisely. This system is designed to help anyone improve—from wherever they are, to wherever they wish to be.

Where is Our Energy?

Our energy flows throughout our physical bodies—in the blood pumped by the heart, the signals of the nervous system, and in every cell. Our energy also extends beyond the physical: science and ancient traditions recognise that energy animates the body and reaches beyond it. The etheric body outlines the physical body a few inches beyond the skin. The aura forms a larger, egg-shaped field that can extend meters out. The aura is like a personal rainbow—a dynamic, ever-changing field of electromagnetic colours that reflects your internal state. Each colour has a specific energetic frequency, and may explain why we feel drawn to certain colours more than others. In earlier times, people could see these fields clearly, much like how we can see the physical body. Some people still have the ability to see these fields, and this ability may be linked to a well-functioning pineal gland.

Maximising Our Energy: Input and Output

Every cell in our body, and everything around us, has a vibrational frequency. We can enhance this energy, or deplete it:
Input of energy: positive and negative inputs
Output of energy: positive and negative outputs

To improve your vibrational frequency, there are four simple principles:

- **Add good energy** - Add in positive fuel, movement, rest, out, or in.
- **Remove bad energy** - Remove negative fuel, movement, rest, out, or in.
- **Stop leaking good energy** - Stop giving too much, or giving to things that are out of alignment.

- **Stop storing bad energy** - Let go and release negative beliefs, programming, and trauma.

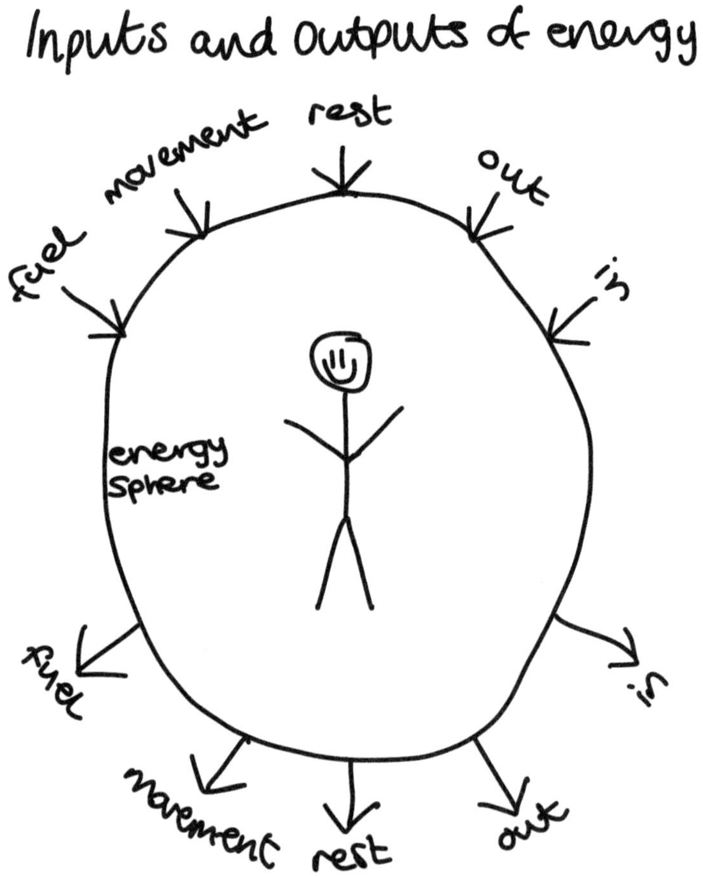

In assessing our own energy inputs and outputs, we become automatically aware of how to increase our frequency.

While simple in concept, applying these principles consistently in daily life takes effort. This book will guide you through how to do this. Begin by becoming aware of where you gain and lose energy. This awareness gives you power—the power to direct and control your own energy. Ultimately, this is the only thing you can truly control. This understanding is central to The Guiding Star System and is key to healing, evolving, and ascending.

A little thought... ★

Interestingly, positive energy output often leads to increased energy input. This is one of life's little secrets: when you spend energy on things you love, that uplift you, or benefit others—you also gain energy, motivation, and joy in return. This forms an overall increase in your energetic frequency.
What do you do that you love and would class as a positive energy output? How do you feel like it gives back to you energetically?

Your Frequency

Your frequency can best be described as your energetic vibration. Everything in the universe vibrates. Even a brick wall consists of particles vibrating at specific frequencies. Atoms are always vibrating, and their rate of vibration is their frequency. Every thought, every bite of food, every movement, emotion, and reaction—all carry frequency. The body, mind, and Soul are interconnected by this vibrational field.

Your frequency can be measured in angstrom units per second (one hundred-millionth of a centimetre). These are units used to measure light waves. Each person has a unique frequency, which can vary across the body but will always have an overall energetic signature. When your frequency increases, you align more fully with your Soul and your authentic Self.

The Frequency Levels of The Guiding Star System

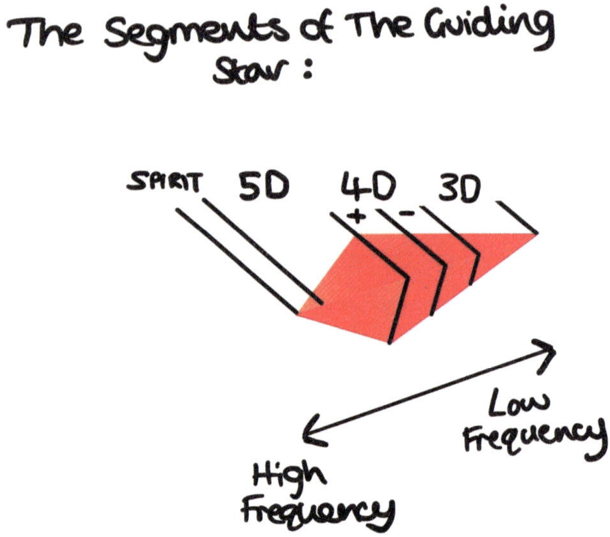

3D

The outside world defines and controls you. Happiness is pursued through money and status. Joy remains elusive. You feel disempowered, ruled by ego, fear, and blame. There is a disconnect from Self and others. Life is reactive and survival-based. Denial. Hiding. Separate. Alone. Poor emotional states. Mood swings between apparent happiness—and unsatisfied and empty. Un-disciplined. Instant gratification. Controlled by thoughts and emotions. Discomfort. No awareness. Lack of power. Looks only outwards to blame, and also for solutions. No looking inwards.

4D-

You begin to question your reality and examine your priorities. A growing awareness links the mind, body, and Soul. You begin seeking, even if your efforts often fall short, you know there is more. Instinct and intuition start to guide you. You realise the need to unlearn, to reflect on your past, and accept that you do not know all the answers. This stage brings discomfort but also curiosity. Functioning. Education. Awakening in the first stage. A thirst for deepening your knowledge in an area of improvement. Seeking deeper than a surface-level meaning. Questioning ego. Holding up the mirror and having an overview glance. feeling of unknown, unease, but also some excitement.

4D+

You feel a growing sense of purpose and connection to your path. You're hungry for knowledge, linking different ideas and seeing the bigger picture. Trust in your intuition deepens. You are evolving, awakening. High functioning. Increasing awareness and vibration. Thirst for answers and further knowledge, and a *knowing* that you are on the right path. You start to remember YOU. Branching out in your topics of further education, and beginning to link them together. Seeing the bigger picture. Beginning to fulfil potential. Increased trust. Intuition is further developing. Looking into the mirror. Questioning and working in depth. You are growing, increasing. Deep meaning. Awakening. The tipping of the scales.

5D

Alignment. Truth. Soul. You live with clarity and authenticity, fully conscious and awake. You recognise unity with all things. Love is pure, unconditional, and flowing. You live in harmony with your energy. Life becomes intuitive, connected, and meaningful. *Clicking* into place. Soul driven. You are your true Self. Clarity. Things make sense. Awareness of connection to everything. Nature, people, universe. Understanding pure love. Strong intuition and power, ability to listen to it, trust in it. Correct allocation of energy in practice. Unity of the energy of the universe. Collective. Purpose and what you are here for. Self-love. Embracing the unknown. Loving, not needing. Connection, not attachment. Being. Just being. All is within. I am.

Centre:

Enlightenment. Pure consciousness. Light. Love. Unity. Divinity. Ego is dissolved. You are Spirit.

How it All Comes Together:

Each point of the Guiding Star connects. Each arm carries an energetic frequency. You can elevate your frequency in any and each area to reach the central hexagon. This centre represents 5D consciousness across all points. Once reached, you may move in and out of this state, but awareness of it remains. Whilst your energy may vary across the five areas, major differences between them are unlikely. For example, you cannot be at 3D in one area and 5D in another because your frequency, as a whole, is unified.

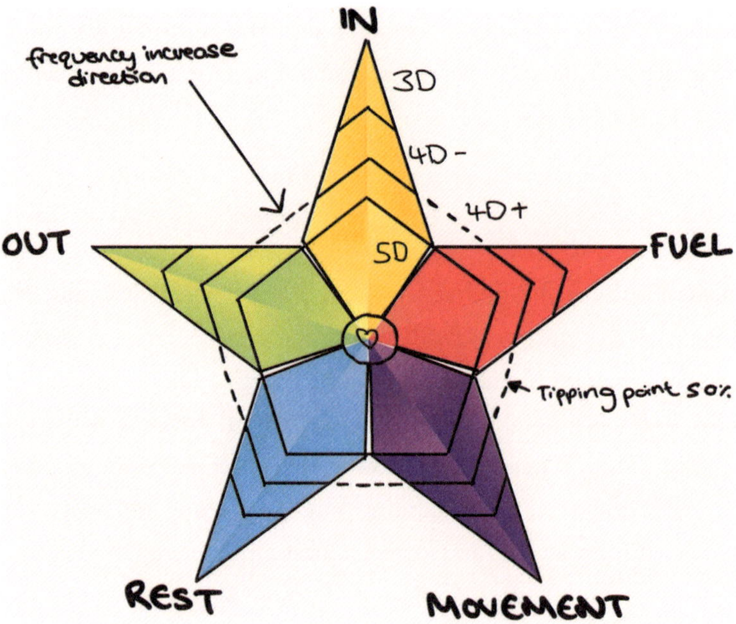

You may be naturally drawn to begin with one particular point. Wherever you start, improvement in one area raises the vibration of the others. The most powerful point is the top of the star—the "in". This governs your entire energy system and cellular behaviour. Once experienced, there is no going back! Enjoy the journey.

Exercise

Take a moment to reflect. Where do you feel you are in the five different sections of The Guiding Star System? Have a look at the levels of frequency to guide your personal assessment. This is one to think about, but not to overthink! Usually the first answer is the one that is the best reflection for you. And, you can always come back and revisit these exercises.

	Where do you currently rate yourSelf – 3D, 4D-, 4D+, or 5D?	**Why have you decided this?**
Fuel		
Movement		
Rest		
Out		
In		

Now, let's take this one further. You have identified above where you feel like you are currently, so now we are going to look at what this is made up of. In the next table, take this point to consider your current energy inputs and outputs. What do you feel gives you energy? And what do you feel drains it?

A little thought… ★

This is where you get to be really honest with yourSelf, and begin the brave journey to becoming all you know you can be. It starts here. You may be including things that you love, such as a person or people, pets, hobbies, travel, etc. As well as things you are noticing that are not love, such as overwork in your job, perfectionism, stagnation, draining relationships, etc. We all tend to overlook the truth when it is painful, as we all naturally avoid pain. Here is your first step to honesty and reflection, to awaken your awareness.

	INPUTS of energy (ascenders/elevators)	OUTPUTS of energy (anchors)
Fuel		
Movement		
Rest		
Out		
In		

Summary

1. We exist in body, mind, and Soul (Spirit).
2. Transference = the transfer of energy from one source to another, in the same form. It takes on that energy.
3. Transformation = the transfer energy from one source to another, and convert or transform it into another form.
4. Receptivity: You are an antenna for both giving and receiving energetic frequency. Have that antenna open to receive the energy sources.
5. Everything has a frequency; the foods we eat, liquids we drink, exercises we do, thoughts we think, feelings we feel, sounds we hear, words we say, things we touch. Frequency and energy awareness and its allocation is the key to energy maximisation in our lives. We now go to explore this further throughout the rest of the book.
6. Everything is linked, always and inextricably, in this vibrational universe.

Trauma

Why Include a Chapter on Trauma?

The first step on any healing journey is to address trauma. Trauma is intrinsically linked to our deepest survival mechanisms. Until we acknowledge and work through our core traumas, they will continue to interfere with healing, evolution, and ascension. We are never fully healed in our lifetime, but it begins with a powerful decision—one we explore in this chapter.

What is Trauma?

Many associate trauma with only extreme events such as physical injury, war, or catastrophic accidents. These experiences are undoubtedly traumatic, yet trauma extends beyond these extremes. It can include witnessing violence, childhood punishment, sexual abuse, bullying, abusive relationships, poverty, racism, homophobia, and many more subtle yet deeply impactful events. Trauma is not the event—it is the internal reaction to an external situation.

What makes something traumatic for one person but not another? People can be involved in and witness to the same environment, circumstances, or event, but not all of them become traumatised. Why is this? Trauma is entirely subjective. It depends on a person's conditioning, nervous system, personal history, and the lens through which they perceive the event. Pioneering trauma expert, Gabor Maté, points out in his book *The Myth of Normal,* that even siblings raised in the same household process shared experiences completely differently. Trauma is about how a person experiences something, not the event itself.

Recognising trauma is the essential first step. We can be reluctant to admit this hard truth to ourselves, and denial can often prevail. In some culture contexts, such as Britain, pride and humour are often valued as coping strategies. Though resilience is admirable, it must be built on a foundation of *acknowledged* pain. Refusing to recognise trauma is often rooted in ego, and a fear of appearing weak. But healing doesn't begin with pride, it begins with truth.

A little thought... ★

Trauma definition within The Guiding Star System: *"Trauma is something that is so distressing to you, that you are wholly overwhelmed by it. Fear. Confusion. Collapse. Threat. Helplessness. Un-processable powerlessness. When something is so distressing that your system cannot process it, the Higher Self may create a protective distance between your Soul (the "in") and your external experience (the "out"). This separation leads to what I call the trauma loop: a state of living disconnected from your true Self, unable to have the desired link with your Soul (with your "in") and live the life that you want. You are alerted to this by the existence of a trigger that takes you back to the pain, informing you to what you need to heal. Until you return to the site of your pain with your own power and free will, the trauma remains unresolved. Trauma is a kind of death within life—but it can result in the re-establishment of Self—and in doing so, activate the connection with Soul."*

Types of Trauma: PTSD and C-PTSD

Trauma can manifest in various forms, and understanding these differences can be crucial for healing. One of the most well-known types is Post-Traumatic Stress Disorder (PTSD), which typically arises from experiencing a single, life-altering traumatic event. This kind of trauma often involves a situation that shatters a person's sense of safety, triggering a cascade of reactions in the mind, body, and Soul. The Self may fragment in response, creating a protective barrier around the Soul to shield it from the intensity of the experience. Think of it like the Patronus charm from *Harry Potter*—a powerful protective shield that guards against darkness. From the moment of the traumatic event onward, there is often a noticeable distance or incoherence between a person's internal systems. This disruption can create lasting effects that influence how they navigate life, relationships, and Self-perception.

Another form of trauma, known as Complex Post-Traumatic Stress Disorder (C-PTSD), is similar to PTDS, but does not stem from one single catastrophic event. Instead, it is from the gradual accumulation of many distressing experiences over time. In cases of C-PTSD, no single incident may be deemed significantly traumatic on its own, but the build-up of numerous smaller, potentially harmful events can create a profound impact.

C-PTSD is often associated with situations of prolonged or repeated abuse—whether physical, emotional, or psychological. This could include enduring a toxic or controlling relationship, experiencing chronic bullying, growing up with a narcissistic caregiver, or facing ongoing sexual abuse. Unlike PTSD, which is often linked to a clear, identifiable event, C-PTSD arises from the slow erosion of safety and Self-worth. The challenge here is that the person suffering may struggle to validate their own experience, as they cannot point to one specific moment that caused the damage. This lack of a clear cause can lead to a deep sense of Self-doubt and confusion, both within themselves and when trying to explain their feelings to others.

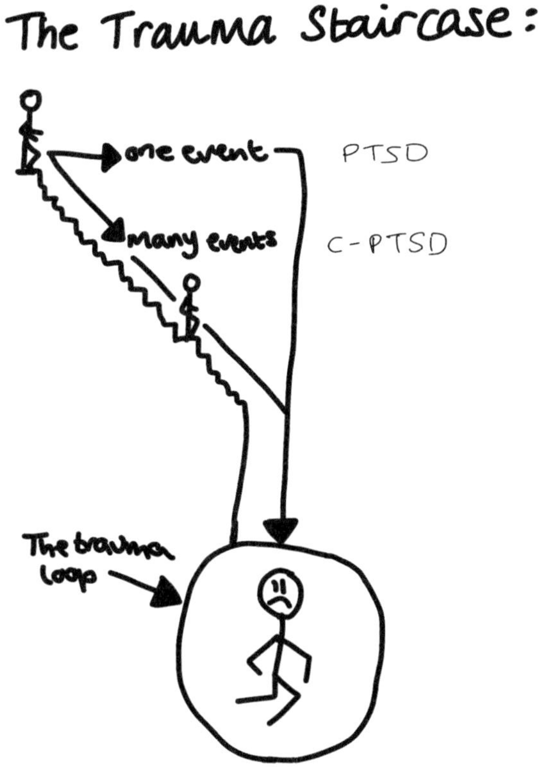

One of the most significant differences between PTSD and C-PTSD lies in how the trauma is perceived and acknowledged. When trauma is the result of one dramatic incident, the person usually has a sense of justification for how they feel—there is a societal understanding that surviving something objectively horrific leaves scars. In contrast, those with C-PTSD often feel conflicted, as they may not even recognise their experiences as traumatic, given that no single event stands out. Instead, the gradual build-up of distressing situations undermines their sense of Self and their trust in their own perception. This insidious wearing down of the Spirit often leads to a strong pattern of Self-criticism and inner shaming.

When a trauma response is triggered, it typically manifests as one of four reactions, commonly referred to as the "Four F's": fight, flight, freeze, or fawn. These responses are primal, instinctual, and deeply embedded within our survival mechanisms. Some people may predominantly experience one response, while others might shift between them depending on the situation. Understanding which response is most common for you can be an essential step towards recognising how trauma is influencing your behaviour.

These trauma responses can also be at the root of many mental health conditions, including anxiety, depression, schizophrenia, and more. Rather than seeing these conditions solely as mental health issues in isolation, it is important to understand that they can often be symptomatic of unresolved trauma. For example, trauma recovery and C-PTSD expert Pete Walker, in his book *Complex PTSD: From Surviving To Thriving*, suggests that schizophrenia can sometimes be an extreme response to trauma, reflecting a profound disconnection from reality as a coping mechanism.

One powerful example of how trauma can mask itself as mental illness is shared in Emmanuel J. Smith's book, *When I Say No, I Feel Guilty*. He recounts the story of a young adult institutionalised for mental health issues, who, after receiving assertiveness training and learning to set boundaries with a bullying parent, was able to enrol in college and move forward with life. This transformation raises a crucial question: how many individuals diagnosed with severe mental health conditions are actually experiencing the long-term effects of complex trauma, compounded by a lack of boundaries and the inability to advocate for themselves?

Teal Swan, a prominent voice in the field of trauma recovery, advocates for a shift in how we approach mental health. Rather than asking someone, *"What is wrong with you?"*, she suggests a more insightful question: *"What happened to you?"* This change in perspective recognises that mental and emotional struggles are often rooted in past experiences rather than inherent flaws. This approach challenges the outdated model of treating symptoms without addressing their root causes. Advancing our understanding of trauma is essential for transforming how we support those affected. By moving away from blame and judgment, and towards curiosity and compassion, we open the door to genuine healing. Trauma-informed approaches to mental health are not just beneficial—they are vital. We must continue to learn from those who have navigated these depths, and from those who, like Teal Swan, have courageously shared their journey of overcoming trauma.

Healing from trauma is not about erasing the past, but is about reclaiming your power from it. It involves recognising how your experiences have shaped you, while choosing not to let them define you. Trauma is not your identity; it is a chapter in your story—one that, with courage and support, you can rewrite.

'Healing from trauma is about reclaiming your power from it."

The Trauma Loop

When you have experienced a traumatic event, it can feel as though you are caught in an unbreakable loop—a relentless cycle that keeps replaying the pain and fear. I call this state *the trauma loop*. It feels like being imprisoned in an impenetrable space where escape seems impossible.

Dissociation is the way the mind distances itself from pain to survive, either during the event itself or when experiencing a flashback later on. While stuck in the trauma loop and a state of dissociation, it becomes challenging to engage with the world, be present in the moment, or experience joy and pleasure. Instead, there is a sense of complete vulnerability, an overwhelming openness to everything, or, conversely, an inability to feel anything at all—swinging between feeling everything or nothing.

You can literally feel everything, or nothing at all.

When the traumatic event has passed, the real work of processing begins. Unlike a physical injury, like a broken bone that heals over time, trauma doesn't follow a predictable path of recovery. Trauma, by its very nature, feels inescapable and leaves behind a profound sense of helplessness and vulnerability. The initial response, rooted in survival mechanisms, serves an essential purpose at the time. It protects the Self by putting up barriers and distancing the core Self from the experience. However, these survival responses can become so ingrained that they persist long after the danger has passed, trapping the person in a loop of unresolved fear and learned helplessness.

When trauma remains unprocessed, it leaves the individual in a state of internal conflict. There is often a disconnect from the Soul—a sense that the Self can no longer be trusted to provide safety and protection. This creates a prison within the mind, where freedom feels unattainable. The person may continue to live, but they do so at a distance from their own essence.

Yet, there is hope. You can break free from the trauma loop by repeatedly learning how to interrupt the cycle and re-engage with life. The gravity of a traumatic experience means it will always leave an imprint. However, when you are ready, you can learn to be the alchemist of your own experiences—transforming trauma into wisdom, resilience, and a deeper understanding of yourSelf. Trauma itself resides at the ego end of the spectrum, but with healing, it can be turned into a source of personal power and insight.

Triggers

When trauma has embedded itself into your physical, mental, emotional, and Spiritual systems, it becomes an integral part of your survival programming. Because trauma affects the entire system, the body and mind become hypervigilant—constantly scanning for any threat that might resemble the cause of the original wound. This is why trauma responses can be triggered by the smallest, seemingly harmless stimuli.

A trigger can transport you right back into the traumatic experience, reactivating all the associated physical and emotional reactions. Sometimes, the trigger can be as minor as a familiar smell—a smell of aftershave similar to that worn by an abuser. It might be the sight of a car that resembles one driven by someone who hurt you, or the sound of a car backfiring, mimicking the noise of a gunshot. Even seeing someone on the street who vaguely resembles a past aggressor can catapult you back into survival mode. These triggers can also cause more subtle responses, and show up as people-pleasing, fear of confrontation, or inability to make the smallest of decisions.

The brain makes these associations instinctively, aiming to keep you safe by heightening your awareness. It is an attempt to prevent the trauma from happening again. However, this protective reflex, while well-intentioned, keeps you locked in survival mode rather than allowing you to move forward and truly live.

This survival instinct, rooted in protection, often clashes with another, deeper instinct—the whisper from your Soul that tells you there is more to life than merely surviving. It is only the bravest among us who listen to this whisper, daring to embark on the journey out of the trauma loop. Triggers, painful as they may be, are also opportunities—your Higher Self signalling what needs healing, much like physical pain alerts you to a wound that requires care. The trigger is not just a reminder of past pain; it is an invitation to transform it.

Recovery up the Staircase

Healing from trauma is not a linear process. Rather than a straightforward ascent, it resembles a staircase—one that you will go up and down many times. Treatment, whether through therapy, personal reflection, or healing practices, creates breaks in the trauma loop, allowing glimpses of a life beyond mere survival. Trauma becomes ingrained so deeply that it will always be a part of you. Once experienced, there is no way to erase it, no path back to a version of yourSelf untouched by it. Recovery means accepting this reality while choosing to move forward anyway.

Just as you cannot undo the past, you also cannot change the fact that trauma may continue to resurface at different stages of your life. Each time you are triggered, you may feel like you are slipping back down the staircase. But with practice, you learn how to find your footing again. Each journey up the steps strengthens your belief in your ability to heal. You start to understand that every descent is not a failure but an opportunity to practice resilience.

Choosing to recover is a decision—a commitment to transforming pain into growth. You can choose for trauma to make you bitter, or make you better. For those who choose bitterness, that journey is theirs alone. For those who choose healing, it is a life's work—an ongoing process of Self-reflection, vulnerability, and the courage to rise again.

Recovery does not have a definitive endpoint; it is a journey of continual evolution and expansion. It is a commitment to living more consciously, learning from each setback, and growing stronger with each ascent. This path is not easy, but it is transformative, revealing the beauty that lies in resilience and the power of reclaiming your own story.

Choosing to heal is one of the most courageous acts of Self-love. It is a statement to the universe that, despite what has happened, you choose to live fully, openly, and authentically. It is not about erasing the scars but honouring them as evidence of your strength.

Shortcuts and Coping Mechanisms

When stuck in the trauma loop, many will reach for shortcuts. These are temporary escapes that provide relief, such as addictions, compulsive behaviours, and extreme stimulation. They can be ways we attempt to bypass the pain. They are understandable and have likely served a purpose. But they are unsustainable, and true freedom lies in facing and transforming the trauma.

How To Get Out of the Trauma Loop

Unhealed trauma creates blocks, constricts your energy, clouds your inner guidance, and keeps your nervous system locked in survival mode. When emotional pain remains unprocessed, it creates unconscious patterns of fear, Self-protection, and limitation that prevent you from fully engaging with the tools of transformation, and will prevent you from the path that The Guiding Star System is able to lead you on. Instead of expansion, you experience resistance. Instead of clarity, confusion. Until trauma is acknowledged and integrated, the system cannot flow freely—because your energy is still tied to the past. Healing opens the channel. It restores safety in the body, trust in the Self, and alignment with the Soul—making expansion not only possible, but inevitable. To break free from the trauma loop and truly thrive, there are six stages:

1. The truth
2. The hammer
3. The ladder
4. The steps
5. The trampoline
6. The key

The Truth

The first and most fundamental step is acknowledging the reality of your situation. The truth begins with realising that you are caught in the trauma loop and that your feelings are directly related to that entrapment. Simply recognising this is a powerful act of Self-awareness. Once you identify the loop, the next step is to understand why you feel this way. What has happened to you? What has left this mark on your Soul?

This process involves facing your personal truth—a truth that is shaped by your unique perspective and past experiences. No two truths are ever identical, as each person interprets their experiences through their own lens. However, for those who have endured trauma that has resulted in Self-doubt, it can be incredibly challenging to establish your truth. Often, you have been conditioned to doubt your own perceptions, told that your feelings are invalid or exaggerated. Admitting the truth may feel like stepping outside the narrative that you have been conditioned to accept.

This stage requires deep introspection and observation. It involves educating yourSelf about trauma and its effects, allowing you to see your experiences from a new perspective. There is immense vulnerability in confronting your own story—questioning beliefs you once thought were solid. It may feel like your entire foundation is being uprooted. Yet, in this vulnerability lies the potential for growth.

Seek out reliable resources—books, podcasts, therapy, and supportive online communities. These can provide insights and validation without overwhelming you. During this phase, distance from certain people who may challenge your new understanding can be necessary. A therapist who specialises in C-PTSD can be invaluable, offering guidance as you navigate this complex terrain. Finding the right therapist is crucial; so, look around until you find a feeling of connection and understanding between you.

Admitting the truth can be profoundly painful. Denial is a natural defence mechanism—pushing the truth away to avoid the shame and guilt it might evoke. Many people go through life never facing the truth of their trauma, fearing the discomfort it brings. Breaking through this denial is an act of immense courage and sets the foundation for healing.

The Hammer

The hammer is one of the most challenging tools to wield because it represents your internal critic—the harsh, shaming voice that holds you in the trauma loop. This inner critic is relentless, deeply embedded, and often ruthless. It insists that you remain within the bounds of your trauma, reinforcing negative beliefs and keeping you stuck.

The hammer's destructive force comes from familiarity. The mind prefers the known, even if that known state is painful. Trauma can create a distorted comfort zone where suffering becomes predictable, and stepping out of it feels too risky. You might convince yourSelf that staying stuck is safer than facing the unknown.

To reclaim the hammer and turn it into a tool for healing, you must first become aware of your inner dialogue. Listen to the stories you tell yourSelf—the Self-blame, the fear, the repeated patterns of Self-criticism. Challenge these perceptions and counter them with your new truth. The goal is to reverse the hammer's force, using it not to punish, but to dismantle the walls that keep you trapped in the loop.

Visualising your best Self can help in this stage. Imagine the version of you that lives freely, unbound by trauma. Envision how that person would think, feel, and act. While you may not be there yet, simply imagining this version of yourSelf plants the seed for transformation.

Redirecting the hammer:

The Ladder

The ladder is your way back to your authentic Self—the connection you had before the trauma, or perhaps creating the connection you had never fully formed. It is not necessarily your final destination, but it represents a tangible step towards reclaiming your sense of Self. Climbing the ladder is a process, not a single leap. Each rung represents a step towards reconnection and healing.

Grieving is a significant part of this stage. Trauma often roots itself in emotional neglect, and part of moving forward is mourning the loss of what you needed but did not receive. This could mean acknowledging how your basic needs were neglected—either by others or by yourSelf—and allowing space for those feelings.

Self-compassion emerges here, often for the first time. You begin to recognise that compassion and nurturing are essential, not indulgent. Giving yourSelf permission to grieve can feel unfamiliar, especially if you were conditioned to see vulnerability as weakness.

Releasing anger is also vital. Trauma can loop unexpressed rage, often internalised as guilt or shame. Allowing yourSelf to feel and release this anger—in a safe, constructive way—validates your experience. You may also find yourSelf redefining your core values as you gain clarity. These values are not static; they evolve as your relationship with yourSelf deepens. Start by identifying three core values that resonate with your evolving truth. Honour them as guiding principles on your journey.

The Steps of Normality

When you first begin to experience life beyond survival mode, it feels incredible. You finally feel a sense of normality—engaging with life in the way you always knew was possible. This does not mean that you will not encounter challenges or difficult emotions, nor does it mean that you find yourSelf back into the trauma loop at times. But now, you have a point of reference—a preferred state where you recognise balance and homeostasis. You learn to notice when you need to realign, and the more familiar this state becomes, the more your recovery and growth accelerate.

Experiencing life in this way feels even sweeter because you know first-hand how it feels to be stuck in the trauma loop. You appreciate the contrast—the polarities between living in survival mode and living in flow.

A little thought... ★

When you are trapped in the trauma loop, and you first find a little break in it, you will feel completely different. To begin with, it may only be for a few seconds, almost forgetting that you were in the loop. When these little breaks occur, the first step is to realise them, and account for the fact that you were present. "*I am here*". Recognise this in any way that you wish. It may happen for a few moments during a walk, having a moment of realisation during your favourite cup of coffee, seeing a beautiful rainbow in the sky. They will usually be little things, where you find yourSelf in mind, body and Soul, all united in that moment. They do happen, and they will happen. They are small engagements of the Soul communicating with you and beginning to guide you.

I am here... :)

The Trampoline

The trampoline is a personal recovery tool—something unique to your own healing journey. Once you have learned how to lift yourSelf out of the trauma loop using your unique tools, you start to bounce back more easily. As you repeatedly practice using the ladder to climb out, you build resilience. Eventually, you learn to skip the ladder entirely, rebounding with greater speed and confidence.

Each time you bounce back, your truth will be tested and perhaps redefined. The old versus new beliefs may clash, but each time you realign, the process becomes quicker—like flicking on a light switch. The more you practice bouncing back, the more robust your inner resilience becomes.

The trampoline represents that moment of recovery when, instead of climbing slowly step by step, you simply spring upward, reasserting your connection to your truth. It becomes second nature, almost automatic, as you learn to trust your own ability to recover.

The Key

The key to higher levels of growth is the acceptance of the impermanent nature of intense emotions. It is the ability to embrace joy and presence while understanding that life's challenges may arise again. This acceptance does not eliminate pain but rather acknowledges that it is transient and manageable.

When you reach this state, you develop an inherent trust in yourSelf. You know that you can move through challenges because you've done it before. This is where you might start to see the purpose behind your trauma. You may begin to realise that, even though it was profoundly painful, something beneficial has emerged from the experience. It could be an increased sense of empathy, inner strength, or simply a deeper appreciation of life.

It's crucial not to rush to this understanding. Forcing yourSelf to find a positive spin on trauma too early can be a form of Self-gaslighting—denying the depth of your pain. Allowing the realisation to unfold in its own time is key. When you finally reach the point where the trauma no longer holds an emotional charge, you can speak about it as just an experience—factual, integrated, and without the weight it once carried.

At this point, you may notice a profound shift in your life—a return to your Soul's path. Trauma, while painful, can sometimes act as an elastic band, snapping you back to where you were always meant to be.

A little thought... ★

It stops here: In taking responsibility for your own experiences, your own value system, your own behaviour and emotions, and your own boundaries, you are taking a stand for your own healing. In doing this, you are automatically taking a stand for the healing of generational and ancestral trauma that resides energetically within you. Your commitment to healing yourSelf, has a healing effect on both past and future generations. This is currently estimated to be 7 years before and after yourSelf, but I see this as an ongoing domino effect, or cascade, throughout the generations. There are many family dynamics that bypass the opportunity for this individual responsibility in healing, which means that there is the passing down of this wounded energy and information to the next generation. But when you heal it within yourSelf, you can end the cycle. Are you currently aware of any patterns that are handed down in your family lines? Are there some that you know have been healed already? Are there some that you wish to heal?

Trauma and Spiritual Awakening

There is a unique connection between trauma and Spiritual awakening. The difference between Spiritual ascension and Spiritual awakening lies in their progression. An awakening is a singular event—a sudden, profound shift—while ascension is a gradual process, built through cumulative experiences. Both lead to the same destination but take different paths.

This parallel between trauma and Spiritual growth can be profound. Trauma can result from a single event (like PTSD) or from a build-up of smaller, repeated harms (like C-PTSD). In a similar way, Spiritual awakening can occur suddenly or as a gradual ascent. Trauma is rooted in the ego, while Spiritual awakening is anchored in the Soul. Yet both are transformative, unforgettable, and often singular in nature.

It is possible for a single, profound Spiritual experience to lift a person out of the trauma loop in an instant, much like how one catastrophic event can create trauma. This experience, however, cannot be forced—it must emerge organically. Similarly, a series of positive Spiritual experiences can gradually elevate a person from trauma, just as C-PTSD can develop from a series of small traumatic events. This positive version of C-PTSD represents healing, evolution, and ascension.

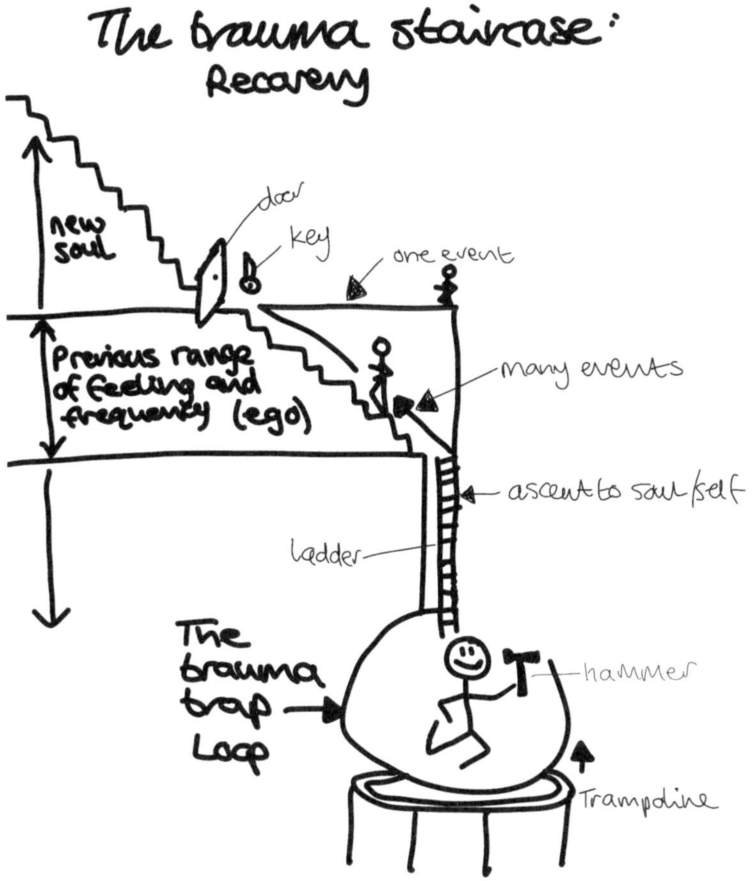

Why Trauma Must Be Treated First

Addressing trauma must be the foundation of any healing journey. Those living with trauma, particularly complex trauma, often remain in a state of nervous system dysregulation. Their mind, body, and Soul are not aligned, leading to a persistent state of hyper-vigilance and survival. The heart (representing feminine energy) and the mind (representing masculine energy) are often disconnected.

Because this state of dysregulation feels normal to someone who has lived with it for years, they may not even recognise the extent of their imbalance. Attempts to heal or ascend may feel like an uphill battle because the nervous system remains fixed in survival mode. Even when focusing on positive change, the body cannot easily align with the desired outcome, making manifestation and personal growth difficult.

People with C-PTSD often live in environments that feel perpetually unsafe. This repeated exposure to stress locks them into a protective state, making any perceived threat—no matter how small—a potential trigger. This chronic state of hyper-awareness drains their life energy, leaving little room for growth or genuine healing.

Some may bury their trauma and channel the unresolved energy into achieving external success, using it as a fuel source to conquer material goals. However, when driven by avoidance, these accomplishments do not lead to true inner peace. The weight of unprocessed trauma continues to drain energy, even when it is redirected toward success.

Healing requires us to confront our trauma, understand its roots, and integrate its lessons. Only then can we move beyond survival mode and step into a life of purpose, connection, and fulfilment.

The Decision of Trauma

The most crucial step in healing from trauma is making a decision—a decision about how you will let it shape your future. Traumatic experiences create powerful memories, often stronger and more vivid than the events themselves. Science now shows that memories are inherently flawed and change each time we recall them. This means that when you replay traumatic memories repeatedly, particularly with an intense emotional charge, they may become increasingly distorted and more painful over time.

When you find yourSelf stuck in this replay—trapped in the trauma loop—you are caught in victim mode. There is no denying the reality of what you endured or the challenge of coping with it. That is not up for debate. However, there comes a point when you must decide: **How long do you want to stay here?**

> There comes a time when you must decide: How long do you want to stay here?

Staying in victim mode means remaining stuck in the ego's desire to use trauma as a justification for not becoming your true Self. The ego will convince you to hold on to the pain, to let it define you. This state is fundamentally different from Self-isolation, which can be a healing, introspective process. Self-isolation, when chosen consciously, allows you to connect with your true Self and reflect on your path forward. It is an intentional retreat to integrate new truths, align with your Soul, and prepare for the next steps in your evolution.

Victim mode, on the other hand, keeps you in a state of powerlessness. While it is completely valid to take time to process and heal, it is equally important to make the choice to move forward when you are ready. Acknowledge your pain, but do not allow it to be the sole narrative of your life.

Summary

Why have I dedicated an entire chapter to trauma in this guidance book? Because trauma, if left unaddressed, can profoundly impact your life, making it feel as though you are merely existing rather than truly living. Trapped trauma acts as a block to healing, hindering your growth and draining your energy. Confronting your own trauma can be daunting—so daunting that many people go through life without ever truly facing it. But, if you can be brave enough to look, there is something to find in it. Life can be beautiful again.

A little thought... ★

I spent years striving for perfection in every area of my life, believing that if I just accomplished enough, I could bypass what I was avoiding. I became skilled at avoiding the one thing that truly needed attention. It didn't matter how well I excelled in any other aspects; until I addressed the root of my suffering, I remained separate from what I was seeking. Addressing trauma is undoubtedly the most critical key to personal growth. It is also the one that is avoided by most, and it is not easy. Letting go of trauma releases the heaviest anchor holding you down and allows you to explore the realms of freedom that you have been longing for.

Are there trauma(s) that you can identify are holding you down? What would it feel like to release them and live life without their restraint? Is this something you are wanting to explore further?

Exercise

This is a promise to yourSelf to establish and keep your top three values. These are the most important principles that you will live your life by, from this moment onwards. What matters to you more than anything, at your very core? Not what is expected, but what really matters to you? This could be a word, a description of your purpose, anything. Give a little explanation if you can. For example, one may be *"Integrity; I promise to always act with integrity towards mySelf and my truth, no matter how challenging the situation may be"*.

What are your three most important core values that you will always honour?

	Core Value
1	
2	
3	

A little thought... ★

I have been looking through my notes, and came across this little thought that I had wanted to remember. A pure moment, captured in pencil and paper! — *"This feeling. I want you to remember this feeling… so calm, so safe. Here is where you really know who you are. This feeling of just being, with no need for anything else. I feel in every cell of my body that everything is alright, and everything will be alright, always. FYI - You've found this by slowing down, and actually stopping for a while, giving yourself what you know you need. And this is also how you get back here."*

Are there any moments that you can recall where you have had a feeling like this where everything became so simple and clear to you? Think about when this was? What helped you to find this feeling?

SUMMARY of The Guiding Star System sections:

FUEL is the feeding, nourishing, and addition of energy to our multi-dimensional being—body, mind, and Soul. It encompasses the transference and transformation of energy into forms we can use to sustain and elevate our human experience.

MOVEMENT is the flow of energy across all dimensions of our being. It represents the actions that generate change in ourselves and our lives—promoting progress and evolution. Movement also influences the frequency of the fuel we seek and the rest we require. It invites us to surrender to external movement beyond our control.

REST is the restoration and slowing of energy within us — including redirection, reallocation, and surrender. Sleep and rest. Introspection and quiet. Peace and rediscovery. Recharging and replenishing of body, mind, and Soul.

OUT is the reflection of our energy allocation and focus. The mirror of our consciousness. The physical canvas on which we paint our lives. It is the visible and physical expression of our relationship to Self and Soul. The embodiment of authenticity and integrity. This is the outside world, the physical.

IN is the direction of our energy, the decision, control, and allocation of our creative Soul power energy. Self. Soul. Our truth, the only truth. Knowing. Being.

Fuel

FUEL is the feeding, nourishing, and addition of energy to our multi-dimensional being—body, mind, and Soul. It encompasses the transference and transformation of energy into forms we can use to sustain and elevate our human experience.

As you move through this chapter, keep reflecting on how each different fuel source we mention feeds your body, mind, and Soul. Some may nourish only one part; others may nourish all three. We are energetic beings, made entirely of energy. The quality of the fuel we consume directly influences the quality of the energetic frequency we bring into life.

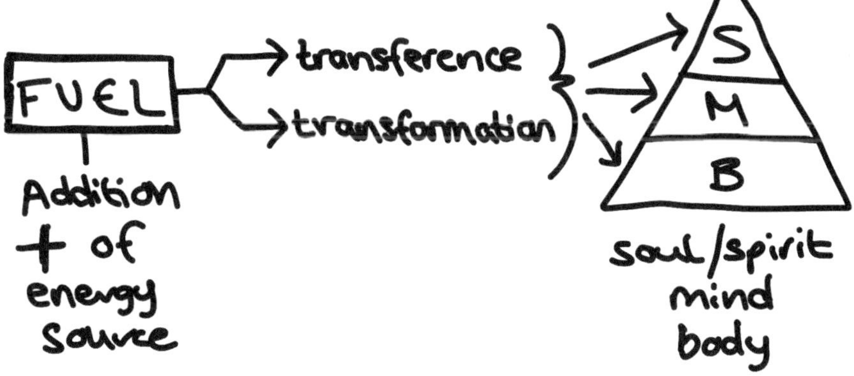

Water as Fuel

Water is a fascinating and vital element. It is the only substance that exists naturally in three states—liquid, solid, and gas—and makes up over 70% of our body. Even more impressively, around 90% of our brain is water. Throughout history, cultures have revered water, recognising it as a carrier of energy, purity, and memory—seen in concepts like "holy water." Although some may regard these ideas as mystical, modern studies now support the idea that water has memory. Each water particle has both a positive and a negative side, allowing them to connect end-to-end, like holding hands in a chain. These chains form circular structures, at the centre of which exists not matter, but an electromagnetic frequency. It is hypothesised that these centres are "coherent domains" that allow water to store memory and information.

Earth's water is continuously regenerated. Rainfall gathers energetic charge from the Sun and atmosphere, and as it falls to the Earth, it collects minerals from forests and rocks. Water's vitality, or energetic quality, depends on its movement. In nature, water spirals and flows dynamically, following a natural, living rhythm. Yet, treated tap water—exposed to straight pipes, chemicals, and stagnation—loses much of its energetic frequency and vitality.

According to Dr. Konstantin Korotkov's GDV bioelectrography measurements, untouched water collected from a tepui summit in Venezuela was reported to be over 40,000 times more "energetically active" than average tap water. Consuming or even contacting this water led to measurable increases in individuals' electromagnetic fields (auras). Whilst this is an observation not yet replicated in peer-reviewed research, it is consistent with indigenous traditions that call these mountains the "Houses of the Gods."

Water's energy can also be observed visually. When frozen, water forms crystals. Water crystals from natural sources and living water forms have hexagonal shapes, symmetry, and beautiful crystals. They are naturally beautiful to look at, and look happy, healthy, and vibrant. In contrast, treated and stagnant water forms deformed, unhealthy-looking, asymmetrical crystals.

Japanese researcher Masaru Emoto conducted experiments exposing water to different words, images, and music before freezing it. His findings suggested that water exposed to positive intentions formed beautiful, structured crystals, while negative exposure resulted in distorted forms. Emoto claims that human consciousness can affect the molecular structure of water, so whilst his own intentions may have affected the results of the experiment, either way, this reveals the possibility of something incredible: that water is incredibly sensitive to the energy and consciousness around it, and that it retains this energy as information within it.

You can try a simple experiment yourSelf: place a small sample of water over a photo, word, or symbol for a minimum of 30 seconds. Then freeze it and observe the crystal shapes that form. The resulting structures often reflect the energy or meaning of what they were exposed to.

Luc Montagnier, Nobel Prize-winning scientist, has dedicated much of his later life to studying water's properties. He believes that the possibility of understanding the frequencies and properties of water within us, and how to manipulate that, could totally revolutionise medicine and healthcare as we know it. He has already concluded that water can retain memory even after multiple dilutions of the original substance, and we wait to see where his research goes from here.

Viktor Schauberger, an Austrian inventor, advocated for the consumption of spring water, untouched by human processing. But for when this wasn't possible, Schauberger designed vortex devices that bring back the life force energy to our water. The vortex mimics the natural spiral movement of water, as all nature works in spirals. The vortex at the centre of the spiral brings the energy of the movement back within itself. When applied to water, it brings life energy back to your water and back to you.

Ancient civilisations seemed to understand this wisdom. They built magnificent fountains, where the dynamic flow of water was believed to amplify its energy, changing the molecular structure of the water and the information that it holds.

This ancient knowledge was behind the use of water to cleanse and heal a person energetically.

How to Use This Knowledge to Increase Your Frequency:

With the knowledge that water is a living entity, and our bodies are primarily water, the way we handle and consume water directly influences our own vitality. Here is a simple three-step method:

1. **Purification** - Purify water back to its natural state, free from chemicals and additives. The best method for this is distillation, ensuring that only pure water remains.

2. **Revitalisation** - After purifying water, revitalise it by reintroducing energetic movement. Use a vortex device, or create a natural spiral manually (you can find DIY vortex guides online). Nature moves in spirals, and spiralling water recharges and reawakens its vitality.

I also add some natural mineral salts to my drinking water to replenish any minerals that have been lost and to aid in my rehydration.

3. **Encoding** - Water is highly receptive to energy. Store your water in glass containers—clear or coloured glass (the frequency of colours will be discussed later). Place the containers on the ground outside for 24-48 hours to absorb Sunlight and moonlight.

Speak positive affirmations, love, and light into the water. Play high-frequency music nearby. You can also meditate with your water, visualising it becoming vibrant and charged.

"Water should be treated like a living being. We are made up of it, and we consume it ... and it unites living beings."

Food as Fuel

We are taught how to eat by our caregivers at a young age, usually based on the eating habits passed down through generations. These habits are deeply rooted in culture and society. For example, in parts of Europe, it is considered rude not to finish everything on your plate, whereas in Japan, it is considered rude *to* finish everything. Eating habits, whilst inherited, are something we can consciously evaluate to maximise our energy.

Food is the most commonly utilised source of fuel for humans. You can often feel the effects of your food choices in your physical body, and whether what you have eaten either nourished you or drained you. Digesting food requires energy, so if you are consuming foods that lack true nourishment, the act of eating itself can drain you. These *false foods* temporarily make you feel full or energised but ultimately deplete your system. This means that food can either add to your energy, or take from your energy.

Reflecting honestly on your eating habits is a challenge to the ego. It requires putting aside long-held beliefs and questioning the truth of them. It is one of the quickest and most effective ways to create immediate improvements in how you feel on a daily basis, and is a great first place to start on your journey to becoming all that you want to be.

How do we approach this? With so much confusion and contradiction in the world of nutrition, it is important to return to something universal: *life energy*. While every human body is unique, all living things share the vital force of life energy. Our task is to fuel and flourish that life force as much as possible. Among all the contradictory diets and advice, one core principle holds true: *eat natural, eat simple, and listen to your body* – "natural" meaning foods as close to their original state as possible.

A little thought… ★

One of the biggest personal challenges I faced was the link between food, money, and waste. I was conditioned to believe that leaving food was wasteful and disrespectful. The result for me was that when I did eat, I often overate. This added further stress to my body. Through conscious work, I was able to identify and challenge these belief systems. Fasting taught me that missing meals would not harm me, and gradually, my nervous system relaxed into new beliefs. There is no longer a need to overconsume. I now approach food with far greater balance and peace.

What is your relationship with food? How do you find your balance? Where do you feel any imbalance may come from? Is there anything that you would like to change?

Intuitive Eating

Intuitive eating is about quietening external noise and tuning into your body's true needs. Technically, you can eat whatever you feel drawn to, as long as it stems from true intuition and not from cravings, emotional coping, or ego-driven desires. Paul McKenna, the renowned hypnotist, popularised a similar concept in his book *Think YourSelf Thin*. His method was not about restriction, but was about awareness. The key rules were simple; eat only when you are physically hungry, eat with full awareness—no TV or phone distractions, chew every mouthful thoroughly (around 20 times), and stop eating as soon as you are no longer hungry, even if food remains.

This approach removes *fear* around food—the fear of scarcity, the fear of deprivation. When you know you can eat again whenever you are genuinely hungry, there is no pressure to finish everything on your plate. This method highlights a crucial point: much of our dysfunctional eating stems from a deep-seated, unconscious fear around survival—a relic from times when food was uncertain.

Food as an Addiction

Food is also one of the most common—and most undiagnosed—addictions. Because we all eat daily, unhealthy eating patterns can easily be masked or normalised. Yet, what we eat and how much we eat dramatically affect our hormones, moods, and overall well-being. Addressing food addiction is complex, as unlike other addictions, you cannot simply eliminate food altogether. Comparing this to an alcohol addiction, it is like asking an alcoholic to visit a bar daily and only have *one* drink. Food addiction often masks deeper emotional wounds or unhealed trauma, so tackling it requires the willingness to confront and heal what the addiction is protecting or numbing.

A little thought...

When I first began intuitive eating, I would start with a short meditation to determine whether I was truly hungry, whether I was actually thirsty, or what exactly my body was asking for. At first, it was difficult to distinguish between genuine needs and cravings; if your intuition tells you to eat three chocolate bars every evening, it's likely not intuition! With practice, it became easier. Learning to listen to your body is a powerful, transformational skill. Sometimes this means facing unexpected desires: After not eating meat for years, I suddenly developed a strong craving for steak. Initially, I resisted, but after many times of this intuitive nudge, I sourced the highest quality, ethically-raised meat I could find, and consumed it with full awareness and gratitude.

Do you listen to your intuition regarding your food? Do you believe that your body has the intelligence to guide you as to what it needs?

The Consciousness of Food

When considering the consciousness of food, all plants and animals contain a consciousness, which we need to transfer or transform into energy. Energy is a form of information, and this information becomes a part of who we are; hence the phrase "you are what you eat".

When considering this, it highlights the importance of eating the best and most vital sources of food, whether derived from plants, or animals, or both. Many have considered their own personal views on consuming animals. However, the consciousness of plants is less understood. Plants may not have a nervous system, but research suggest that some can energetically *sense* harm. They can anticipate injury, and have an innate desire to survive, which may cause them suffering.

As humans, we are consuming forms of consciousness continually. Our survival depends on it. How we choose to consciously fuel ourselves is a very individual decision, one which will take an alignment with our own personal truth. What you fuel yourSelf with, you take on energetically, to become a part of you. This knowledge can help you decide what is best for you, ongoing.

We are not yet advanced enough to fully understand the consciousness of the life forms we consume, and all food sources come with advantages and disadvantages. They are all *impure* sources of energy in the way that they require our energy in order to break them down and digest them, although some less than others. Ancient civilisations possessed knowledge of energy systems far beyond our current understanding. Many ancient structures—aligned with the stars, Sun, and moon—are believed to have had power-generating properties, tapping into cosmic energies to charge our energetic frequencies and fuel us, leaving less requirement on the consumption of food. This would offer a level of energising that far surpasses any other form of fuel in terms of its transfer and transformation of energy, as it is much purer and more available.

Until we reclaim this level of understanding, we remain reliant on the Earth's circle of life—plants, animals, fungi—to sustain us. In the meantime, we can answer only to ourselves and our own truth. And pick the very best sources of food that we can.

A little thought... ★

We are put on this Earth fully reliant on the gifts of the Earth to nourish our bodies. Our option is to consciously choose the highest quality forms of fuel available to us—those that best support our frequency, vitality, and connection to life. We take in energy from this, and we choose how we spend it. When we spend our energy authentically, we not only elevate our own frequency but we raise the collective frequency of consciousness; like raising the water level of a lake—every boat is lifted. In living authentically, in choosing our fuels consciously, we become part of the cycle of giving back as we receive.

Are you conscious of the fuels that you use for your body? Are you aware of the energy that you take on from them? How do you most love spending your energy, in a way that also gives back?

The Adaptability of the Human Body

The human body is an extraordinary and intelligent organism, constantly working and adapting in remarkable ways to ensure our survival. This adaptability includes the body's ability to utilise different foods it is given as fuel. The food we are fed during childhood, as our bodies are growing and developing, becomes our *default* or *original* food source. This does not mean that it is the healthiest option; it simply reflects what the body has adapted to using. Because of this, when making changes to our diet, we must proceed gradually, even if the changes are toward much healthier, higher-frequency foods. Shifting too rapidly can shock the body, placing it into a state of stress or survival mode. From birth through puberty, our bodies are incredibly malleable, adapting to the circumstances we are given. As we age, we must listen more carefully to our body's evolving needs. Change is possible at any age—but it must be approached with patience and respect for the body's natural intelligence.

15-Year Purification

Linda Goodman, in her inspiring book *The Forgotten Codes of the Universe*, shares an ancient Hatha Yogi teaching: a 15-year purification process achieved through gradual reduction of food groups, allowing the body to adapt without distressing it. The cycles are as follows:

- **First five years:** Eliminate red meat.
- **Second five years:** Eliminate white meat, fish, and eggs.
- **Third five years:** Eliminate all underground vegetables and dairy.
- **Fourth five years:** Transition to a fruitarian diet, focused on fruits, tomatoes, and nuts, with occasional bread and cereals as needed.

Throughout the entire process, one day per week is dedicated solely to consuming fruit and fruit juices—both known for their cleansing and restorative properties. This practice not only detoxifies the body but also retrains it to use fruits as a primary energy source. The more efficiently your body can transfer and transform energy from food, the less food it requires.

The purification of your body allows it to work at its best and most efficiently. If you are reading this and are drawn to enhancing the purification of the body over the long term, this may be a good place to start. This is no quick-fix diet, and it will become a way of life if it is something that you choose.

A little thought... ★

In ancient times, once the body was properly purified over many years, it was possible to become a *waterarian* or even a *breatharian*, gaining fuel from pure water, fresh air, and minimal food. This is where sources of fuel other than food are prioritised and maximised in order to provide energy by charging our cells. Today, with the pollutants and chemicals in our environment, this might seem impossible—but as I write this, I am sitting in Cripple Creek, Colorado, at 10,000 feet elevation, surrounded by pure mountain air and fresh spring water; so perhaps it is still within reach, in some places!

Have a think about how you purify your body? Do you do anything currently? Are you drawn to advancing your purification, and if so, which suggestions appeal to you?

Understanding the Filtration System

I once believed that the body would simply take what it needed from any food or supplement and eliminate the rest without issue. This was a belief that the body would act as a filter for whatever I put in it. In reality, the body's filtration and detoxification processes require a significant amount of energy. The filtration systems of the body—primarily the liver, kidneys, and lymphatic system—are extraordinary in their efficiency, but can be overburdened and get backed up. Especially over time. The more work you save your body by providing clean, high-frequency fuel, the less energy you require from filtering it, leaving you more energy for healing, growth, and higher-level functioning. Fruits and vegetables, in their natural forms, come with built-in filtration and energy transformation systems. Consuming them allows you to inherit their filtered energy directly, with minimal effort required by your own body.

Absorption

True nourishment comes from what the body can absorb—not just what it consumes. The body readily absorbs substances that are natural and aligned with its own biological structure. You cannot cheat your body with artificial shortcuts; your intelligent body knows the difference. The purer your body and your fuel sources, the higher the level of absorption and the smoother the energy transference within you.

Absorption is also influenced by stomach acid, which is designed to both break down food and destroy harmful bacteria. To preserve stomach acid strength, it is important not to consume excessive liquids during meals, as this dilutes the acid and hampers digestion. Natural foods, especially fruits and vegetables, are rich in both nutrients and water, making them particularly easy for the body to *transfer* and *transform* into energy.

The Power of Soil

The soil in which our food grows greatly impacts its energetic and nutritional quality. Modern mass-farming methods have overworked the soil, depleting its minerals and vitality. Chemical sprays and artificial growth methods further lower the frequency of the food produced today. In contrast, 100 years ago, food grown organically by farmers who cared for the Earth, contained significantly higher nutrient density and life force. Organic food today may appear more expensive—but when you consider its vastly superior energetic and nutritional value, it is actually a much greater investment in your health and vitality. Nothing beats growing your own food, fed from your local soil, with your own love and care, but if that is not currently possible, then sourcing organic food and taking high-quality natural supplements, is the next best thing.

The Alkaline Diet

An alkaline diet honours the original sources of food that the human body was naturally designed to thrive on, before hunting. These teachings, championed by healers like Dr. Sebi and Yada the Awakening, centre on consuming seeded fruits and alkaline plants in their original, unaltered form. This means from when before man started to alter them to make the manufacturing process easier or more profitable, including the cross breeding of fruits and vegetables and scientific intervention. Alkaline foods, sometimes referred to as "God-made foods" or "source foods," are naturally high-frequency, and the fruits produce seeds and therefore can reproduce. This is beautiful high-frequency energy to *transfer* and *transform* into the human body. Today, many common fruits and vegetables have been selectively bred for appearance, sweetness, and convenience, often at the expense of their original qualities and frequencies. Seedless grapes, oversized bananas, uniform supermarket apples—these are products of human intervention, not nature.

When you taste naturally grown fruits, you experience a different quality—stronger, purer, and less artificially sweet. Eating alkaline, original-source foods raises your energetic frequency and brings you closer to natural vitality, you are feeding yourSelf on an energetic level. It is entirely possible to seek out and include more of these foods in your life, reclaiming the energetic integrity of your diet.

A little thought… ★

When I travel to a country that has original source fruit, grown and ripened naturally in the Sunshine, it tastes so different. As I write this, I am currently in the Gold Coast of Australia; the bananas are smaller, as they originally were, and they have black seeds inside them. All of the fruit and vegetables are Sun-ripened and juicy. Everything in the grocers just tastes so much more "full of life"! Also, the fruit doesn't taste too sweet, but remains so full of flavour and colour. I would love to be able to eat like this every day.

Do you taste the difference in this type of quality fuel? Do you have regular access to food that makes you feel like this? And if not, how can you make it a part of your life?

Know Your Food

Where does your food come from? When you begin to understand the energetic frequency of what you consume, you can harness it as a form of energetic input. Consider the difference between eating plants grown organically and ripened by natural Sunlight versus those cultivated with chemicals under artificial light. The growth process and treatment of anything you put into your body will directly affect your energy systems.

If you choose to eat meat, reflect on the contrast between consuming meat from animals that have been artificially inseminated, pumped with antibiotics, and raised in confined, industrial conditions—versus animals that were free-range, organically raised, and naturally conceived. The energy and life force of the animal at the time of its death also matter. There is a significant energetic difference between an animal that dies in a state of terror within an abattoir and one that is hunted in the wild.

As a society, we have become disconnected from the origins of our food. We once grew and raised our own food; now we often have no relationship with it at all. Whatever your choices around food, let them be rooted in your core values and integrity. Many people avoid examining their beliefs around food because doing so requires deep Self-reflection—and that is rarely easy. I am not advocating for perfection, nor suggesting everyone must grow their own food. But cultivating awareness and making conscious changes, however small, can create profound shifts in your energy, health, and make an incredible difference to your body, energy and life.

"You are what you eat"- this is true for us as well as our food source... What did that apple fuel itself with? Know what you are putting in your body.

Know Your Body

Throughout your life, your relationship with food will evolve. The way you nourish yourSelf will shift in alignment with your body's changes, your learning, your emotional landscape, and your level of Spiritual awareness. We can only live in the present moment, and the right way to eat for you will vary depending on your life and your needs at any given time.

There is no one-size-fits-all approach. Yes, some principles apply universally—such as avoiding processed junk foods—but the deeper optimisation of your physical body through food also requires you to consider your mental, emotional, and energetic states. It asks you to assess your knowledge versus your inner knowing. To reflect on whether your needs are physical or arising from something subtler.

An example of this will be during periods of deep emotional growth, ego death, or Spiritual upheaval, where you may be called to nourish yourSelf differently. Certain foods may support the emotional or energetic layers of your experience—even if they are not typically considered "healthy." Instead, certain foods, textures, or even temperatures may hold an energetic resonance that supports you in moving through those layers of transformation. A warm grounding stew might soothe during grief, while light fruits and fresh herbs may feel expansive during times of clarity and renewal.

The key lies in cultivating awareness. Truly knowing yourSelf means recognising how your body, mind, and Soul work together in cycles and rhythms, and listening not only to physical cravings but to the deeper energetic messages behind them. Sometimes the craving is for comfort, sometimes for strength, sometimes for release. By honouring these subtly inner cycles, you transform food from mere fuel into a sacred ally.

When you approach nourishment with this depth and honesty, a meal becomes medicine, frequency, and guidance. It can ground you when you are unravelling, lift you when you are heavy, and energise you when you are ready to expand. This is the essence of eating in alignment with the Self: to allow food to participate in your journey of transformation, rather than to control or restrict it.

A little thought...

Learning how to fuel my body correctly has been a deeply personal and often challenging journey. Years ago, I committed to a vegan diet, and at the time, my reasons were many and meaningful. However, I have a natural tendency to be ungrounded, always running around and busy. This disconnection contributed to multiple episodes of adrenal fatigue. I had been operating on adrenaline, which was further fuelled by adrenaline-inducing foods. Eventually, this caught up with me. Over time, I became familiar with the signs of this imbalance. At its core, it reflected a deeper denial of emotional processing that I had not yet faced. Through inner work and healing, I have cultivated greater Self-awareness. I now understand that maintaining balance is a lifelong commitment. And to help me in keeping this balance, I have chosen to reintroduce meat into my diet. My body craves it, and I feel a marked improvement when I honour that call. In the past, I was plagued by guilt, shame, and inner conflict—sometimes just from the thought of eating meat, let alone acting on it. Today, I understand that this practice supports my physical body in a way that is specific to my own needs and current stage of development. I also trust that as I evolve and master my internal balance more fully, this requirement may fall away.

Herbs

Herbs have been revered across many thousands of years for their profound energetic and medicinal properties. From the temples of Egypt to the healing sanctuaries of Greece, and through the vast, intricate systems of Traditional Chinese Medicine and Ayurveda, herbal wisdom has long been understood as a bridge between the natural world and human healing. To the ancients, plants were not just physical remedies—they were living beings carrying unique energetic signatures, each with its own Spirit, vibration, and purpose, to fuel us in the exact way that we needed it.

Every herb contains a concentrated energetic imprint—its own special properties, shaped by the soil it grew in, the climate it endured, and the cycles of the Sun and moon it absorbed. The subtle, intelligent energies of herbs work on multiple levels: physical, emotional, mental, and Spiritual.

Herbs can be used in a variety of forms: tinctures, teas, salves, essential oils, infusions, and even energetic preparations such as flower essences. One of their gifts is that many retain their beneficial properties when boiled, making herbal teas an accessible and powerful way to extract and deliver their healing essence. In traditional societies, herbalists understood that the body's needs were never separate from the mind or the Soul. Those once labelled *witch doctors* or *wise women* held deep, intuitive knowledge of how to match the right plant to the right person—prescribing not only for physical symptoms but for energetic misalignments, emotional blockages, and Spiritual disharmony. What a way to support your fuel system!

Herbs invite us to slow down and re-enter a reciprocal relationship with nature—one in which we listen as much as we harvest. Whether you feel drawn to work with a handful of simple kitchen herbs or to study ancient pharmacopoeias in depth, this is a path that strengthens both intuition and connection. There are many excellent books, teachers, and courses on this subject, and if it resonates with you, I encourage you to follow that calling.

A little thought... ★

I love sourcing herbs and food from local farmers' markets and supporting small-scale, sustainable producers. Seasonal eating is designed to support our innate cyclical nature—not only supporting the body's energy, but also bringing variety, freshness, and greater vitality into your meals. Subscription boxes for organic seasonal local produce can be a beautiful way to introduce yourSelf to new ingredients and reconnect with what the land is offering in real time. I've discovered so many new plant varieties this way—and the learning process has been joyful and nourishing, and the few odd dishes have at least given an experience!

Do you ever use herbs in your cooking? Are there particular ones that you are drawn to or use regularly? How can you expand on this for your benefit?

The Input and Output of Energy from Food

The food you consume will either provide you with energy and vitality, or it will act as a drain. This is the true measure of whether something is beneficial for you. While humans share many similarities, each body is unique. What energises one person may not suit another. Your body is the most amazing equipment. If you listen to it, your body will tell you what it needs and when it needs it. Take care of it and, in return, it will take care of you.

Some Food Guidance

Understanding that everything you consume carries energy, and that you are taking that energy into *your* system, is a foundational truth. The key is learning to determine what works best for *you*. When you find foods that nourish you and support your energy, that is a powerful step forward. Your body will learn to thrive from quality inputs, creating beneficial long-term effects on your health and vitality.

Here are some practical, easy-to-follow principles for fuelling your body with food:

1. **Educate yourSelf.** Become aware of what you're eating and what is truly good for you. The landscape of food has changed drastically in the past 50–100 years. Know your sources and make informed choices.
2. **Make changes gradually.** Don't shock your body. Allow it time to adapt. Work with it, not against it, and learn to listen throughout the process.
3. **Eat unprocessed foods** in their natural, whole form. (Non-GMO, organic).
4. **Include a variety of raw, alkaline, organic plants**—with a full spectrum of colours to provide diverse nutrients and energies.
5. **Keep your meals small.** A good rule is to eat until 80% full, and that no meal should be larger than your two fists combined.
6. **Eat an organic apple a day, including the seeds.**
7. **Cut out or minimise sugar and alcohol.** Every major dietary philosophy agrees on this point.
8. **Embrace good fats.** They support energy, brain function, and cellular health.
9. **Grow your own food** as much as possible. Even small efforts reconnect you to the source of your nourishment.
10. **Have one day a week** where you consume only fruit or drink pure, fresh fruit juice—stored only in glass.
11. **Seeded grapes and key limes** are among the most cleansing and healing foods. Consume them often and with gratitude.
12. **Enjoy your food**, but stay mindful of the line between enjoyment and dependency or addiction.
13. **Natural minerals are magic!** Sea moss, shilajit, and high-quality mineral salt are excellent sources.
14. **Support your nutrition** with high-quality supplements, herbs, and fresh juices.
15. **Purification can transform your life,** but your internal world must be ready to receive it.
16. **Do your best, and let go of perfection.** It does not exist. Treat yourSelf occasionally, and when you do, enjoy it fully.
17. **Listen to your body.** It is always communicating with you—learn to hear what it's really saying.

As Linda Goodman beautifully said; *"Never forget that what you eat and what you think is what you are. The food taken into your body is what gradually... slowly, but surely... forms your thought patterns. And your thoughts, both conscious and subconscious, are in absolute control of your body's health or lack of it."*

Food is not just nourishment—it is *fuel.* It is a form of energy that we consume multiple times a day, and it plays a central role in shaping our overall frequency. The food you choose determines what energy your body takes on, what your cells use to function, and ultimately, what you become. The process is one of transference and transformation.

A little thought... ★

I have found, in my own journey, that when something doesn't feel right—whether in your body or your life—you are naturally drawn to one of the key areas we explore in this book. That first area of focus often becomes the gateway to awareness, and ultimately, to personal responsibility. For me, it began with food and nutrition. It was the first path I was called to explore in order to heal. I could clearly see the connection between fuelling my body with the right nourishment and enabling it to function optimally. I understood that when I gave my body what it truly needed, it could respond with greater energy, clarity, and vitality. That was a great starting point for my conscious journey—and it might be the place to start or continue yours too?

Air as Fuel

Of all the elements the human body depends on, air is the most vital. It is the fuel source we require most frequently—we can survive without food or water far longer than we can without breath. Oxygen enters the body through the lungs and is transferred into the bloodstream, where it is pumped throughout the entire body. It fuels countless biological processes and systems, supplying the energy we need to live, move, and think. During physical activity, our demand for oxygen increases as our energy output rises. Have you noticed that you are not hungry when exercising? That's because your body is using oxygen as its dominant fuel source in that moment, shifting its energetic needs.

It is not just the use of the oxygen that makes a difference, but also how we take it into our bodies that can make all the difference. Humans can breathe through both the nose and the mouth, but nasal breathing provides distinct benefits. It filters, humidifies, and regulates the flow of air, and it significantly increases nitric oxide production—enhancing the body's ability to absorb oxygen. Nasal breathing calms the nervous system, supporting vagal nerve health and improving heart rate variability (HRV), a key marker for stress resilience and emotional well-being. In contrast, mouth breathing—especially when triggered by shock—activates the sympathetic nervous system and the fight-or-flight response. Nasal breathing, on the other hand, supports a parasympathetic state, which promotes calm, digestion, and healing. Training yourSelf to nasal breathe during exercise is powerful. Start by walking in nature while consciously breathing through your nose, gradually increasing intensity over time. You can even train yourSelf to nasal breathe during sleep by gently taping your mouth at night.

Fresh Air

The air we breathe, when sourced from fresh and pure environments, carries a heightened energetic frequency and greater potency in both transference and transformation. It fuels not just the body, but the energy systems of our entire being. Florence Nightingale, an early pioneer of holistic healing, recognised the importance of fresh air in recovery and well-being. She once stated, *"It is the unqualified result of all my experience with the sick, that second only to their need of fresh air is their need of light."*

Clean, fresh air is charged with life force energy—the same energy we have explored throughout this book, and the same energy that flows within us. It is a natural gift from Mother Earth, designed to sustain and nurture us. Breathing pure air not only increases our energetic intake, but it also improves the detoxification capacity of the lungs. When air is clean, the lungs don't need to filter through as many pollutants, and can more effectively release what no longer serves the body.

Fresh air is best received through the nose. The nose, which also houses our sense of smell, is finely attuned to detect the presence or absence of purity in the air. Truly fresh air has no scent—any noticeable odour often signals the presence of something foreign. This is another way our bodies intuitively help us navigate what supports us and what does not. Air pollution is a growing issue, especially in urban environments, and is closely linked to rising respiratory ailments. The quality of the air you breathe is part of the environment you choose to live in—and changing it, even in small ways, can significantly affect your health and well-being.

Breathing is not unique to humans. Trees, too, breathe—and in doing so, they mirror and support our own respiration. We are in a symbiotic relationship with them: we exhale what they need, and they exhale what we need. Through the process of photosynthesis, trees draw in Sunlight, carbon dioxide, and water, and transform them into sugar for fuel, releasing oxygen as a by-product. This exchange is a perfect example of Earth's harmonious design.

Beyond oxygen, air also carries life force energy and serves as a conductor of electromagnetic frequencies. This energy is primarily charged by the Sun, but also by the Moon and planets. Air has the extraordinary ability to carry multiple frequencies at once, keeping them distinct—just as different radio stations travel through the same airwaves, without merging. This quality helps explain its broader Spiritual symbolism; it is the element of communication, the pathway for sound waves and signals. It connects all living beings—humans, animals, plants, and ecosystems—and links us to the broader energies of the cosmos. Air is what unites us. And like many of the most powerful forces in life, it often goes unnoticed—hidden in plain sight. There is a beautiful paradox in this: that something so essential, so constant, and so energetically potent, is also so subtle. This is the mystery and magic of air—its esoteric simplicity, and its invitation to deeper awareness.

When you learn to harness breath as a source of energy, you can direct that energy intentionally. Your body's inner intelligence will guide you to where it is most needed—whether physical, emotional, or energetic. Breath becomes a sacred ally in healing, integration, and expansion. Through conscious breathing, you can strengthen your connection to the Self, access higher states of consciousness, and explore the infinite realms of the subconscious. It supports the mind, the body, and the Soul—bridging the seen and unseen, the known and the unknown.

> **A little thought... ★**
>
> To optimise your environment, introduce more plants into your home—especially varieties renowned for their ability to purify and revitalise the air. Spider plants, snake plants, and English ivy are particularly effective, though almost any healthy green plant will contribute to your well-being. These living beings are not merely decorative; they are active participants in your environment, constantly working to cleanse toxins from the air, release oxygen, and harmonise the subtle energies of your space. Plants have their own frequency, and their presence can subtly elevate the vibration of the energy in your home.
>
> Do you have plants in your home? How do they elevate the energy of your home space? Are you planning to expand your plant family?!

Breatharianism

Breatharianism is a great example of the utilisation of air being maximised as a fuel source. This is the belief that the life force energy of the air can fuel and nourish a person, so that food can be dramatically reduced or eliminated. I am not suggesting this at the extreme, but the following examples illustrate some of the incredible possibilities from expanding our awareness of the power of the breath.

Elitom El-Amin is a breatharian who lives on very little—if any—food. Raised in Ohio on the standard American diet, he once consumed excessive portions and frequent meals. His transition to breatharianism was gradual, beginning with the elimination of meat and heavy foods, which noticeably improved his health and energy. He then adopted weekly fasting, increased physical movement, and began meditating regularly. Eventually, he reduced his food intake to one meal per day—

80% raw—and ultimately to just once every other weekend. Elitom credits meditation and connection to breath as the core of his transformation. He believes breatharianism is not something to be forced, but a natural step that arises as consciousness expands. Living primarily on breath, he describes himself as operating from a higher frequency—where food and drink would only reduce that vibration. More than two decades into this lifestyle, he remains healthy, vibrant, and thriving—challenging the limits of modern scientific understanding.

Another powerful figure in this realm is Devon, known as *The Black Airbender*, who also lives a breatharian lifestyle. Drawing energy from the air—of which he particularly credits gases like nitrogen and carbon—Devon utilises nasal breathing, ancient scalar technologies, and breath-based movement. I had the privilege of experiencing a private breathwork session with him in Bali. His presence was so calm and centred. The session included extended breath practices and subtle techniques like *eye breathing*, that left me deeply grounded and energetically uplifted. I loved it!

Breathwork creates an increased oxygenation of the brain, which leads to enhanced mental clarity, focus, and emotional well-being. Studies—such as those by Zaccaro, Piarulli, and Laurino—have shown that reducing breath to fewer than 10 breaths per minute decreases anxiety, depression, and confusion, while increasing calm, alertness, and overall comfort. Breathwork not only boosts oxygen levels; it helps create the internal conditions necessary for healing. Trauma, stored emotion, and incomplete experiences can be processed more efficiently in this elevated, oxygen-rich state. Breathwork practices are rooted in ancient traditions, offering a gateway to transformation. Whether active or passive, breathwork includes a wide range of techniques—from deep, intentional patterns to the simple awareness of breath during meditation. All forms carry power, and I encourage you to explore further if you feel called.

Wim Hof, known as *The Iceman*, is a pioneer in demonstrating the full potential of breath as fuel. He discovered this ability during profound personal trauma, through surrender and deep inner work. By harnessing breath, he has achieved feats once thought impossible, including conscious control over aspects of the autonomic nervous system—previously believed to be entirely involuntary. Under scientific conditions, Wim has shown that humans can override these systems through breath and intention. His practices merge breath, consciousness, and cold exposure to access deeper states of awareness and resilience. Wim's connection to the breath became a lifeline to his Soul—a source of healing and liberation. His journey, from homelessness to global recognition, is a testament to the power of inner alignment and the breath as a sacred tool. Through his teachings, he empowers others to explore these capabilities for themselves—proving they are not unique to him, but accessible to all who seek them.

I give these examples to illustrate the power of air as a fuel source, I am not suggesting the extremes are my recommended prescription for everyone! But awareness of these amazing possibilities expands our awareness and makes us appreciative of something that we likely take for granted on a daily basis. There is such power in the utilisation of the breath.

A little thought...

The autonomic nervous system governs unconscious processes like heart rate, digestion, sexual function, and breathing. It has two main branches: the sympathetic (fight, flight, freeze, and fawn) and the parasympathetic (rest, digest, rejuvenate, and reconnect). The breath is a rare tool that bridges these two systems. It is both automatic and voluntary, making it a powerful point of intervention. Conscious breathing enables us to transition from stress states (sympathetic) into calm and healing states (parasympathetic). After moments of emotional or physical stress, returning to the breath is how we invite balance back into the system.

In cases of trauma, the challenge often lies in the nervous system becoming stuck in a prolonged sympathetic state. When the experience is incomplete or unresolved, the body cannot return to the parasympathetic state of rest, recovery, and safety. This was my reality for many years. I spent so much of my life trapped in this heightened, survival-driven state. In using breathwork, something shifted. Through moments of accessing the parasympathetic nervous system—if only briefly—I was introduced to an entirely different state of being. It was unfamiliar and yet somehow familiar too. As I gradually reintroduced this state into my life, becoming more comfortable with it, it began to feel like a place I did not want to leave.

However, in response to this, I began doing everything in my power to avoid returning to the sympathetic state—it became my new fear. It was a form of Self-protection. I was afraid that if I went back, I wouldn't be able to return to peace again. I had lost not only my sense of Self, but all trust in my ability to protect and guide mySelf. This remains one of my greatest healing edges: to trust that I *can* move into sympathetic states when needed, and also *know* how to bring mySelf back. That it is not a permanent place. That I am no longer helpless within it. When you learn how to consciously engage the parasympathetic nervous system, you gain access to a powerful Self-regulation tool. You learn that this peaceful state is always available to you—and that you can return to it, over and over again. That is real freedom. That is the sovereignty of the nervous system. And for those healing from trauma, it is everything.

Sound as Fuel

Sound is a form of energy, made up of vibration. It moves in waves and travels primarily through air, though it can also pass through liquids and solids. When a soundwave comes into contact with its surrounding medium—whether air, water, or solid matter—it causes that medium to vibrate, enabling the sound to travel. We receive sound into the body via our ears, which act as instruments of vibration transference. The human ear can detect sounds ranging from 20 to 20,000 Hz (hertz)—a measurement of vibrations per second.

Many ancient traditions and Spiritual texts speak of sound as the origin of creation. The Bible tells us that God spoke the world into existence. In Indian belief, the world was Sung into being through three cosmic songs. Hindu mythology references the blowing of the conch shell, initiating the first wave of creation. These all point to the same idea: sound is sacred, and its vibration is a formative force of life itself.

Interestingly, sound travels far faster through water than air—about 1,500 metres per second in water compared to 340 metres per second in air. This is because water has as denser molecular structure. Underwater sound remains mostly underwater, which is why you may not hear much when your head is above the surface. But submerge yourSelf, and the sound becomes amplified. Try it for yourSelf! What's most important is this: **sound alters the frequency of water**. We've already explored how words and vibration affect water's molecular structure—and since our bodies are predominantly water, sound has a profound impact on our physical and energetic states.

Sound can elevate consciousness, restore harmony, and create coherence in the energy systems of the body. One powerful example is the Solfeggio frequencies—also known as the *holy tones* or *God notes*. These frequencies have been used for centuries in Spiritual and healing practices, resonating with the fundamental energetic laws of the universe. They were rediscovered and added to in the 1970s by Dr. Joseph Puleo through a combination of Pythagorean mathematics and biblical numerology. They are known as the Solfeggio scale, and they include nine frequencies:

- **174 Hz** – New: Physical healing, pain relief, comfort
- **285 Hz** – New: Cellular regeneration and immune system support
- **396 Hz** – Liberation from fear, guilt, and ego
- **417 Hz** – Facilitates change, clearing past trauma
- **528 Hz** – Transformation and miracles; DNA repair; stress reduction
- **639 Hz** – Connection and harmony in relationships
- **741 Hz** – Expression of truth, alignment with Soul purpose
- **852 Hz** – Awakening to Spiritual order
- **963 Hz** – New: Activation of the pineal gland and Spiritual awakening

Fascinatingly, all these frequencies reduce to the numerological values of 3, 6, or 9—the sacred numbers referenced by Nikola Tesla—*"If you only knew the magnificence of the 3, 6, and 9, you would have a key to the universe."*

One way to use sound as a tool for energetic alignment is through **binaural beats**—two slightly different frequencies played in each ear. The brain responds by blending them into a third tone, unifying the hemispheres of the brain and often stimulating the pineal gland. This can create coherence in the brain, enhance focus, and deepen Spiritual experience.

In 1983, the CIA conducted experiments with Robert Monroe, who was a pioneer in exploring altered states of consciousness. He headed the Monroe Institute to explore expanded consciousness using **Hemi-Sync** (hemispheric synchronisation) technology. By introducing separate frequencies to each ear, the brain is forced to reconcile the difference, leading to enhanced awareness and access to deeper brainwave states. These methods were once classified but are now publicly accessible and absolutely fascinating, and I invite you to explore more of Monroe's work if this is something that interests you.

When sound is projected into matter, it creates precise geometric patterns—visible evidence of the structure and order that underlies vibration. This phenomenon, often revealed through cymatics (the study of visible sound), demonstrates that sound is not random but inherently intelligent. Every frequency carries a unique blueprint, and when it meets matter, it imprints its design.

Many ancient cultures appear to have recognised this truth. The sacred symbols etched into temple walls, the mandalas in Eastern traditions, and even the geometric patterns in Islamic art may not simply be aesthetic choices, but visual translations of sound frequencies. These images are strikingly similar to cymatic patterns produced today with modern technology. Could it be possible that ancient civilisations encoded their knowledge of sound and vibration into these symbols, preserving them as timeless maps of consciousness and healing?

If so, these sacred codes may serve more than decorative or Spiritual purposes—they may be keys, reminders left for us to remember the language of frequency. Symbols such as the Flower of Life, the Sri Yantra, or labyrinth patterns could be multidimensional scripts, designed to initiate shifts in awareness or align us with higher states of consciousness. When contemplated, meditated upon, or placed in our environment, they may interact with our energy fields—recalibrating us toward harmony, balance, and wholeness.

Sound itself is one of the purest forms of healing. Our cells, organs, and tissues all vibrate at specific frequencies, and when disharmony occurs, it manifests as illness or imbalance. Sound can retune the body, bringing coherence where there is distortion. Sound has always been central to healing traditions. Shamans, for example, use sacred songs—like the **icaros** in Ayahuasca ceremonies—to shift cellular vibration, clear trauma, and guide healing journeys. Sound does not just accompany these ceremonies: it facilitates them. It can lift someone out of a *bad trip*, ground them in their experience, or help them move through what needs to be released.

There is growing interest in using sound frequency in modern healthcare. In Hindu tradition, it is believed that vibrations from a conch shell can kill disease-causing bacteria—a simple but powerful example. At the **Pyramids of Chi** in Ubud, sound healing sessions inside pyramidal structures amplify sound waves, creating deeply immersive healing environments. These sessions, using instruments, bowls, and sacred sounds, have brought transformative results to many participants.

Imagine a future where medical diagnosis includes energetic scanning, and treatments are prescribed in the form of frequency—tailored to each individual's energetic blueprint. Sound may well be a key to *healing*, as well as *vitality*, and potentially even *immortality*.

Music

Music is vibration, emotion, and connection. It has evolved alongside humanity for thousands of years. Ancient cultures used music ceremonially, with purpose and reverence for its healing power. Singing bowls, gongs, chanting "Om" and "Ong", are ancient tools still used in modern sound healing. Today, music still moves us—but it can also influence our energy in ways we may not fully realise. Whether it is the melody, beat, harmony, or lyrics—we each connect with sound in deeply personal ways, and we will connect in a way which is unique to us. We love what we love. Music can be profoundly energising and uplifting to us, and is a relevant fuel source for consideration.

Reggae is a wonderful genre of music to illustrate this. It has been long established for being played at the pace of a resting heartbeat, is said to provide a "heart massage," especially when played through deep sub-bass speakers. The uplifting lyrics further support healing and harmony. And I can confirm, the vibes of reggae parties have always bene good for my Soul!

Even genres like hip-hop are beginning to transform and recognise the power of the frequency that they radiate. Artists like Dee-1 are pioneering an emerging genre that has been given the name "Spiritual rap"—music designed to uplift, educate, and elevate listeners through both sound and lyrical content, whilst retaining the hip-hop styles. He's gaining recognition from major names in the industry, and this evolution is just beginning.

As a fan of UK Garage—especially the upbeat "girlie garage" style—I dream of this genre being revived with Spiritual and uplifting messaging. That two-step beat pattern carries such joy and resonance.

Sound is one of the most accessible and powerful forms of fuel available to us. It surrounds us constantly. It moves through us. It can heal. It can awaken. It is vibration, and it is sacred. As Linda Goodman explains: *"A sound, spoken or musical or otherwise, once sent into the ethers, never ceases to exist. It just keeps rising on higher frequencies (like the dog whistle humans cannot hear, but dogs can) – until the average human ear can no longer detect the sounds. But they are still out there… somewhere."*

Your Personal Sound

The sounds you create are utterly unique to you, and act as a form of expression. Whether speaking, singing, crying, humming, or laughing—each expression is a vibration of your frequency. These are your sounds, your truth, your offering. They hold within them an ability to represent you, but also to act as a fuel source for yourSelf and those with whom encounter them.

The spoken word has long held power. Every word vibrates at a frequency, and carries energy and information—affecting both speaker and listener. The words you speak to yourSelf are the most potent of all, shaping your inner reality and frequency. They are a choice, and you can become aware of your words, both internally and externally, and make changes for your benefit. Hearing your own voice saying the words that you need to hear is such a powerful fuel source.

Our own words have a greater effect on our own body, whether they are directed towards our Self or something else. They are made from our physical body, so the vibration of these sounds vibrates through us more than anything. As we just discovered, our bodies consist largely of water, and sound travels most effectively through water. Be mindful of the energy in the words around you. If you are often drained by the words of others, notice the pattern.

Crying and screaming are primal sound responses to emotional intensity. They release energy from the body and signal our state to others. We often feel a sense of relief afterwards. Yet, many are taught to suppress these expressions—especially in adulthood—leading to unhealthy coping patterns. Screaming into a pillow, or while alone in a car, can be a profound emotional release. Try it—it works!

Humming is a powerful Self-soothing tool. It creates internal vibration, activates the parasympathetic nervous system, and invites calm and safety. In times of extreme trauma or breakdown, people often instinctively hum while curled up—creating a cocoon of vibration that stabilises the nervous system. Humming is a sacred, intuitive form of healing.

Singing is another beautiful vibrational fuel source that we have access to. You don't have to be good at singing, to know that it feels good to you! The ability to sing is a beautiful gift, that can be so powerful. The feeling that you can get from some people's unique singing voice, just hits differently. Some even have the ability to make the sounds of their singing resonate with millions of people, as it can fuel us in the way we feel that connection.

A little thought... ★

I have always loved wind chimes, and there are always some hanging in my garden. The gentle, spontaneous sounds they create bring beauty, presence, and a certain magic to my home and outdoor space. Their song arises only when the wind chooses to stir them—making each note unique, each moment unpredictable, and each harmony perfectly in tune with nature's own rhythm. Their tones are shaped entirely by the movement of the air, yet they always seem to carry an energy of upliftment, lightness, and peace.

These delicate harmonies don't just sound pleasant—they hold a frequency. A positive, soothing vibration that subtly nourishes the environment and everyone within it. This is the quiet power of sound: it influences us constantly, whether we are conscious of it or not.

It's worth reflecting on the soundscape that surrounds you in daily life. What sounds bring you joy, calm, and inspiration? Which feel intrusive, draining, or unsettling? How do these sounds influence the energy of your environment—and, in turn, your own inner state? And more importantly, what do you have the power to change, enhance, or invite in? Your sonic environment is as much a part of your energetic field as the light, colours, and objects you choose to keep around you. By curating it consciously, you create harmony both within and without.

Light as Fuel

When we think of light, we usually think of what we can see—the visible spectrum of electromagnetic radiation (EMR). This is light radiated into a visual range, which is interpreted by the eye and understood by our consciousness. However, the full light spectrum extends far beyond what the human eye can perceive. Still, the visible portion is the one most relevant to our day-to-day human experience, and notably, the only range of light that can travel underwater.

Light travels much faster than sound because it does not require a medium to move through—it is an oscillation in space. Though often described as a wave, light also behaves as a particle, measured in photons. It is effectively a by-product of energised atoms. When these atoms release excess energy and return to a lower or *ground* state, they emit light. In this way, light is a manifestation of energy in motion.

If we relate this to the concept of the unlearning spiral, our original Soul state—pure and radiant—is at the centre. Our healing journey is a return to this grounded, original state. And just as an atom emits light when it releases excess energy and settles into its most balanced form, so too do we radiate more light when we release what is no longer needed and realign with our true essence.

In Spiritual terms, light represents the divine, the sacred, and the intelligent. It is illumination—symbolic of insight, clarity, and truth. Light can be the bridge between *knowledge* and *knowing*. In Buddhism, light is said to accompany transcendence into Nirvana. Jesus said, *"I am the light of the world"*. This all underscores the Spiritual power and divine truth inherent in light. It illuminates our path and leads us back to Soul.

We each possess what is known as a light body. Your aura is an external reflection of your energetic field, while your chakras represent the internal energetic map. Together, they form the light body. Much like how combining all colours of visible light results in pure white, our chakras and aura combine to create our unique energetic radiance.

Our primary source of light is the Sun, but we also receive light from the Moon and the stars. Sunlight has profound benefits for the human body—it boosts vitamin D, improves sleep, supports immune function, reduces inflammation, enhances mood, helps regulate blood pressure, and promotes longevity. Sunlight is a potent form of energetic fuel, supporting not only physical health but also emotional and Spiritual well-being. Some even suggest that Sun exposure on the genitals amplifies these benefits—so if you dare, let the Sun shine where it rarely does! The Sun constantly offers energy, fuelling all life on Earth and guiding us not just in the 3D world, but toward expanded 5D consciousness and Soul alignment.

Light is a form of energy, and it carries information. Some individuals are gifted with the ability to work with light language—a vibrational form of communication interpreted through sound, movement, symbols, writing, or dance. This transmission of energy brings Spiritual wisdom into the physical world. These gifts are said to be available to anyone open and ready to receive them.

A little thought...

I love natural forms of light, and find myself drawn to them. Living in the UK means I experience a full spectrum of seasonal change. Whenever the Sun shines, I am out in it. In winter, I find deep comfort in fire. As a fire sign in both Western and Chinese astrology, this feels natural to me. There is something profoundly energising about open flames. When I don't have access to a fire, I surround mySelf with candles. I hang Feng Shui crystals in my windows to catch and scatter rainbow light throughout my home when the Sunshine comes out, even momentarily. I even hang them in the trees in my garden, inviting the spectrum of light to dance and energise my outdoor space. These subtle interactions with light bring joy, harmony, and vitality.

How do you interact with different light sources in your home? Does this alter if you have different seasons? Is there anything that you can do to enhance this source of energy in your environment?

Colour Fuel

Colour is simply light at different frequencies. It brings variety, emotion, and vibrancy into our lives. Each colour carries a measurable frequency, expressed in terahertz (THz), and a wavelength measured in nanometres (nm). These differences explain why we are naturally drawn to some colours more than others—we resonate with their energy. Language reflects this energetic truth through familiar expressions:
"Feeling blue." "Green with envy." "In a dark place." "It's all golden." "Red with anger."

When we perceive colour, it is the result of light interacting with an object and scattering its wavelengths. What we see is the reflected light, interpreted as colour by our brains. The spectrum of colour is continuous—not sharply divided—each hue blending into the next. Although we categorise colours, the boundaries are soft and expansive.

Sir Isaac Newton's experiments revealed a hidden colour between violet and blue: indigo. Though not distinguishable to the naked eye, it was identified as a unique frequency that only few could see. Because of its subtlety, it was later removed from many modern colour charts—but it remains significant in energetic systems like the chakras, where both indigo and violet play distinct roles.

Food has less to do with calories, and everything to do with frequency. Fruits and vegetables absorb energy from the Sun and the Earth. They are, in essence, living embodiments of light and colour. As a plant grows, it draws in Sunlight and transforms that energy into vibrant, tangible forms—manifesting in colours of fruit and vegetables. When we consume these foods, our bodies do not just absorb the physical; they absorb the energy. That energy is then transformed and radiated back through us—reflected in our etheric body and aura. This is why eating a full spectrum of colour-rich, natural foods supports balance not only in the physical body, but in the energetic body as well.

If we are not regularly feeding ourselves a full rainbow of light and colour through our food and lifestyle, it's inevitable that imbalance will occur. Over time, a lack of vibrancy in our diet can lead to a lack of vibrancy in our energetic field. The aura, while ever-changing and reflective of our inner state, responds clearly to imbalances. When colour and energy are out of sync, this may manifest physically as being underweight or overweight—not due to calories, but to a lack of frequency alignment. With this understanding, it is easy to see why traditional diets often fail. They focus on the quantity instead of the quality of vibration. They treat food as a physical object, rather than as energy. When we begin to see food as light, as colour, and as frequency, we shift into a more holistic and Spiritually aligned way of nourishing the Self.

Let's Look at the Different Frequencies of Colour:

COLOUR	FREQUENCY (THz)	WAVELENGTH (nm)	FOOD EXAMPLE
Violet **(indigo)**	668-789 (Highest frequency)	380-450	Red onion, beetroot, red cabbage, blueberries, blackberries, plums, purple sweet potato
Blue	606-668	450-495	Damson plums, blue tomato, blue spirulina, blue potato, blue lotus flower
Green	526-606	495-570	Lettuce, Cucumber, cabbage, green melon, green pepper, avocado, lime
Yellow-Golds	508-526	570-590	Pineapple, mango, yellow peppers, papaya, apricots, bananas, lemon, gold melon, peaches, oats and grains, ginger
Orange	484-508	590-620	Oranges, carrots, sweet potato, pumpkin, turmeric

Reds	400-484	620-750	Tomatoes, strawberries, raspberries, red peppers, red apples, rhubarb, cherries, cranberries, pomegranate, grapefruit, watermelon
Pink (pale red)			
White	A mix of all possible colours of the visible spectrum.		Potato, fish, white meat, cauliflower, garlic
Black	A complete lack of colour.		Black beans, black rice, black garlic

A little thought... ★

This may seem like a lot of information, and a lot of possible ways you can implement this into your life. It can help if you save this table and refer to it any time that you wish. Having got to this point in the book, it would be a good point to reflect on what your diet is currently like in terms of the colours and frequencies that you are absorbing into your body.
What colours do you eat the most of? Are there any gaps in the colour spectrum? How can you make some changes to your daily life to expand into this?

Colour Bathing

Much like Sunbathing, colour bathing involves absorbing energy—but instead of Sunlight, it is the frequency of a specific colour that you are choosing to immerse yourSelf in. This is a form of chromotherapy, or colour therapy, and it has gentle yet powerful healing and balancing effects on the body.

Colour bathing works by surrounding yourSelf with the light frequency of a particular colour—usually through coloured light bulbs or filters. The light can be applied to targeted areas of the body that need support, or to the soles of the feet while lying down, allowing the frequency to be absorbed into the whole system.

Some modern wellness innovations now even include full-spectrum showers that bathe the user in coloured light. A session of just 30 minutes per day can bring visible results in vitality, balance, and mood.

Nature itself offers the most accessible and intuitive form of colour bathing. The Japanese concept of forest bathing, or *Shinrin-yoku*, captures this beautifully. It is the practice of walking quietly among the trees, breathing in the forest air, and letting nature recalibrate your system. Surrounded by the expansive spectrum of living green—symbolic of vitality and heart energy—you naturally begin to absorb the frequency of life itself. The leaves, the grass, the shifting shades of green all provide subtle and potent nourishment to the energetic body.

Green is not the only colour nature offers in abundance. The vast blues of the sky and sea provide a different kind of restoration—tranquillity, relaxation, and emotional release. The next time you are at the beach, try focusing on the horizon—the line where the sky meets the ocean. Soften your gaze, relax your breath, and take in the frequency of calm. You will also be receiving the healing light of the Sun at the same time. It is no surprise that time in the forest or by the sea leaves us feeling lighter, clearer, and more aligned.

Love, too, amplifies our experience of colour. As Linda Goodman so beautifully wrote:

"All those who deeply love seem to be fine-tuned to the colours of the spectrum, because they're vibrating to a higher frequency. Reds are redder, blues are bluer, and yellows are more brilliant. In fact, all the senses are thus heightened by love. Fragrances are more hypnotic, music more inspiring, food tastes better, and the sense of touch is more intense. Twin Souls vibrate to an even higher frequency than other lovers or mates, and can often see one another's halos or auras." Love, light, and colour all interweave as forms of frequency—and each one, when embraced consciously, becomes a powerful fuel for the Soul.

Crystals as Fuel

Crystals have been revered across ages and cultures, honoured by many ancient civilisations not just for their beauty, but for their power. These remarkable formations occur naturally all over the Earth, formed through geological processes involving heat, pressure, and time. As elements heat and cool, their molecular structures stabilise in a process known as crystallisation, creating the distinct, ordered patterns we recognise as crystals.

Crystals are a paradox in form—delicate in appearance, yet incredibly strong in structure. Their exact energetic properties depend on their type, origin, and the specific conditions under which they were created. Each crystal carries with it *encoded energetic information*—a kind of vibrational memory. They are repositories of the frequencies, environments, and even intelligences present during their formation. This makes them far more than decorative objects; they are conduits for energy, awareness, and ancient wisdom.

Many believe crystals embody the intelligence of Earth itself—holding energetic imprints from ancient civilisations and times long forgotten. The ancient Egyptians integrated crystals into every facet of life—from healing to ritual and burial. It is commonly said that they buried their dead with crystals to carry into the afterlife, but this may only scratch the surface. Perhaps these crystals were intended to serve as energetic keys—carriers of wisdom to be accessed again in future lives or other incarnations.

Crystals may act as reminders of Soul-level knowledge tied to the cycles of Earth and humanity. As Linda Goodman wrote: *"Crystals and pure, unalloyed metals possess the highest proportions of aesthetic substance of anything in inanimate Nature. Alloys do not possess a cohesive wholeness, because they emanate two types of vibrations. This is why the ancient alchemists, Egyptian healers, and seers used only highly refractive crystals and pure, unalloyed metals in their work. Their faith in these cannot be called mere superstition because today's modern electrician has also found that batteries and circuits require pure, unalloyed metals – and the crystal is used as a detector in wireless telegraphy because it is sensitive to the vibrations of the ether."*

This connection between crystals and energy isn't mystical alone—it is scientific. Crystals are used in technologies today, from watches to wireless systems, because they are sensitive to vibration and stable in frequency. The same qualities that make them invaluable in electronics are what make them so powerful for energetic healing and Spiritual alignment. When used with intention, crystals become a fuel source—offering energy, clarity, healing, and alignment. They are not passive objects, but active participants in our journey of remembrance and transformation.

The information on crystals is incredibly vast, but here are some of my favourites, and what they can be used for. If this is something you are interested in looking into further, then there are some wonderful old books out there, and Judy Hall is a great author.

CRYSTAL	COLOUR	USES	ENERGY
Clear quartz	Clear	Amplifies energy, enhances clarity, supports manifestation, and balances all chakras.	Known as the "master healer," it resonates with pure light, amplifying intentions and raising overall vibration.
Selenite	White	Cleanses and purifies energy, promotes peace and mental clarity, and is excellent for aura and space clearing.	Carries a high, ethereal frequency that connects to angelic realms and clears stagnant or heavy energy.
Citrine	Yellow	Attracts abundance and prosperity, boosts confidence, promotes joy, and clears negative energy.	Radiates the frequency of Sunlight—uplifting, energising, and aligning you with the vibration of abundance.
Rose quartz	Pink	Encourages Self-love, compassion, emotional	Emits a gentle, heart-centred frequency that softens the aura and

		healing, and harmonious relationships.	opens pathways for love and forgiveness.
Amethyst	Purple	Supports Spiritual growth, calms the mind, aids meditation, and helps with protection and sobriety.	Holds a calming, protective frequency that elevates consciousness and connects to higher guidance.
Moldevite	Green	Accelerates Spiritual transformation, deepens intuition, and clears old patterns.	A rare, high-frequency stone that acts as a catalyst for rapid Soul evolution and energetic upgrades.
Black tourmaline	Black	Provides powerful protection, grounds energy, shields from EMFs and negativity.	Anchors you to the Earth's grounding frequency, creating a stable energetic shield.

A little thought... ★

How you use crystals is a personal choice. They are great just to have around you in your home, or you can use them with your meditations, keep them in your bag, wear them in jewellery, or any other ways that you can think of. It is said that the energy of the crystal should not be in direct contact with you continually, like wearing a piece of jewellery all the time, as you can become used to the energy that it brings. Crystals that I work with come in and out of my conscious awareness, and are changing all the time. I do have my absolute favourite star-shaped clear quartz crystal from the Lemurian age, which I absolutely love, and this has even travelled the world with me, so it is close to me nearly all the time! I am also continually learning more and expanding my crystal collection in line with deeper knowings.

Fuel of the Mind – Knowing and Knowledge

In the earlier chapter, foundational concepts, the difference between *knowledge* and *knowing* was introduced. In understanding that the knowing and embodiment of knowledge is the deeper level, then *knowing* as a form of *fuel* arises—a deep desire for truth. On the learning journey, you move from absorbing knowledge to arriving at a place of inner knowing. In this process, knowledge becomes nourishment for the mind—fuel for thought, growth, and evolution.

We live in a world saturated with information. The 3D realm constantly bombards us with input. The information we absorb—what we allow into our awareness—becomes a part of us. When we are conscious and discerning, we can choose what to let in and what to release. Information does not just come through books or conversation—it is embedded in every choice we make. It is present in the television shows we watch, the background noise we allow while working, the films we consume, and perhaps most significantly, the news.

We do not always choose what information is made available, but we do choose what we engage with, both consciously and subconsciously. And that choice matters. The information you choose to consume has a direct impact on your electromagnetic field. It becomes part of your frequency. Books, conversations, podcasts, films, social media accounts—all of these carry energies. They influence your thoughts, which influence your beliefs, which shape your reality. This isn't metaphorical—it's energetic truth. When you become aware of this, you begin to curate what you allow in and become intentional about your mental and energetic input.

A little thought...

I made the choice many years ago, that I was not going to watch The News. This is not because I don't care about the world, but is because I choose not to feed negative systems with my energy. What you give your consciousness to, you give your focus and energy to—and energy feeds all things. Instead, I choose to

subscribe to social media channels that report good news, uplifting stories, and examples of what I want in my consciousness. I listen to podcasts that expand my awareness and guide me toward growth and evolution. In this way, the information I consume becomes fuel—raising my frequency, not lowering it.
What do you have in your life that you maybe haven't realised before? What do you choose to fuel your mind? And what changes can you make to improve this?

Ways to Get to Know Your Fuel Better

Understanding your own fuel—what energises you, sustains you, and elevates your frequency—is a deeply personal and evolving journey. There are many tools and insights available to support this Self-discovery. Here are some powerful ways to deepen your awareness of how you fuel your body, mind, and Soul:

- **Study Ayurvedic principles**—The ancient wisdom of Ayurveda teaches that each person has a unique dosha constitution (Vata, Pitta, or Kapha). Balancing your doshas through tailored food and lifestyle choices can help optimise your fuel.
- **Consider saliva and blood testing**—These tests can offer insights into hormonal imbalances, vitamin deficiencies, stress markers, and more—revealing the deeper layers of how your body is functioning.
- **Test for food intolerances or allergies**—Unidentified sensitivities can drain your energy and disrupt your system. Identifying them can bring clarity and relief.
- **Look into gut health testing**—Your gut is your second brain—and a vital part of how your body digests, absorbs, and transforms fuel into energy.
- **Explore genetic testing**—Your DNA holds valuable information about how your body functions, including how you metabolise certain foods, respond to exercise, and manage inflammation or detoxification.
- **Explore your hormonal cycles**—For women, this may mean syncing with the lunar cycle; for men, it often aligns more closely with the

solar cycle. Learn how your natural rhythm influences your energy, clarity, and drive—and how to honour it.

- **Cultivate body awareness**—Tune in to how your body feels after different foods, environments, people, or choices. What energises you? What depletes you?
- **Track your energy patterns and mood over time**—Keeping a daily journal of energy, mood, sleep, and food can reveal hidden patterns and help you better understand what truly supports or depletes you.
- **Observe your breath and breathing habits**—Breath is one of your most immediate sources of fuel. Are you breathing shallowly or deeply? Nasally or through the mouth? Your breath tells you a lot about your current state.
- **Explore somatic practices and body-based therapies**—Practices like somatic experiencing, bodywork, or trauma-informed movement help release stored energy and increase connection to your body's internal fuel and intuition.
- **Assess your environment and energetic hygiene**—Your surroundings either nourish or drain you. Consider your exposure to noise, clutter, EMFs, toxins, or negative influences.

A little thought...

With learning and progression, it is natural to go through many different phases. I once has a supplement obsession after I discovering the concept of minerals! Another phase I went through involved over-testing and anxiously monitoring my body—particularly my adrenal function. I found mySelf repeatedly getting tests, worrying constantly about the results, and ironically, putting even more strain on the very system I was trying to heal. Looking back, I can see it had become an *avoidance tactic*. I wasn't yet ready to face the world the way I truly wanted to. I hadn't built the courage to make the changes I deeply longed for. At that time, I was profoundly unhappy—but rather than confronting that truth, I channelled my energy into controlling something measurable. This avoidance eventually manifested as dysfunction in my physical body.

It is important to remember that your body is always changing. Test results can vary significantly within hours, or depending on your emotional state. Any test—blood, saliva, genetic, hormonal—is just a snapshot in time, and typically focused on one small part of the body. When looking at any form of physical monitoring, always remember to step back and see the whole picture. You are not just a body. You are body, mind, and Soul—fully integrated. The real wisdom comes from learning to listen to *all* parts of yourSelf, in harmony.

Summary

1. **Fuel is not just food.** What you consume includes light, breath, thought, sound, colour, and belief. All of these are forms of energetic nourishment, and each one contributes to your vibrational signature.
2. **All fuel is energy in transformation.** Every form of fuel we consume initiates a transference and transformation of energy—whether physical, emotional, mental, or Spiritual. What we absorb becomes part of us. We are conductors, constantly converting external energy into the essence of our being.
3. **Everything holds a frequency.** Food, water, colour, sound, air—each one carries a vibration. Awareness of these frequencies and how we allocate them is key to our energy ascension.
4. **Receptivity is power.** The more attuned we become to the energetic qualities of what fuels us, the more open we are to receiving what truly nourishes us.
5. **Quality is everything.** The frequency of the fuel source determines its impact. The more refined and conscious the source, the more life force it gives. Self-love demands high-quality fuel, and Self-love is a fuel in itself.
6. **Unlearning is part of the path.** As we work through our unlearning spiral, we shed old attachments to false or toxic fuel sources. This process is essential for returning to our true frequency.
7. **Knowledge becomes knowing.** On this journey, the accumulation of knowledge is only the beginning. As it integrates, it becomes

knowing—and knowing is fuel. Truth and Self are energetic sources in their own right.

8. **Fuel needs evolve with you.** Your energetic and physical requirements change with the seasons, your emotional cycles, Spiritual growth, and life phases. Honour the impermanence—what fuels you now may shift, and that is ok.
9. **Emotional and relational energy are fuel too.** The people in your life, the emotional environments you dwell in, and the conversations you engage in all act as energetic inputs. Surround yourSelf with relationships that uplift and energise you.
10. **Trust your inner guidance.** There is no perfect plan—only what is right for *you*, right now. Stay curious, experiment, observe, and listen. Self-trust is your most powerful diagnostic tool.

"You are what you fuel yourself with."

"You are what you fuel yourSelf with – the choices you make in terms of how to fuel your body, from the water you drink to the thoughts you think, will determine the frequency of what you are and what you become." – *Me*

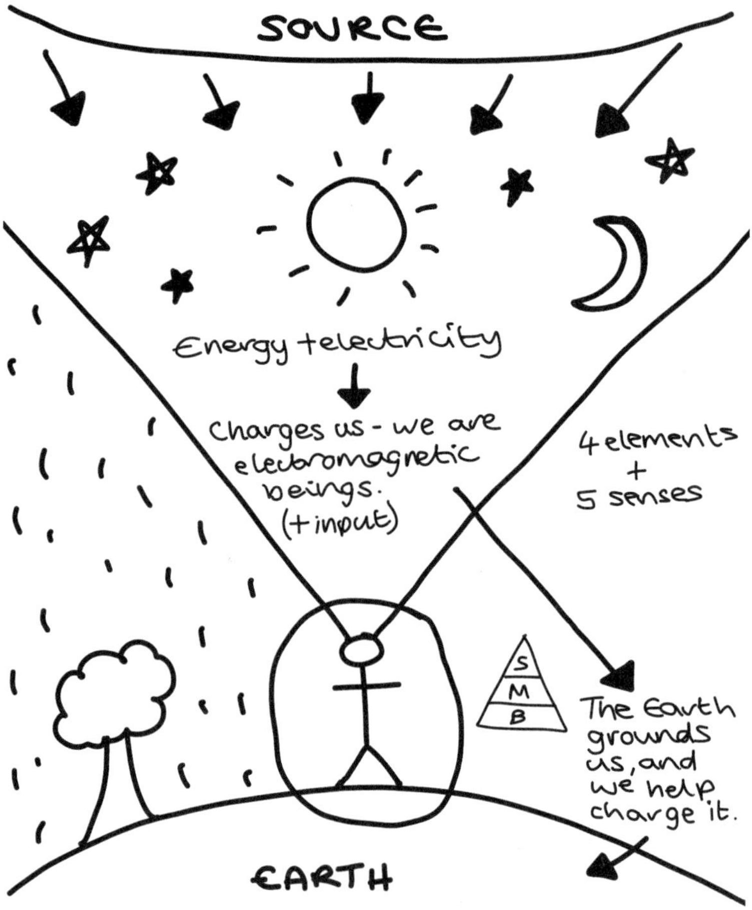
SOURCE
Energy + electricity
Charges us - we are electromagnetic beings.
(+ input)
4 elements
+
5 senses
S
M
B
The Earth grounds us, and we help charge it.
EARTH

Exercise

FUEL SOURCE	My inputs of fuel energy + that charge me (4D+ to 5D)	My inputs of fuel energy – that deplete me (3D to 4D-)	How my highest Self would fuel themselves (5D)	Changes I am going to make to my fuel inputs
Water				
Food				
Air				
Sound				
Light				
Colour				
Nature				
Love				
Other practices				

A little thought... ★

The Coherence of Nature: As I sit here writing, I'm on the edge of the beautiful Boulder Reservoir in Colorado, surrounded by the purest elements of nature. It feels like the perfect place to reflect on the *coherence of nature*—the way everything in the natural world works in harmony to restore and realign us. Even a single element of nature—Sunlight, Earth, water, or air—has a positive energetic influence on the body. But when these forces are combined, their power is amplified. Right now, my feet are grounded on the Earth, touching wet rocks and soft mud where the land meets the water. I'm gazing across a still, expansive body of water fed by mountain streams. These waters have travelled naturally from rainfall through the peaks, touching rocks, trees, air, and mineral-rich land before arriving here—charged, alive, and vibrant.

Around me are trees and grasses in deep, vital greens—stretching so far it feels like I can see the whole Earth. The air is clean and crisp, untouched by pollution, and I can feel it nourishing me as I breathe it in. All I hear is the gentle ripple of the water, the breeze moving through the trees, and the rhythm of my own breath. It's one of those moments where I wish I could stay. The symphony of elements being absorbed through every sense of my physical body: recalibrating me. Within minutes, I feel reset. Time slows down. My nervous system softens. My body returns to its natural frequency.

Nature is built on an intricate, intelligent web of coherence—so profound and multidimensional that the human mind may never fully grasp it. But we don't need to intellectually understand it to benefit from it. We only need to experience it, to be in it, and to let it work through us. These natural forces realign not just the body, but the mind and Soul. Their influence is deeply personal, and what you experience is unique to you. It is meant for you. And that is more than enough.

Movement

> **MOVEMENT** is the dynamic flow of energy within us across all dimensions of our being. It represents the actions that generate change in ourselves and our lives—promoting progress and evolution. Movement also influences the frequency of the fuel we seek and the rest we require. It invites us to surrender to external movement beyond our control.

As you move through this chapter, reflect on the ways movement supports your energy, and how it changes depending on what you are fuelling yourSelf with, or the rest you have received. Some forms of movement may energise the body, others may shift the mind, and some may open the heart or stir the Soul. Movement is both a conscious choice and a surrender to life's natural currents—it is how we grow, adapt, and evolve.

Movement of the Physical Body

The body was designed to move. In physical form, the body is a tangible representation of our Soul here on Earth, allowing us to interact with the 3D world we inhabit. It has the ability to move in a wonderful variety of ways. When we think of physical movement, we often think of exercise, fitness, strength, or flexibility.

In any form of training—whether a sport, a gym practice, or another discipline—movement is practiced, refined, and eventually internalised. Repetitive movement strengthens neural connections, shifting action from the conscious mind to the subconscious, where it becomes fluid and automatic. As this process deepens, the body is able to move with more precision, and the mind becomes free to refine, rather than learn.

There are so many types of physical movement and exercise, and they can all help strengthen the vital relationship with us. In the foundational concepts chapter, the body—mind—Soul relationship was introduced, along with the ideal hierarchy of the three systems to create harmony within. Some forms of physical movement underpin this hierarchy perfectly, as the body's relationship with the mind is enhanced, and the mind's relationship with the Soul is enhanced. Building this relationship is key to creating and keeping the inner harmony that we desire. Here is some more detail on a few key areas of physical movement:

Walking is the most natural and accessible form of human movement—an innate rhythm we are born to follow. It is so woven into daily life that we often overlook its power, yet this simple act holds profound physical, mental, and energetic benefits. Far from being "just exercise," walking is an opportunity to restore balance, connect with the body, and recalibrate the mind.

When done regularly—especially in natural environments—walking becomes a form of moving meditation. Each step stimulates circulation, strengthens the heart, supports healthy joints, and tones the muscles without placing strain on the body. It reduces stress hormones, encourages creative thinking, and fosters emotional clarity. The gentle, rhythmic movement also soothes the nervous system, signalling safety and calm, while the shifting scenery draws attention away from mental chatter and into the present moment.

Nature amplifies these benefits. Walking among trees, along the shore, or across open landscapes offers an exchange of energy with the environment—breathing in cleaner air, absorbing Sunlight, and grounding through contact with the Earth. Science supports what ancient traditions have always known: natural surroundings recalibrate our energetic frequency, helping us return to harmony.

In studies of the world's Blue Zones—regions where people live the longest, healthiest lives—walking is a consistent lifestyle thread. It is not forced, but integrated naturally into the rhythm of daily life. Errands, visits to friends, or moments of reflection often happen on foot, turning movement into a joyful necessity rather than a chore.

Increasing your daily steps, especially in spaces you enjoy, is one of the simplest yet most impactful ways to improve well-being. Whether it is a purposeful morning walk to set the tone for your day, a gentle evening stroll to digest and unwind, or a spontaneous wander when inspiration calls, each step is an act of Self-care. Over time, walking can become a grounding ritual—a way of honouring the body, quieting the mind, and reconnecting with the Soul.

A little thought...

I walk every day, often on the beach near my home, in all kinds of weather! I love it, and I thought nothing of how easily I get to do this every day. But while travelling in Bali, I noticed how difficult it was to walk as freely—the roads are not built for pedestrians, and the beaches are tucked into bays. This prevented me just being able to walk, unrestricted, for as long as I wanted. It drew my attention to how important it was for me. I turned to yoga instead, and did many practices, but it didn't replenish me like walking. I realised just how essential walking was to my equilibrium. It is something that I will always include in my daily life, and will not take for granted again.
What about you—How do you incorporate walking into your life? Do you feel like you need as much as I do?! Do you have a planned route, or do you just walk freely?

Stretching is a gentle yet profoundly transformative form of movement. It does far more than lengthen muscles—it restores harmony to the entire body-mind system. By improving flexibility, increasing blood circulation, enhancing joint mobility, and supporting muscular balance and alignment, stretching works as both a preventative and restorative practice. It also has a powerful effect on the nervous system, calming overactivity and creating an internal sense of safety.

As a lifelong gymnast and coach, stretching has been a cornerstone of my physical and mental well-being. Over the years, I have learned that your body will only stretch as far as your nervous system allows. Many people believe they have reached their flexibility limit because of muscle tightness, when in truth, it is the body's safety system holding them back. The nervous system perceives a certain range as *safe*, and beyond that, it will trigger protective tension. This is why relaxation is key—when we learn to breathe, soften, and trust the process, the body naturally begins to open.

Relaxing into stretches trains the nervous system to release tension, expand its range of *safe* movement, and foster inner calm. This is particularly powerful in somatic stretching, which consciously connects mind, breath, and movement. Somatic work can reach deeply into the places where trauma is held in the body—often stored in the fascia, hips, shoulders, or other protected areas. Unresolved trauma leaves energetic and emotional imprints in tissue, subtly shaping posture, movement patterns, and even how we carry ourselves in the world.

Through patient, mindful stretching—especially when combined with breathwork—we can begin to unlock these hidden layers. The body remembers, but it also knows how to release when given the right conditions. Each stretch becomes more than a physical act—it becomes an invitation for the body to let go of what no longer serves, restoring both freedom of movement and freedom of Spirit.

Yoga is an ancient practice that weaves together body, breath, and stillness into a single, harmonious flow. Its origins trace back thousands of years, carrying with it the wisdom of Self-mastery and the remembrance that the body is not separate from the mind or the Soul. At its heart, yoga is not just about physical postures, but about union—returning to the Self through conscious presence.

There are many forms and lineages—Hatha, Vinyasa, Kundalini, Yin, Restorative—each offering a different doorway to the same truth: that wholeness is found when we are fully here, in this moment, inhabiting our body with awareness.

For those who have experienced trauma, dissociation, or a sense of disconnection from their physical body, yoga can serve as a gentle yet powerful bridge home. Through mindful movement, intentional breathing, and moments of stillness, it re-establishes a sense of safety within the body. Over time, this practice can rebuild trust between body and mind, allowing the nervous system to soften, the breath to deepen, and the inner landscape to feel less like a place to escape and more like a place to dwell.

Yoga invites you to listen—to feel the subtle messages of your muscles, joints, breath, and energy. It asks you to move with compassion for yourSelf, to notice where you hold tension, and to allow that tension to release not only in the body but in the deeper layers of your being. In this way, yoga becomes not just a physical discipline, but a practice of Self-reclamation—anchoring you back into your own presence, and gently awakening the Soul's memory of unity.

Pilates is another powerful form of movement, rooted in precision, control, and deep connection to the body's core. Created by Joseph Pilates in the early 20th century, this practice focuses on small, intentional movements that engage the deepest layers of muscle—particularly the stabilising muscles of the abdomen, back, and pelvic floor. While breath is used to support the movements, the primary focus lies in cultivating control, stability, and alignment throughout the entire body.

Through regular practice, Pilates strengthens the relationship between body and mind, helping you to move with awareness rather than habit. It not only builds strength and tone but also improves posture, joint health, and functional movement patterns—making everyday tasks easier and more graceful. The emphasis on alignment supports a balanced structure, preventing injuries and allowing energy to flow more freely through the body.

Pilates also invites a meditative focus, as each exercise requires full presence. The mind learns to communicate more clearly with the body, and the body learns to respond with precision and efficiency. Over time, this harmony enhances both physical confidence and inner resilience, creating a stable foundation from which all other forms of movement can flourish.

Resistance training—whether using weights, resistance bands, or simply your own bodyweight—is a cornerstone of building physical strength, stability, and resilience. The principle is simple yet profound: if we do not use our muscles, we lose them. This becomes increasingly important as we age, when natural muscle mass begins to decline. Strength training not only maintains and builds muscle but also supports bone density, joint health, and a robust metabolic function.

The benefits extend far beyond the physical. Regular resistance training has been shown to enhance cognitive function, sharpen focus, and improve mood through the release of endorphins. It often brings a renewed sense of confidence and Self-esteem—proof that you can lift, move, and carry more than you once believed. Over time, this physical strength becomes a reflection of inner strength, building a sense of discipline, determination, and trust in your own abilities.

Strength in the body can mirror and support strength in the mind and Soul. The act of progressively challenging yourSelf—lifting a little heavier, holding a position a little longer—translates into your approach to life. You become more willing to push through resistance, not only in the gym but in your personal growth. In this way, resistance training becomes more than an exercise—it is a physical expression of your ability to meet life's challenges and grow stronger because of them.

Cardiovascular exercise—simply described as "getting out of breath"—is a vital component of physical well-being. It strengthens the heart, lungs, and circulatory system, allowing the body to move oxygen more efficiently and nourish every cell. Over time, this improved oxygen delivery boosts energy levels, enhances stamina, and supports a greater sense of vitality in daily life.

Cardio does not have to mean punishing workouts or high-intensity routines; it simply needs to be regular and intentional. Walking briskly, dancing, cycling, swimming, hiking, or even playing can all raise your heart rate and offer cardiovascular benefits. The key is consistency and finding forms of movement you genuinely enjoy—and what you enjoy, you are far more likely to sustain.

Beyond the physical, cardiovascular exercise supports mental health by releasing endorphins and reducing stress hormones. It can clear mental fog, lift your mood, and provide a moving form of meditation. In moments of rhythm and breath, your mind can quiet, and your awareness can return to the present moment. Regular cardio can become a way of actively circulating energy through the body, breaking up stagnation, and supporting the flow of life force.

When approached with mindfulness, cardio becomes more than exercise—it is a practice of honouring the body, energising the mind, and fuelling the Spirit with the breath of life.

Flow State

Repetitive movement has a unique ability to bypass the noise of the conscious mind and access the deeper layers of the subconscious. This is where the thinking mind begins to soften, and instinct, intuition, and presence start to guide the experience. Many athletes, dancers, martial artists, surfers, and Spiritual practitioners describe this as entering a "flow state"—a moment when everything aligns, distractions fade, and time itself seems to slow down or dissolve. In this state, there is no separation between the one moving and the movement itself. Action and awareness merge into a single, fluid experience. The body knows what to do, the mind trusts it completely, and the Soul feels utterly at home.

Flow state is a heightened state of consciousness. In these moments, you are tapping into 5D awareness while fully grounded in 3D reality. Your perception expands, your energy aligns, and for that moment, you are both the creator and the creation. It is a living meditation. This is one of the ultimate states of unification, and once experienced, it is something that stays with us. It is something we can all aim for, but ironically, it can never be the aim of our chosen physical movement, as the mere "trying" takes you away from the natural introduction to the flow state. It instead is a natural by-product of all that we have spoken of, and whilst achieved through physical movement, is a profoundly Spiritual experience.

Physical Movement and Mental Health

The mental health benefits of movement run deep. While science celebrates the endorphin release that accompanies exercise, the real magic lies in the way movement interrupts negative thought patterns, shifts our focus, and re-establishes trust in ourselves. It is a physical reminder that change is always possible. Every time you show up for yourSelf through movement, you are strengthening an inner muscle of Self-esteem—not the fragile, ego-driven kind, but the steady, Soul-rooted kind. Progress is not always measured in visible results; sometimes, the act of showing up *is* the transformation.

Exercise is also a living metaphor for Self-challenge. Each time we move, we are invited to confront our perceived limits and gently, or sometimes boldly, push beyond them. With conscious intention and Self-love, physical training becomes far more than a means to shape the body—it becomes an act of reverence for the vessel that carries our Soul. By strengthening, nourishing, and caring for this vessel, we create a stable, vibrant foundation from which we can live our truth.

Exercise is often central to trauma recovery. Movement in the body releases emotional blocks and reconnects us to our awareness. Boxing, for example, helps individuals channel aggression, express boundaries, and reclaim physical space. Different types of exercise resonate with different aspects of the psyche. We tend to gravitate toward what feels familiar or safe—often reflecting our current internal state. But growth comes when we challenge ourselves to try new forms of movement and explore unfamiliar territory.

A little thought... ★

There are so many different forms and combinations of exercise and physical movement. Each and every one of us will connect with these differently and will naturally be drawn to some over others. Getting a good variety is key, and having the courage to explore your abilities—whether within one of your already chosen activities, or in exploring something totally different.

What exercises do you have in your life? Why do you feel drawn to these particular things? Do you desire to expand and challenge yourSelf with exercise somehow?

Movement of Mind

Your mind is something that continually develops and evolves as you live. Your Soul, however, remains the same throughout your journey. You can move further away from it or closer to it. You can retrieve new parts of it, rediscover forgotten wisdom, or uncover deeper truth—but your Soul remains constant, while your body and mind change and develop.

Within the movement of mind comes the *movement of knowledge*—and with it, the evolution of what we *know*. This is the openness to learning, to challenging your existing beliefs, to welcoming new information and fresh perspectives. It is a willingness to allow continual expansion. This flow of knowledge creates the movement and development of your inner landscape. As you take in new insights, your worldview shifts. Your beliefs evolve. Your lens on life becomes more refined. What you choose to consume—intellectually, mentally, and Spiritually—shapes the systems of belief you live by.

This includes the movement through phases of knowing and knowledge, the conscious evolution of thought, and the impact of the mental fuel you give yourSelf. As we explored in the previous chapter, the mind is shaped by what it consumes.

Emotional Movement

The concept of emotional movement refers to the natural process of allowing emotions to flow through you. Every emotion carries a charge—a specific energetic signature—and when that energy is acknowledged and accepted without resistance, it can move through you and into completion. In doing so, the energy is freed, and what remains is the lesson. The emotional charge no longer lingers, and it does not become embedded in your system.

Emotional movement also relates to your personal growth and development—the continual shift toward emotional mastery. This means learning to observe your emotions with honesty and clarity, seeing them for what they are without judgement. This is a form of energetic movement within your consciousness, a movement through the spiral of unlearning and toward greater truth and Soul alignment.

Emotions are designed to move. They are intended to pass through the body, mind, and Spirit in response to experience. When this process is allowed to complete, the energy of the emotion is transformed, and its lesson is integrated. However, when a strong emotion—especially one perceived as negative—is not fully expressed or resolved, it can become trapped in the body. This often happens during a trauma response, where the individual is triggered into a reaction, unable to respond out of choice. When this happens, the emotional energy becomes stuck. The body, mind, and Spirit are left holding the incomplete experience.

Your subconscious Self will continue to bring up similar memories, feelings, or even repeated life scenarios, trying to complete the process and learn the original lesson. This is why certain events may play on repeat in your mind. You might replay a situation from the past, imagine how it could have gone differently, or anticipate how you might face something similar in the future. These are signs of incomplete emotional movement.

The more you resist these unresolved emotions, the stronger they become. The energy behind them is not trying to harm you—it is trying to complete itself. There is no avoiding the lessons meant for you, and often, the thing you least want to face is the very thing your Soul is urging you toward.

Healing and ascension are both rooted in completing these unfinished emotional experiences. They are often held in the body as memories, trauma, or anxiety. When you fully allow yourSelf to move through them—physically, emotionally, mentally, and Spiritually—you release their grip. They become part of your wisdom, no longer your burden. They are lessons passed and embodied. But do not be fooled—there will always be more. You are not here to complete everything. You are here to grow, and there is always another step.

"When hate and fear are both conquered, the will is then free and capable of immense power. This is the message of your own nativity, hidden in the silent stars. Listen to it." – Linda Goodman

A little thought…

I know that when you find yourSelf stuck in emotions, the way through is not always clear. Confusion usually clouds the answers, even though they are always there. How do you get to these answers? How do you move through these emotions? These are skills that we develop with practice, and practice can, of course, be messy. I love journaling to start the process, followed by a mediation on what I have written. If I am not yet able to sit with this, then going for a walk or run always helps me. But, when I am ready, I always ask the *why*? Why did this happen? Why did it cause me to feel like that? When did I first feel that feeling? Why did it hurt me then? Go deeper. When you are ready to ask, the answer is always there, and it is likely to create the necessary movement that you are seeking.

Movement to Soul

The movement toward Soul is the direct path to your true Self. This movement is the deepest journey we can make. As we explore throughout the Guiding Star System, there are many ways to arrive here. We will look at those different routes more later in the book, as learning multiple tools to get you there gives you the choice which is best for you. The paths may look different, but the destination is the same.

When knowledge deepens into knowing, it enters alignment with the Soul. Knowing is no longer intellectual—it is embodied. It becomes part of who you are. As knowledge moves into the space of knowing, it passes through your personal values, your experiences, and your connection with Self. This creates a fluid, living belief system that grows in alignment with your Soul. Knowing is not fixed. It is in constant movement—always checking itself against inner truth. The more you tune into knowing, the more you align in authenticity.

Let us now consider movement toward Soul in light of the learning journey and the unlearning spiral—two essential maps for understanding this sacred path that we looked at in the foundational concepts chapter:

The Learning Journey and Movement

We each progress through life on our own individual paths, with movement as our constant companion. Movement is something we cannot fight—it is inevitable. Whether subtle or radical, internal or external, every human is experiencing movement at all times. The *pace* of this movement is often reflected by how committed we are to our growth, how open we are to change, and how willing we are to embrace the lessons life places before us.

As we journey through life, we experience many phases, many deaths and rebirths. Most will move through the broad stages of birth, childhood, adolescence, adulthood, old age, and eventually death. This natural movement through time is inseparable from the movement of the mind, and ultimately, the movement toward Soul. Interestingly, we are *naturally closest to our Soul* at the beginning and end of life. At birth, our consciousness is new—unencumbered by conditioning and still closely linked to source. At death, our awareness begins to turn inward again, reuniting with Spirit as we prepare to return to it. The more we can align with Soul *during* this in-between journey, the more meaningful our experience becomes—not only for ourselves, but for the world around us.

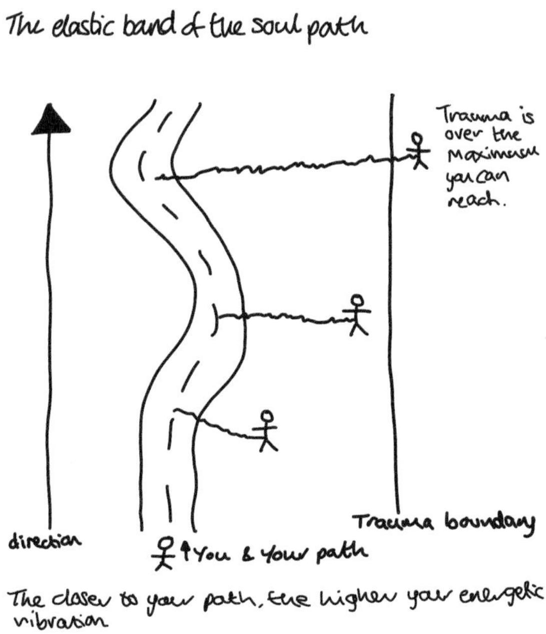

The Unlearning Spiral and Movement

As we looked at earlier in the foundational concepts chapter, the unlearning spiral begins with you as a pure Soul at birth, as the central point. The line of the spiral represents the timeline of your life, and is the life you have lived so far, and the forward movement of life so far in the sense of development. And the spiral represents the biggest decision we will ever make for ourSelf in our lifetime:

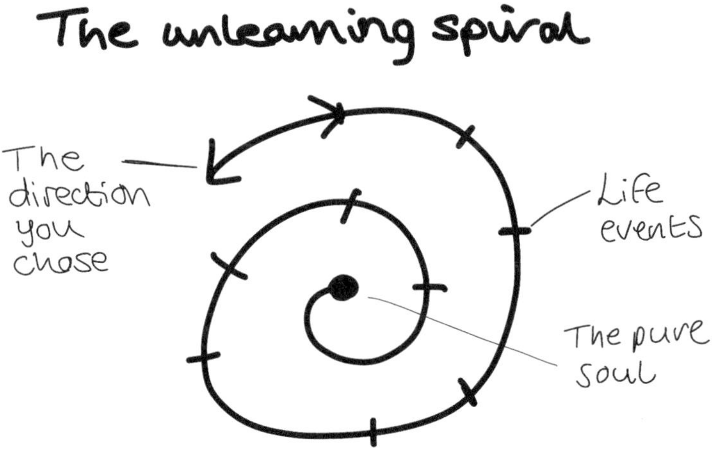

Movement and The Ultimate Decision

The most powerful movement you will ever create in your life begins with a single decision. And this decision is the same for every human being: **Will you own the full truth of who you are? Will you step fully into your Self and your power?** This is the moment everything changes. It is the point of pivot on the unlearning spiral. It can arrive in many ways—a sudden realisation, a firm decision, or a loud declaration. Are you truly ready to take full responsibility for discovering and honouring your true Self—no matter what that journey brings?

This decision requires a lifetime commitment to Self-awareness, honesty, and responsibility: a continual evolution process. To walk this path is to acknowledge that you are the creator of your reality—and to commit to walking through every lesson meant for your Soul. Yes, it is a bold, challenging path. It is not the easy road. It is not the popular road. But it is the road of truth. And once you have glimpsed at the connection with your Soul—you can never unknow that. This choice is the ultimate movement. It will shake and shape every area of your life. It will dismantle illusion and bring you home to truth. And from this space, everything becomes possible.

A little thought... ★

What if you understand this question fully—but you're just not ready to answer it? That's ok. I was there too. I knew all the right answers. I understood the truths. But I didn't yet have the energy, the Self-belief, or the upgraded internal framework to act upon them. And that is an important place to be—one of preparation. This question requires a certain energetic frequency just to receive it, let alone live it. If you want this life, but it still feels just out of reach, the work lies in healing. In restoring the connection to Self. In building belief and resilience. In upgrading the system from the inside out. Everyone's timing is different. The most important step is acknowledging the question—understanding that there *is* a way through, even if you are not there yet.

Have you made your decision yet? We look at the ways that the journey of this decision unfolds later in the book, but keep in mind that it only becomes relevant alongside the moment of this decision.

"The most powerful movement begins with a single decision: to own the truth of who you are."

Movement in the Physical World

Movement in the physical world is one of the most visible and impactful demonstrations of energetic shift. When we create movement in our external reality, we disrupt stagnation and transform inertia. Feelings of boredom, frustration, or unease often stem from a lack of movement in some area of life. You may have the most beautiful dreams and plans—but without action, they remain dormant. Taking action in the physical world is a powerful declaration. It is an act of responsibility, of applying your energy to your creation, and an expression of gratitude for the opportunities you have. Physical-world movement can take many forms: starting a new exercise class, changing your work environment, moving house, or travelling to new places. These shifts hold different energetic weights, but they all generate momentum and change.

A little thought... ★

Personally, I find that when life becomes too comfortable or routine, I like to shake it up. Sometimes this means something small, like going to a new restaurant. Sometimes it means booking a solo trip somewhere I have never been before. As I write this, I am sitting in Uluwatu, Bali, just a few days into a three-month trip I have gifted mySelf this in order to work on this book. This is me taking responsibility, creating movement, and honouring my purpose. I have also made massive shifts in my life before leaving to come here—including changing careers, moving homes, starting new studies, and letting go of old relationships. All of these were movements towards my truth.

What movements towards your truth do you feel that you could make? What would this feel like? When was the last movement you created in your physical world?

Movement and Freedom

Your ability to create and allow movement is intimately linked to the freedom you grant yourSelf—physically, mentally, emotionally, and Spiritually. These layers are all connected. The flexibility of your physical body is deeply tied to your nervous system, which reflects your mental and emotional state, and your connection to Soul.

True movement thrives in a state of safety. You cannot be in a state of creation and love while operating from fear and survival. In these lower states, you will instinctively restrict movement. Any sensation of restriction is a message from your energy system, pointing to where healing is needed.

Only in freedom can we meet our true Self—and from this space, experience love. Love is the natural state we were born into, the centre of the unlearning spiral. To move back to this place is to come home.

The Movement of Letting Go

Every individual has their own narrative, often formed in the face of pain or survival. This story—our identity narrative—becomes entangled with our ego. It becomes our justification for being stuck, for staying safe, for avoiding change. Letting go does not mean saying that what happened to you was ok. It means deciding that it will no longer control or define you. It is not your fault, but it is your responsibility now.

Letting go is the energy of acceptance. It is where we shift from being at the mercy of our past to becoming a conscious co-creator of our future. The moment you release your attachment to the story, you create space for movement within and elevation of energy, frequency, and Self.

This process often brings up fear. The ego will protest. It will tell you that you need to know how, when, and what. But those are not your responsibilities. The energetic exchange here is powerful: you release your current identity to receive your true one. This is the part-death of ego that initiates evolution. That is real courage. As Carl Jung said, *"[t]here is no coming to consciousness without pain. People will do anything, no matter how absurd, in order to avoid facing their own Soul. One does not become enlightened by imagining figures of light, but by making the darkness conscious."*

The art of surrender comes from allowing yourSelf to relax into a feeling of knowing and familiarity within creation and existence. This is the art of being and allowing it to come to you. Surrender does not mean let go and do nothing. It means to remain fluid and flexible, and follow the call of the universe. Flexibility in how it is delivered is what invites it into your life.

Movement and Polarity

The human experience is designed to be rooted in polarity. There is a spectrum of everything that we do, think, and experience. The polarity runs through all three forms—body, mind, and Soul. Positive and negative, light and dark, good and bad, love and hate, ego and Soul. Everything exists somewhere along a spectrum of polarity, and all are open to movement. Much like the gradient running through shades of white to black, we often find ourselves somewhere in the grey area, but life is the experience of both. Evolution comes from the free movement inbetween when required, but somewhere in the middle usually lies your personal ideal. Here are some examples of polarities:

Masculine – Feminine
Light – Dark
Ego – Soul
Positive – Negative
Love – Fear
Humility – Arrogance
White – Black
Good – Bad
Movement – Stillness
Ebb – Flow
Happiness – Sadness

The interesting thing about polarities is that they are inherently linked—they are joined on a spectrum. One would not exist without the other, as one would not be experienced without the contrast of its opposite. If we did not experience both extremes, we would not be able to recognise or value either. While some polarities are often labelled as *negative*, these experiences are usually necessary to appreciate and grow into the positive end. It is in the discomfort that we find transformation.

The human experience is meant to move through the entire spectrum of polarity and absorb the lessons within each point. These lessons are felt and interpreted through our emotions and inner awareness. As we evolve through our life experiences, we tend to gravitate toward a place on the spectrum—a conscious middle. This is where knowledge of both extremes supports the balance we seek. This mediumship is not about neutrality, but about wisdom through experience. It is the place where harmony is birthed through understanding.

Movement with the Earth

The Earth is in continual movement. Its motion creates natural cycles and polarities—night and day, seasonal transitions, and shifting weather patterns. These energetic movements profoundly affect all living things that depend on the Earth for their survival: humans, animals, plants, and the entire energetic ecosystem. The Earth is a constant provider, nourishing and supporting us at every opportunity, including through the fuelling of our intricate energy systems. The changing seasons reflect the Earth's own rhythm of movement and rest. Each season gifts us different energies, different mineral requirements, and natural produce to best nourish and support us through that phase. In this way, the Earth responds to our energetic needs in perfect timing, if we choose to align with its natural rhythms.

Our circadian rhythms—our internal body clocks—are directly influenced by the movement of the Sun and the moon. The Sun governs our daily wake-and-sleep cycles, aligned with masculine energy. The moon, tied to feminine energy, flows with monthly cycles. Though modern life can disrupt these patterns, we are still energetically wired to them. When we consciously return to alignment with these natural movements, we find harmony, ease, and increased energetic efficiency. We shift from resistance into flow.

The stars above us at any given moment reflect the energies most active in our lives at that time. Our unique Soul makeup—imprinted with star energy at our time of birth—interacts with these stellar frequencies in individualised ways. As above, so below. The Sun determines the day, the moon determines the months, the stars determine the years, and the Soul as Self.

The moon has influence that extends far beyond poetic symbolism. Its gravitational pull is strong enough to move ocean tides, guide the opening of oysters, and orchestrate countless natural phenomena. The bond it has with water is undeniable—and considering our bodies are largely composed of water (over 90% in the brain alone), it's no surprise that lunar cycles influence our moods, dreams, and energetic states.

Expanding our view even further, we look to the movements of the planets. Every 26,000 years, all the planets align on the same side of the Sun—a cosmic reset point of energetic alignment. To the ancients, planets were "wandering stars," and their positions were seen to influence the energy of our own "wandering rock," Earth.

A little thought... ★

Right now, as I write this, Earth is moving through the Age of Aquarius. While there is some debate among astrologers about the exact timing of these age transitions, there is general agreement that we are already immersed in this new energy. Aquarius, an air sign, brings with it a breath of fresh air—lightness, clarity, innovation, and awakening. This is a time of increased awareness, collective consciousness, and a return to integrity. A time of sharing wisdom, rising in truth, and breathing life into a new version of the world. We will be in this Aquarian Age for more than 2,000 years. It is a slow and graceful, energetic upgrade for the Earth and all her inhabitants. It truly is a remarkable time to be alive—to witness and participate in this great collective shift.

Can you feel the world changing and awakening right now? Does it seem a little different? How do you want to show up in it?

Summary

1. All movement—whether physical, mental, emotional, or Spiritual—initiates a transference and transformation of energy. Energy flows from one form into another, and the movements in our lives determine where and how that energy is allocated. We are the conductors of the energy we choose to move with.
2. Every movement carries a frequency. Whether we move in harmony or in resistance, the frequency is transmitted. Some movements—like those of the Earth—are beyond our control, while others are the result of our conscious choices. Energy ascension begins with awareness and alignment to these movements and frequencies.
3. Receptivity: The more attuned you become to the energies that move through, with, and for you, the more fluidly you can navigate them. This expands your ability to act with power where you can, and surrender where you must. This is not just about receiving, but about flowing with life. Receptivity to lessons increases your rate of transformation—and your ability to manifest from the energetic into the physical.
4. Your quality of life is shaped by the movements you allow and create. Fuel and movement are intricately connected, and the choices we make in both determine the frequencies we embody. The physical movements we honour, and the mindset we choose, are reflections of the relationship we have with our Self.
5. As we move through the unlearning spiral, we release attachments that block us from flowing toward our highest Self. Every layer we shed allows for a more authentic movement through life.
6. Knowledge will naturally evolve into knowing when we commit to the journey. All movement, whether conscious or unconscious, ultimately points us toward our truth and Self. This understanding comes as a part of the journey from knowledge to embodied knowing.
7. The Mind Continuum—from ego to Soul—is not a fixed position but a spectrum. We continually shift across it in different areas of our lives. The movement along this continuum is the dance of growth.

A little thought...

You will inevitably move through phases that reflect your current state of awareness. At one point, I found mySelf obsessing over different forms of movement—jumping from one to the next, driven by the unconscious desire to *complete* things. I was treating life as a tick-box exercise, chasing happiness through societal expectations and conditioning. And unsurprisingly, it never truly satisfied me.

Unravelling these patterns has been a long journey. I had a lot to unlearn. And I am still learning. But by choosing to live more authentically, I've begun to discover the truth of happiness. Now, my movements—whether tiny baby steps or giant leaps—come from within. The pace doesn't matter. It is the direction that does.

How is your direction right now? How aligned do you feel? Do you put expectation on yourSelf? Is there anything that you desire to change?

Exercise

MOVEMENT	My inputs of movement energy + that give to me (4D+ to 5D)	How my highest Self would make changes (5D)	Changes I am going to make to my movement (4D+)
Physical movements of choice… Walking, stretching, strength, cardio			
Physical movement for fun, play, and connection			
Movement of mind – knowledge and learning			
Movement of emotions			
Movement to Soul			

A little thought... ★

"Your chosen movements of creation and trust in Self, alongside flowing with movements in which you have no control, are what determine your life and lifestyle here. Moving through your un-learning spiral and along the path of the learning journey are advancements in movement towards Self, via the lessons that you are required to learn, in order to be all that you know you can be." - ME

Rest

REST is the restoration and slowing of energy within us — including redirection, reallocation, and surrender. Sleep and rest. Introspection and quiet. Peace and rediscovery. Recharging and replenishing of body, mind, and Soul.

As you move through this chapter, consider how different forms of rest serve your body, mind, and Soul. Some forms may offer physical recovery, others may calm the mind or open space for emotional or Spiritual integration. We are not designed to run at full speed without pause. Rest is not a weakness, it is an intelligent, nourishing part of our energetic rhythm.

Rest is a part of life that we often fail to prioritise, despite its vital role in our health and happiness. It is an integral part of The Guiding Star System that we are building through this book. Sleep is essential for living — physically, mentally, and Spiritually. It governs healing, regeneration, and resetting. But rest is not limited to sleep. True rest also includes downtime, space, and stillness — time for the body, mind, and Soul to simply *be*. Meditation, grounding, silence, spaciousness — these all count as rest.

In today's world, one of the biggest challenges we face is the ability to rest the mind. Our overstimulated systems are constantly bombarded by phones, screens, notifications, and noise. Learning to disconnect, reset, and let the body restore itself has become an essential — even radical — act of Self-love.

"The rain falls and fills the lake. One who honours rest becomes radiant." – Ancient Indian proverb.

Rest in Sleep

During sleep, the body undergoes profound repair and recalibration. Physical movement becomes still, allowing the deeper mechanisms of healing and regeneration to activate. In this state, the body resets—regulating vital hormones like insulin, producing antibodies to strengthen the immune system, and activating the brain's cleansing system (the glymphatic system) to wash away toxins that accumulate during the day. It is like an office being cleaned overnight—the clutter can only be cleared when the workers step aside. In the same way, sleep gives your body the space to restore balance and prepare for the next day's demands. Without it, you are not only tired, but carrying the *unprocessed mess* of the day before into tomorrow. Over time, this backlog disrupts both physical health and emotional equilibrium.

Sleep, then, is not simply rest—it is a sacred function of maintenance, repair, and renewal. It is the body's natural rhythm reminding us that stillness is as essential as movement, and that true vitality comes from honouring both.

Despite vast research, science still cannot fully explain *why* sleep is so essential, or how it has survived this far down the evolutionary process — only that it is absolutely non-negotiable, and vital. And I believe that sleep is vital for the body, the mind, and the Soul — I will explain why: When we sleep, we mostly enter a state of amnesia. In this altered state of consciousness, we lose awareness of the 3D physical world. The part of us which dreams is not the physical body or the mind — it is the Soul. It's this deeper part of you that journeys into the unseen, reconnecting to the energy from which it came, and reshaping the filters that colour your waking life. Simply put, sleep is Soul returning to the Spirit world — a recalibration and remembrance of all we forget through the act of birth. It is an aid in the evolution of the Soul, as in the state of sleep, the Soul gets to remember what the mind does not. One of the world's leading sleep researchers and pioneers in highlighting the importance of sleep, Dr. Matt Walker, describes sleep as the most *"under-appreciated"* key to overall health. This may be why.

The Stages of Sleep

There are four main stages of sleep — each one deeper than the last. Like steps on a staircase, each stage is passed through in sequence. As we fall asleep, we descend through the stages:

- **Stage 1**: Light sleep, often a continuation of recent thoughts. Short, less emotional dreams.
- **Stage 2**: A deeper version of stage 1, still relatively mundane and tied to recent memories.
- **Stage 3 & 4**: Deeper sleep. Physical repair and neurological cleansing occur here.
- **REM**: Emotionally vivid, bizarre, often profound dreams. The most Spiritually resonant stage.

Each sleep cycle takes about 90 minutes. As the night progresses, we spend longer in REM, and our dreams become more surreal and symbolic. These deeper dreams often carry insights and shifts that subtly influence our waking lives.

REM sleep, the most profound state of dreaming — where the magic happens. In this dream state, the brain's electrical activity looks almost identical to that of someone who is awake, but instead of being in the external world, we are in the inner world — navigating a deep state of Spiritual and energetic recalibration.

REM sleep intelligently comes hand-in-hand with a form of physical paralysis, to prevent us from acting out our *dreams*. However, as with all functions, there are examples where this mechanism has failed. When this happens — as in cases of parasomnia, sleepwalking, or some night terrors — the results can be dramatic, as there is no control feature preventing us from literally acting out the depths of our dream world, without any conscious awareness.

To illustrate this, I will provide an example of one of the earliest legal cases involving sleepwalking, *Massachusetts v. Tirrell* (1846). In this case, the defendant was acquitted of murder due to acting within a *"trance state"*. The courts recognising that they were not in awareness or control of their actions whilst in this state.

A more recent and well-known example is *R v. Parks* (1992), where the defendant drove to his in-laws, killed one, and severely injured the other — all while sleepwalking. He then shortly woke up, and unaware of what had happened, but noticing he was covered in blood, he drove himself to a police station. He was totally unaware of his own severe injuries. He was found not guilty due to lack of conscious control. These cases illustrate just how distinct our subconscious states can be from our waking selves.

A little thought... ★

I have often reflected on the true purpose of sleep and all of its intriguing mystery. What if the progression through sleep stages is a journey — one that takes us deeper into the infinite subconscious, offering access to our Spiritual guidance and wisdom? What if sleep is like our Spiritual "pep talk", our return to Spirit, in which we can get a little rest and recharge, before coming back to human 3D life again? Think of this idea as like half-time in a football match: a little well-needed break, a re-assessment of what is required back on the pitch, and a good bit of coaching and guidance!

Can you remember feeling much better after sleep? Have you had any instances where a good sleep has helped an illness or recovery? Can you recall any Spiritual guidance you have received during sleep?

Dreams

Dreams are a by-product of rest and sleep, and are experienced in an altered state of consciousness. For many years, it was believed that dreams only occurred during REM sleep. We now know that dreams can arise during every stage of sleep—they're simply more frequent and vivid during REM. Even in stage one, our lightest sleep, we can enter dreamlike states. This stage has often been likened to hypnosis, which we will explore later.

One of the most fascinating shifts across the sleep cycle occurs in the physical changes in our body; there is a gradual reduction—and eventual halting—of serotonin production by the time we reach REM. Serotonin, a mood-altering chemical that helps regulate our emotions in waking life, is not required in the dream world. This absence creates a space for unfiltered subconscious exploration, untethered from the mood-based constraints of 3D life. This may be to enable the processing of our 3D experiences, as dreaming plays a vital role in integrating and organising new information. Pioneering researchers in sleep and dreams, Zadra and Stickgold, observe in their book *When Brains Dream*, that *"[s]ince 2001, over 1,000 scientific papers have appeared, extending our knowledge of how sleep stabilises, enhances, integrates, analyses, and even alters our memories—processes that vastly improve what we know and how we understand it."*

Linking this to the *unlearning spiral* that we looked at in the foundational concepts chapter, our memories—along with the conditioning and experiences that shape them—are deeply affected by how we process sleep. We continually take on new information in our everyday lives, and that forms part of our own internal memory and filing system. How that new information is filed and linked with our other files, will determine how we access it in our waking world. Sleep does not just restore us; it shapes our internal filing system, subtly reshaping our sense of Self and all that we operate from.

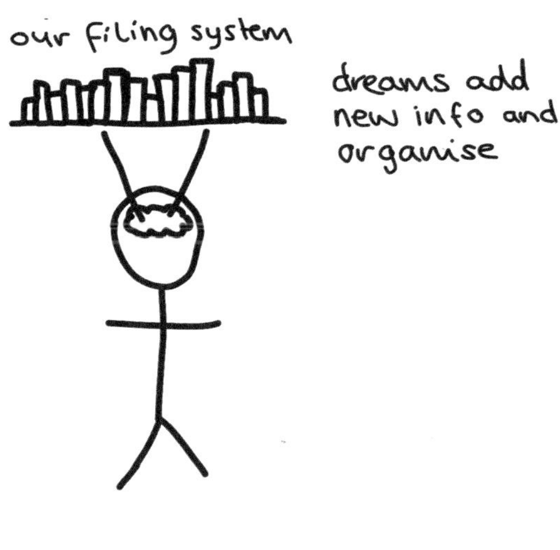

In this way, dreams become a bridge between ego and Soul. They act as messengers, filtering information from higher consciousness down into our waking reality. Rarely do they hand us direct answers to life's questions. Instead, they gently recalibrate our perception over time, helping us evolve.

A little thought... ★

From sleep, we may remember the occasional dream. But in relation to the amount we dream and how long we spend asleep, it is only ever a tiny percentage of what has occurred. This form of amnesia may be similar to the amnesia that we experience during birth? (Like a protective layer of amnesia between the veil of consciousness that separates human 3D living and 5D spirit world). Before birth, we are in Spirit form and have access to all the answers, and are all we could ever wish to be. But the amnesia that we experience in birth and in sleep, may be aiding our Soul's experience in the 3D world; by allowing us to *learn* and *live* the lessons that we have chosen for the development of our Soul?

What do you feel is true for the purpose of sleep? Do you feel that our lack of consciousness and memory has a Spiritual benefit to it?

Emotions are central to both our waking lives and our dreams, acting as markers of weight and meaning for our experiences. During sleep, we are given the chance to process and reduce the emotional charge associated with difficult memories. This is one of sleep's most profound healing functions. The profound psychoanalyst and sleep researcher, Ernest Hartmann, suggested in his book *The Nature and Functions of Dreaming*, that the safety of the sleep state allows the brain to integrate traumatic experiences into our memory systems—separating the physical body from emotional turmoil, while still allowing the feelings to be worked through.

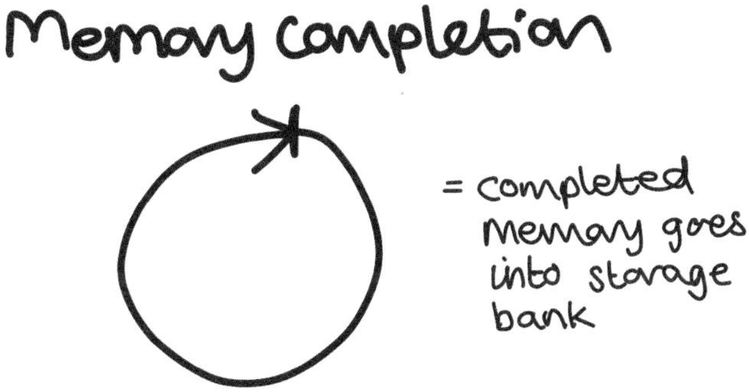

This is especially relevant in trauma. Zadra and Stickgold explain how those with PTSD often experience a disruption in REM sleep. Their dreams replay trauma in vivid, emotionally charged flashbacks—rigid, unchanging, and creatively frozen in time. Unlike the usual distorted and symbolic dreams we usually experience, these traumatic dreams lack flexibility. The trauma becomes stuck in the psyche. This is similar, but more complex, in those with C-PTSD, who carry a catalogue of emotionally charged experiences rather than a single defining event.

The sense of helplessness at the root of trauma freezes the memory in place, making it difficult to resolve. REM sleep, in its natural state, typically includes a shutdown of noradrenaline—a stress hormone that heightens alertness. However, in trauma survivors, this hormone is often still active, reflecting the ongoing replay of trauma and a disrupted ability to fully surrender to healing. Although science is yet to fully confirm the extent of healing through dreams, I believe it is foundational. In PTSD, the dream state replays the exact trauma. But instead of working through it, the dream doesn't complete, it repeats. In this, the dream and our subconscious is trying to show us what still needs to be processed.

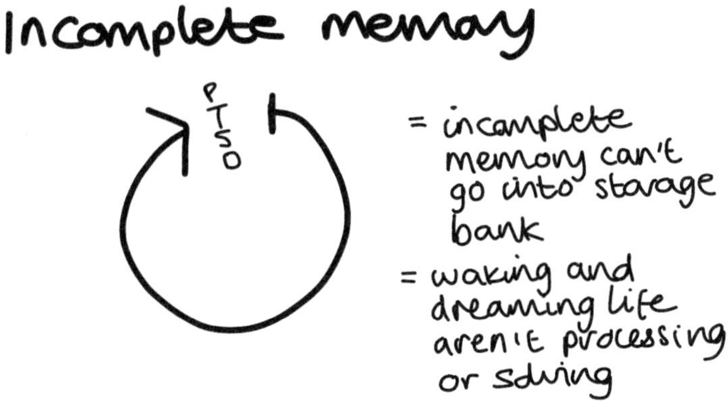

Recurrent dreams, especially emotionally intense ones, often signal that a lesson remains unlearned or unresolved. These dreams do not just reflect old material; they highlight the present moment's most important focus. Calvin Hall, psychologist and dream expert, described dreams as *"the embodiment of thoughts"*—a mirror of our personality, beliefs, and all that we are.

Ancient civilisations honoured dreams as portals to divine wisdom. In all major religions, dreams were once seen as sacred—a form of divine communication. Modern society has largely dismissed their power. As children we are often told that *"it was just a dream"*, which trains us to ignore one of the most natural, Spiritual tools we are innately equipped with.

When we arrive on Earth as babies, we initially have no awareness of our physical bodies and remain energetically connected to the Spiritual realm. It is perhaps no coincidence that infants sleep so much, given the possibilities we have explored. Likewise, toward the end of life, people often sleep more—again suggesting that the closer we are to Spirit, the more of this reconnection and Spiritual support we require.

A little thought... ★

This topic is absolutely fascinating, and I now see that this was what I was experiencing, when I was very unwell, with M.E. I was unable to recognise it at the time, but looking back, I was sleeping for approximately 20 hours per day. There was nothing physically wrong with me in terms of western medicine, but I was absolutely beyond exhausted. On reflection, it was my Spirit and Soul that needed recovery as opposed to my physical body. I needed the contact and guidance that I could only receive from these other realms, even though I was blissfully unaware of it then. It was giving me the strength and guidance to navigate the physical world again.

Have you ever felt a strong connection to sleep like this? Has it ever helped you recover from illness or dis-ease? Even if you were not aware of it at the time, but looking back now?

Dreams often contain elements from our daily lives, woven into strange, symbolic forms. Could it be that our subconscious filters through what matters most to us in that given moment, and brings us guidance accordingly? And when we gain greater command of our waking 3D world, perhaps dreams shift from processing trauma to supporting Spiritual expansion and creation? Many inventors and creative geniuses throughout history credited their dreams as sources of ideas and breakthroughs. These were not coincidences—they were the result of mastered 3D-5D awareness, making space for higher consciousness to work through them.

In dreams, we surrender our free will. Dreams strip away our control—and in doing so, teach us how to surrender and trust again. During REM, both serotonin and noradrenaline are shut down. The ego-based, 3D systems of logic, planning, and impulse control are reduced. We enter a state of surrender and connection to higher wisdom—Soul consciousness. This surrender is essential. It is not just a lack of control; it is trust in something far greater.

"The activity of the Soul we call fantasy is free from all the rules of reason."- Karl Scherner.

Dreams show us who we are, without the mask of ego. They are a mirror. We are both the dreamer and the dream. The world that surrounds us in the dream is generated entirely by us—and so it is in waking life. **And this is the big realisation: our dream world is just a reflection. And so too is our waking world.** What we focus on becomes our dream—and our reality. This is true on both planes.

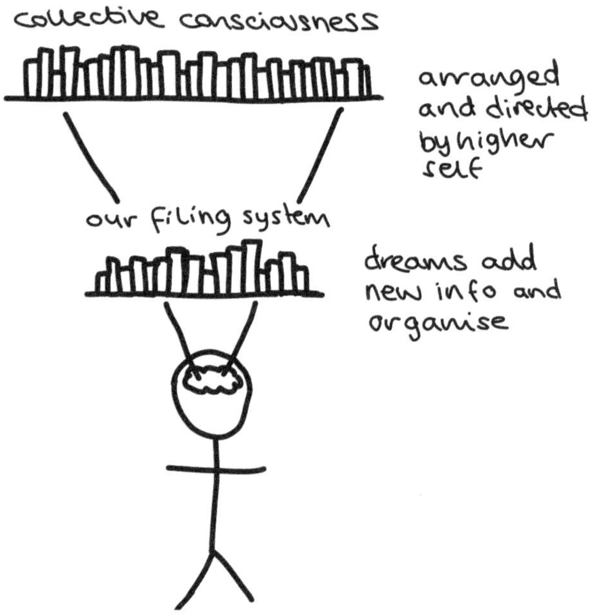

Dreams are the movement of knowledge into knowing. They help us evolve through experience. Carl Jung believed that dreams guide us toward balance, delivering unconscious material for us to integrate into a fuller version of Self. He also recognised the ancestral nature of dreams and the existence of a collective subconscious that connects all human beings.

The Society for Psychical Research, established in 1882 in the UK, has studied many phenomena—including dreams, apparitions, and telepathic communication. Their findings support what many ancient cultures already knew: we are connected to each other through a shared energetic field. Whether we call this field collective consciousness, source, or Spirit—it is a dimension we all have access to, especially when the ego is at rest and the Soul is awake, such as in sleep.

A little thought... ★

As your consciousness moves through higher states, it vibrates faster and becomes less dense—less tethered to physical reality. Dreams are the perfect everyday example of this, that we can all relate to. In dreams, we are often already in an astral form—out of body, but *spinning* too fast to be visible in the physical world. Some Spiritually sensitive individuals are able to raise their frequency in waking life enough to briefly perceive this astral form, accessing gifts of heightened frequencies and sensitivities. We look at this later in the *in* chapter, but interestingly these gifts are all accessed via some state of rest.

Lucid Dreaming

Lucid dreaming is the ability to become aware that you are dreaming, while still within the dream itself. This awareness marks the beginning of a lucid dream — where you consciously recognise that your current state is, in fact, a dream. There is a deeper layer to this experience, where one is not only aware but able to exert free will within the dream, influencing its events, direction, or interactions. The most common form of control tends to be over the Self, rather than the external elements of the dreamscape.

Lucid dreaming can offer profound benefits. It can help solve complex life problems, promote emotional healing, support physical recovery, release phobias, and contribute to personal and Spiritual growth. This deepened engagement with consciousness is powerful. However, as with all forms of conscious expansion, it exists on a spectrum. With the light comes shadow. Those who frequently experience lucid dreaming may also face lucid nightmares — disturbing dreams from which they struggle to wake. Another related phenomenon is a false awakening, where you believe you have returned to waking reality, only to discover you are still dreaming. These experiences can be disorienting and sometimes scary, and should be given the respect that they deserve.

To wrap up the lucid dreaming section on a softer note, I was once told about a woman who had mastered lucid dreaming to such a degree that she could invite any sexual partner into her dreams, to satisfy her how she wished. Whether or not she had—or even wanted—a romantic relationship in the 3D world, I'll never know. But the concept certainly opens up some fascinating questions, and the possibilities are endless!

Dream Incubation: Using Dreams to Our Advantage

There's no denying the importance of dreams and how significantly they can impact our lives and our state of rest. But how can we actively engage with them for our benefit? How can we intentionally align with their energetic potential? Thomas Edison, Salvador Dali, and multiple Nobel Prize winners have credited dreams with their breakthroughs. This is a vastly untapped area of human potential. The practice of dream incubation — the deliberate use of dreams to access guidance or insight — dates back to ancient Mesopotamia, and was further developed by both the ancient Greeks and Egyptians. Dream incubation involves setting a clear intention to dream about a specific topic or to receive an answer to a pressing life question.

Exercise

If you are interested in exploring the phenomena of your dream world, there are a few ways that can be helpful to start. You can begin by keeping a dream journal by your bed, to track the dreams that you have. Look for repeated themes and symbols that are relevant to you, and try to remember and re-cognise its significance. It can be helpful to have the guidance of generic meanings, but remember, whichever book or source you may choose to guide you, it is your personal interpretation and meaning that ultimately matters. Any awareness within a dream can open up the facility to a lucid dream. But as a starting point, I recommend dream incubation. Here is a simple method that you can try:

1. Choose a night when you feel relaxed and present.
2. Identify the issue you want insight into, and condense it into one clear sentence.

3. Ask yourSelf honestly — are you truly ready to receive the answer? Are you willing to let go of the attachment or fear that's keeping this problem in place?
4. Focus on how it would feel to be free of this issue. Then write down:
5. *"Thank you for showing me that…"* followed by the solution or feeling that you desire.
6. Fold the paper and place it under your pillow.
7. As you drift off, repeat the phrase to yourSelf and focus your energy on it.
8. Upon waking, write down anything you remember from your dreams.
9. Reflect on any imagery, symbolism, or emotions that may relate to your original request.

A little thought…

Tired but Wired? This phrase perfectly describes the frustrating state of needing rest, yet being unable to access it. It is when the body is clearly exhausted, but the mind will not quieten down enough to allow sleep or relaxation. This often precedes burnout, adrenal fatigue, and nervous system dysregulation. It is the warning sign that I look for to show me if I have become out of balance, or have missed the earlier signs. It sounds paradoxical — if the body is tired, surely it should rest? But this contradiction reveals something deeper: disconnection. When we are ungrounded or disconnected from Self, the systems of the body lose coherence. The intelligence of the body becomes disrupted by the noise of the unintegrated mind.

For me, this realisation was a turning point. All the times I felt deeply exhausted yet unable to rest were moments I was ungrounded and not fully in my body. I wasn't connected to me. Recognising this gave me insight into the true roots of rest, and its relationship with grounding, safety, and Self-connection. If we cannot feel safe in our environment or in our body, the systems of rest cannot activate.

I learned to begin this reconnection process by walking in nature and becoming aware of my breath whilst doing so. My pace of walk can be adjusted to ensure I get that reconnection – sometimes I need to walk quickly for the first part of the walk, and reduce it slowly. After this, I can then relax into the body, and use

stretching, full body massages, and Epsom salt baths.
A personal question for you now, and one that I'd like you to think about in depth: How do you create safety in yourSelf when you need rest? How do you nourish that part of you? Think of the times when you've felt truly rested, or perhaps the opposite, and how you have got yourSelf to that restful place? Then, go one step further: How can you cultivate more of this feeling in your life?

Non-Sleep Rest

Rest isn't only found in sleep. True rest can also come through conscious disconnection from the noise of the 3D world — a purposeful redirection of energy away from mental stimulation and habitual patterning. This kind of rest requires stillness in the mind, and often emerges when we are focused on something gentle, simple, or quiet — something that doesn't add to the chaos of our inner world, but instead calms it.

We often trick ourselves into thinking we are resting when we are actually escaping. Binge-watching TV, doom-scrolling on our phones, drinking lots of alcohol, engaging in unhealthy dating dynamics, or endlessly playing video games — these are not restorative. They are distractions, numbing us from pain or pressure we feel unequipped to face. These behaviours are not to be judged, only to be understood. They are survival strategies, often rooted in fear — and all fear is learned. If it is learned, then it can be unlearned. This recognition is the first and most powerful step toward changing your relationship with restoration and true rest. It is also why true non-sleep rest can feel so difficult, especially at the start.

A little thought… ★

I had internalised the belief that rest was weak, even wasteful. I believed every moment had to be productive — and that rest could only be earned. I went into my healing journey with the same intensity. One example was when I started my walking. I walked twice every day — beach, forest, wherever I could — and I did love it. But before long, I started turning it into a task. I added longer distances. I listened to podcasts and audiobooks as I walked. I stopped noticing the birdsong. I stopped feeling the ground beneath my feet. I was missing the whole point. Then came the realisation: I needed to walk for only *ten minutes a day in nature, with no distractions whatsoever, just me and me.* It was uncomfortable to put this into practice, at first. Why was it so hard just to be with mySelf? But over time, that ten-minute walk became my sanctuary. I realised — if this feels difficult, it is likely to be because your connection to Self is weak in that moment. Life in the 3D world pulls us from our centre. We are constantly learning how to return to our connection. And through trial, error, and practice, we learn what reconnects us. For me, it's travel. In recent years, I have gifted mySelf longer periods away — one month in Scotland, three months in Australia, two months in Colorado, two months in Bali, and shorter trips to Portugal, Ibiza, Switzerland, Spain, Portugal, and London. The nomad in me thrives in those expanses of space and introspection. Rest, in its truest form, is the space where true acceptance lives. You find a true state of rest within Self. It is where we stop running, stop pretending, and surrender into our own presence. It is the absence of tension. It is truth. It is being.

Ask yourSelf – what are your personal views on your resting? How do you allow yourSelf to rest? When do you stop yourSelf from resting in the way that you need?

"Rest is not weakness; it's an intelligent, nourishing part of our rhythm."

The Brain on Rest: The Default Mode Network

When the brain isn't focused on a specific task, it shifts into what's known as the **default mode network (DMN)** — this can be likened to the brain's resting state. It is a kind of mental background hum, where the mind wanders freely in the familiar. When we concentrate intently, parts of the DMN shut off. But when we rest, those parts light up again.

The DMN is not static — it shifts and adapts, depending on your internal world. That is why trauma, conditioning, and suppressed emotions deeply affect how the DMN operates. If you are someone who always needs to stay busy, your DMN might be carrying unprocessed pain.

When we stop avoiding ourselves, we invite completion. The DMN flags unresolved experiences and tags them for deeper processing — sometimes during waking rest, sometimes in dreams, and particularly in REM sleep. This is how the mind helps us heal. It finishes what was left open. It frees what was trapped. But only if we give it the stillness and space it needs to begin. It can be so challenging to find this stillness if you are in a pattern of always being busy and rushed. If this sounds like you, then here is something that you can begin to start small:

Exercise:

Start your morning, every morning, with 5-15 minutes of peace! Just after you have woken up, stay in the stillness with no interruption from phones, emails, or tasks. Just notice and feel what comes up – it may surprise you. If you find this beneficial, then you may increase the time, or develop this into a meditation practice.

A little thought... ★

When I first began allowing mySelf to slow down, I noticed something I had long been avoiding: the flood of unprocessed emotions. My subconscious had simply been waiting for a moment of quiet to speak. Rest had always felt unsafe for me, because in stillness, those unprocessed experiences would surface. Avoiding rest became a defence mechanism—I could keep moving, keep distracting, keep busy, and avoid what I did not want to face.

But healing required something different. Healing meant allowing mySelf to stop running, to sit with what arose, and to trust that I could face it. As I began to process these memories, something remarkable happened. My Default Mode Network—the part of the brain most active in states of rest and reflection—began to shift. Instead of replaying trauma, it started presenting me with clarity. Instead of exhausting me with old stories, it began offering insight, integration, and perspective. What once felt like a threat transformed into a source of nourishment. This was when I learned that stillness is not the enemy, but the doorway. Rest is not a void, but a sacred space where the body and mind reorganise themselves, making space for healing, wisdom, and new creation.

Meditation

Meditation is an example of non-sleep rest. It is an ancient practice that stills the body and allows us to separate from the mind and its constant stream of thoughts. This offers a form of rest that supports our three forms of being: we are resting the physical body in stillness, we are resting the mind from outside stimulation, and we are creating a connection to Soul, which is a form of pure rest in itself. The Soul gets to rest when we tune in to it. With less external 3D stimulation, the focus turns inward. The *out* fades, and the *in* becomes illuminated.

This practice has been embraced by many civilisations long before modern science could understand its benefits. For years in Western culture it was seen as something "woo-woo", but as is so often the case, what was once dismissed is now being rediscovered — because the truth of its power is undeniable.

Meditation naturally shifts the brain into lower theta brainwaves while maintaining consciousness — the space where creativity, healing, and transformation reside. It creates the internal conditions for you to experience something, before it physically arrives, and for the nervous system to believe that what you seek is already yours.

There are countless techniques for meditation, but most begin with the breath — guiding you into presence. With continued practice, you access the part of you that can *observe* your thoughts, rather than be consumed by them. In that moment, you remember: *you are not your thoughts*. You are the observer.

Meditation creates rest, and as with all polarity, rest breeds movement — in this case, Soul movement. That internal shift, that rising frequency, that contact with your Self — that's where the magic is. Meditation opens up a space that used to be filled with busy mental noise. And the moment that space is created, it is filled — not with more thoughts, but with the intelligence of your Soul, with what your Higher Self knows you are ready to receive.

A little thought... ★

My own meditation practices have evolved to become more ceremonial and intentional. I sometimes light candles, use crystals and incense, and surround mySelf with essential oils. I speak aloud — thanking and then directing. This is my form of connection. And as with all things in this book that spark something in you: you will find your own way, the best way for you. Practice will then make it familiar. And familiarity will make it scared, for you.

Do you have meditation as a part of your daily routine? How can you introduce or strengthen your practice? What benefits have you experienced from meditation?

Hypnotherapy

Hypnotherapy is often regarded as indefinable due to the vastness of its results, but as a brief attempt, I would say that it is a bit like meditation on steroids! It offers all of the same attributes for body, mind, and Soul, in the form of a non-sleep rest, but amplified in its depth and potentially-transformative properties.

The word "hypnosis" comes from the Greek *hypnos*, meaning sleep, and *agogos*, the path leading to it. Hypnotherapy can be understood as a bridge state — a conscious bypass into the subconscious mind. It has long been described as a *"trance state"*, and many ancient civilisations used ritual, rhythm, and flame to help people access it. This work is deeply powerful because it allows direct access to the subconscious by moving past the critical control faculty (CCF) — the filter that stands guard between the conscious and subconscious mind.

One of the most celebrated figures in the field was Milton Erickson. He approached hypnotherapy not through commands or instruction, but through gentle trust. He used stories, symbols, and metaphors — tools that spoke the language of the subconscious and Soul. Symbolism bypasses the ego's defences, so it is more naturally received by the deeper parts of us. It's also why our dreams rarely show us literal memories; instead, they present symbols that point toward the emotional truth. Erickson understood this well. And in doing so, he revolutionised the way hypnotherapy was practiced — through trust, suggestion, and surrender.

He believed — as I do — that every person's subconscious is governed by their Higher Self. And that this *always* knows what is best for a person. It will only guide a way that they are ready for, based on their current level of consciousness. There was no pushing, no coercion. Just a deep trust in the process of inner wisdom.

A little thought... ★

I'll admit, when I began my psychotherapy training, I was sceptical of the hypnotherapy module. I had only ever seen stage performers on TV making people bark like dogs, so needless to say, I was starting on a back foot! But, the moment I began to experience it and work with it, I realised just how powerful it truly is. I have used it professionally and personally, and some of the results are nothing short of transformational. I believe that it is a deeply under-utilised tool for healing, reprogramming, and awakening — one that ancient cultures understood far better than we do now.

What are your thoughts about hypnotherapy? Have you ever used it or considered using it? What would you use it for, if it could help you with anything?

If you would like to know more about hypnotherapy, please have a look on the social media pages and website for The Guiding Star System. Full details are at the back of the book.

Grounding

Grounding — or "Earthing" — is a greatly restorative form of rest and reconnection. It is the act of reconnecting physically and energetically with the Earth. The Earth has a natural frequency of 7.83 Hz, known as the Schumann Resonance. This frequency is our biological baseline, our energetic home, and the state in which our bodies can truly find a state of rest. Our bodies are designed to be in contact with this frequency — bare feet on grass, bodies lying on the ground, hands in the soil, skin against bark. For most of human history, we lived in alignment with it.

Now, we've built a world that separates us from it; we wear rubber-soled shoes, live in high-rise buildings, lay carpets and fake grass, surround ourselves with Wi-Fi, appliances, and devices emitting disruptive electromagnetic fields. Our connection is interrupted — and so is our energy. The result of this is build-up of synthetic charge in our systems, which increased inflammation in the body, and a gradual departure from our natural state of harmony and health.

The antidote is simple; touch the Earth. Stand barefoot on grass. Walk on a beach. Swim in the sea. Sit with your back against a tree. Submerge yourSelf in nature and feel the recalibration begin. Grounding is not just about the body — it is a full-system reset. It is a form of rest for the body because during these times, our body is not working to alter unnatural frequencies within it — it can rest in its natural frequency. This also creates the natural state of peace for the mind and reconnection to Soul energy.

Trees are the masters of grounding. Their roots stretch deep into the Earth, their trunks unmoved by storms. They adapt, endure, and *remain.* When you sit against a tree, back supported, feet on the grass, you feel steadied by their wisdom — and are invited to remember your own.

Ancient Indian healing practices knew the benefits of grounding, and often used it to help treat illness. This involved burying the person up to the neck in the rich Earth, near a fire. The body was warmed by the fire and healed by the frequency of the ground. It was a full energetic recalibration. And it often worked. Grounding is one of the most powerful, accessible forms of rest and reconnection available to us. It is stabilising, replenishing, and real. When done with awareness, it can be medicine for the Soul.

Fasting

Fasting is the conscious practice of going without—usually food, and sometimes even liquids or water. This acts as a form of rest on the body – rest of the complete digestive system and constant processing and neutralising of foods and liquids. The quieting of the mind is required in order to keep to the fasting practice. And in resting the mind and body, the connection with Soul is naturally strengthened.

Interestingly, fasting is one of the few things that all major religions agree on and promote in some way. There are many different versions of fasting, but all bring with them a clearing, a restoration, and a regeneration of all levels of being: body, mind, and Soul. And perhaps my favourite thing about fasting is that it requires nothing physical. It is about reducing, or taking something away. It costs nothing. And its benefits can be incredible.

On a physical level (including the effects on the brain), our bodies were designed to go without food for periods of time. Our primary fuel source is glucose, but when that runs out, and hunger sets in, the body activates its ketogenic system, drawing energy from stored fat. This intelligent biological response switches us into survival mode, upgrading us in many ways—sharpening mental alertness, increasing physical strength, and boosting GABA (a calming neurotransmitter). All of this puts us in peak condition to find food and water.

This system has been largely forgotten in modern society. We are used to eating often, and our egos panic at the first sign of hunger. It is not always easy—especially not when you are surrounded by food or people eating. Fasting challenges your beliefs about how much and how often you *need* to eat. But your body, your choices, and your growth are yours to own. What you avoid now will always meet you later in some form. Fasting is an invitation to face yourSelf. If it calls you, please do your research, take it slowly, and allow your body to reawaken its ancient wisdom.

The magic number is 16 hours. Once you have passed that point—which is easier to achieve when part of that time is spent asleep—you are already shifting into a different state. This is commonly known as intermittent fasting. Around the 17-hour mark, you enter a state called autophagy, where the body begins deep cellular cleansing, clearing out viruses, damaged cells, and anything that no longer serves. Only the strong survive.

At 24 hours, the intestinal stem cells begin to reset, offering a powerful reboot to the gut. And by 36 hours, blood sugar drops significantly, placing the body in a heightened fat-burning state. A 36-hour fast followed by a 12-hour eating window can be a powerful method for fasting and releasing a default frequency that no longer serves us. When approached with respect and in a safe way, fasting brings the body back to its natural blueprint.

A three-day water fast brings about a full reset of the immune system, boosting stem cell and white blood cell production. These effects are not achieved through one-off efforts— the true benefit lies in consistency, so it makes it most beneficial to schedule your fasting periods, and honour them. Once you experience the clarity and vitality that follows, the motivation to do it should not be an issue.

Fasting can be profoundly supportive for anxiety, in part due to an increase in BDNF (brain-derived neurotrophic factor), which helps calm the nervous system. It also supports gut repair and systemic cleansing, which both feeds directly into mental and emotional well-being.

In modern society, an abundance of food is tied to wealth and power. Many celebrations are built around indulgence. Fasting, in contrast, teaches Self-discipline. It is a sacred pause. A space to remember your power. When you are fully in alignment, even if briefly, it gives you perspective on where you are, what serves you, and what does not. It is within this space that the deepest lessons can be seen, felt, and integrated. Your cells begin to resonate with clarity, vitality, and truth—including your intuition.

A little thought... ★

My longest fast has been five days on water alone. It felt like magic. I had an old ankle injury that healed completely, and I experienced an overwhelming sense of well-being and clarity. I felt peaceful, calm, and completely present. It was as though time slowed down. I did need plenty of rest, and I made space for that. I have found a lighter way of fasting that I find particularly good for me, and that is eating only original seeded fruits, for a day or two. This can work well before or after a water fast, or as a stand-alone practice. It doesn't offer all of the benefits of water fasting, but is a great cleansing rest and reset on your system.

Is fasting something that you have in your practices? Is it something that you would like to add in to your routine, or enhance in some way? If reading this has sparked your curiosity about fasting, I'd recommend researching more into it before starting your first fast.

Fuel – Movement – Rest: Energetic Union

So far, we have explored three core components of The Guiding Star System: fuel, movement, and rest. In their simplest form, these three work in a sacred cycle. The fuel you choose powers the movement you create, and when that exchange is balanced, rest becomes effortless and deeply restorative. When your fuel supports your movement, and your movement is aligned with your frequency, your rest naturally optimises itself. There is no need for the body to waste energy correcting imbalances—it can simply flow.

This trinity forms the energetic engine of your existence. When these are in harmony, your baseline frequency elevates. You begin to move through life with more ease, presence, and power. However, even when people have experienced the benefits of these practices, it's common to fall out of alignment. Why? Because of unresolved energy blocks in the outer layers of the Self—those tied to the lower chakras, the ego, and the traumas that still ask to be integrated.

Disruptions in this union often show up as distorted relationships with these elements. Fuel becomes addiction. Movement becomes punishment. Rest is avoided. Ego, vanity, shame, and depletion take hold where healing, flow, and alignment could live. These distortions are signals—beautiful, valuable messengers—inviting you inward.

When you understand the dynamic interplay between fuel, movement, and rest, you begin to understand the energetic nature of your entire life. These three are the foundational practices for reclaiming your power, returning to your Self, and raising your frequency from the inside out. We now get to explore this in the remaining sections of the book.

A little thought… ★

Dissociation is itself a form of "rest" from the pain of trauma. Addictions operate the same way. They offer a temporary rest period from the internal chaos. But this kind of rest is not a healing rest—it's a pause button on a wound that will keep playing underneath. True rest comes when the energy tied up in that trauma is consciously acknowledged, felt, and then released and reintegrated into the whole Self.

Internal Family Systems (IFS), or "parts work," created by Richard Schwartz, provides a beautiful framework for the reintegration of your different parts. It teaches you to honour the parts of yourSelf that have helped you to survive—and to redirect their energy toward something healing and constructive within you. If this speaks to you, I deeply recommend exploring his work.

"True rest is the space where acceptance lives."

Rest – Summary

1. **All rest offers transference and transformation.** It is the sacred space in which energy is restored, repaired, and realigned. Rest opens the channel to source energy and its infinite wisdom. How that energy is best received will always depend on your Soul and personal incarnation of Spirit. Rest flows through all dimensions of our being: body, mind, and Soul.
2. **Every form of rest alters your frequency.** Rest represents a shift in consciousness—it is a moment of being beyond the active, thinking, doing state of 3D. While some forms of rest, like sleep, are vital for survival, others—like meditation, stillness, or creative flow—allow deeper Soul connection. These are not optional luxuries. They are essential for energetic longevity and expansion.

3. **Your best rest will always occur at your natural energetic frequency.** When you rest in alignment with who you truly are, the effects ripple outward, recalibrating your whole system.
4. **Rest is often avoided by those who fear stillness.** Stillness connects us to Soul and Self, and for some, that is where painful truths or long-avoided messages live. The ego resists rest because rest invites truth—and truth dissolves illusion.
5. **Rest to recover. Reflect. Repair. Rejuvenate. Renew. Recharge.** It is not laziness. It is preparation for expansion.
6. **Rest is an invitation to receptivity.** When you rest, you surrender to a higher consciousness. Whether consciously or not, rest downloads insight, recalibrates energy, and opens new possibilities. Becoming aware of this makes it even more powerful.
7. **Quality of life is directly linked to the quality of your rest.** It is not just about fuelling your energy or moving it forward. You must also allow it to slow, settle, and realign. As with all things, balance is key—and your ability to rest determines how you show up in the 3D world.
8. **As we spiral through the unlearning process, rest offers the integration.** Rest is where lessons crystallise, emotions settle, and Soul wisdom returns to the surface.
9. **Rest is a sacred bridge from knowledge to knowing.** It is through rest that truth is revealed, and the Self returns to alignment. The Soul finds its peace only in truth.

"The only rest for Soul is in its own truth, and aligning with that truth, no matter what." – Me

Exercise

REST	How do you currently rest and rejuvenate?	What changes do you want to make to maximise your rest?
Rest of physical body		
Rest of mind		
Rest of Soul		

The Distinction Between *Out* and *In*

Before we move into the next sections—*Out* and *In*—it's worth taking a moment to understand the distinction between them. Put simply, the *Out* chapter explores your external world: the physical and tangible – including your physical body, people, places, circumstances, and experiences that manifest around you. The *In* chapter focuses on your internal landscape: your thoughts, emotions, connection, energy, and Soul-level awareness.

The key principle to hold in mind is this: your external world is a projection of your internal world. What you see and experience on the outside is a reflection of what is happening within.

Imagine your internal world as the soil, and your external life as the garden that grows from it. If the soil is nourished, healthy, and balanced, the plants that grow will be strong and vibrant. But if the soil is depleted, neglected, or filled with weeds, the garden will struggle to thrive—no matter how much effort is put into the surface.

The *In* and *Out* are always connected. Energy moves from within to without. When you shift your internal world—through healing, Self-awareness, and alignment—you will notice that your outer world starts to shift too. People respond to you differently. Opportunities arise. Your environment reflects your new frequency.

Understanding and honouring this connection is essential to creating lasting change. You do not have to chase the outside world to make your life better—you align the inside, and the outside will follow.

These chapters are deeply interlinked, as one is a reflection of the other. The guiding principles that influence both aspects are explored in the chapter titled *The Meeting Point of Out and In*, where we look at the harmonisation between these two realms. True alignment occurs when there is coherence between what is happening within you and what is being reflected outside of you.

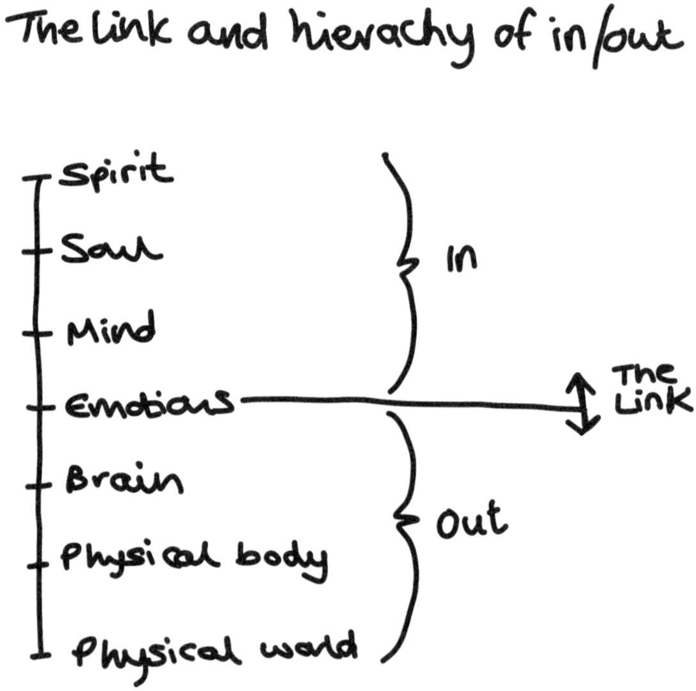

Out and In: The Brain and the Mind

To simplify, the brain is the physical structure—the tissues, cells, neurons, and fluids that comprise the organ itself. These are tangible elements you could touch (though you probably wouldn't want to!). The mind represents the non-physical functions of the brain. It encompasses thoughts, energy, and the complex systems of consciousness. Although they are intangible, their existence is undeniable. The key difference lies between the physical and the non-physical, between *cell* and *energy*.

A fascinating thing about the mind is that for the majority of the time, our minds operate unconsciously, controlling our thoughts and behaviours without our awareness. This is a necessary function that allows us to manage the constant influx of sensory information. If we had to consciously process every piece of information we encounter, we would be completely overwhelmed. Instead, the mind stores repeated information in the subconscious, like a storage bank, creating automated responses and behaviours to make functioning easier. Imagine having to learn that fire is hot every single time you encounter it, or having to relearn how to drive a car every time you get behind the wheel! Life would be infinitely more difficult.

Our subconscious stores both inherited and learned information—lessons, traumas, childhood behaviours, and innate desires. Experiences that elicit strong emotional responses are prioritised in our systems until we process them and reduce the emotional charge. The subconscious also incorporates ancestral, generational, and past-life influences. All this accumulated data shapes our reactions and choices, striving to keep us safe and protected. This subconscious programming significantly influences our daily lives, mindsets, and overall well-being. It is essential to understand this process and learn to become mindful and consciously guide your own mental programming. By becoming aware and taking charge, you can fully unlock your potential, harnessing the power of your mind.

A little thought... ★

There is currently no scientific consensus that consciousness originates solely within the brain. Emerging research suggests that it may not be confined to one place at all — some studies explore the heart's electromagnetic field, the gut's vast neural network, and even the intelligent responsiveness of cell membranes.

The precise seat of consciousness remains one of science's greatest mysteries. Yet it is also an invitation — a question that invites you to pause and feel into your own truth. Where do you sense your consciousness lives? Is it in the quiet of the mind, the beat of the heart, the depth of the belly, or something vaster that flows through every cell?

The Stars!

Sun Signs, Moon Signs, and Ascendant Signs. Your Sun sign—sometimes incorrectly called your star sign—relates to the position of the Sun at the exact moment you were born. The Sun moves through the twelve zones of the zodiac stars, each corresponding to a constellation. For example, my Sun was in Sagittarius at the time of my birth, meaning I was born under the Sagittarius zodiac. The Sun can shift signs at any point during the day, not just at midnight, so if you were born on the cusp, it is worth checking if the sign you have been told is accurate.

The Sun sign represents your personality and how you project yourSelf to the outer world. It is the visible, external part of you—how others see you. As my favourite author Linda Goodman explains: *"The Sun is the most powerful of all the stellar bodies. It colours the personality so strongly that an amazingly accurate picture can be given of the individual who was born when it was exercising its power through the known and predictable influences of a certain astrological sign… The Sun isn't the only factor in analysing human behaviour and traits, but it's easily the most important single consideration."*

The Sun sign aligns with the themes of the *Out* chapter of this book. It represents what we are born into—our energetic personality blueprint, our raw characteristics, and the outward identity we begin life with. These traits, along with ancestral genetics, form the foundation of our human experience from day one. Over time, it is possible to outgrow or evolve beyond certain traits of your Sun sign, particularly the more challenging ones. Much like karmic cycles, they can be transcended—depending on your growth, healing, and the relationship you cultivate with your *In*.

Your Moon sign, on the other hand, corresponds to the moon's position at the time of your birth and represents your inner Self—your Soul, emotional landscape, and intuitive nature. It reflects who you are when no one is watching. Your moon sign governs your instinctual responses, feelings, and subconscious reactions. It is the inward you, and its essence resonates through the *In* chapter.

Your Ascendant sign (also known as your rising sign) is calculated from the exact time and place of your birth. Imagine the moment you were born and looked up at the eastern horizon—whichever sign was rising at that precise time is your ascendant. The ascendant sign greatly influences your reasoning, decision-making, first impressions, and spontaneous reactions. It is how you immediately react to the *Out,* not when you have had time to contemplate your reaction. It is often referred to as the mask you wear when meeting the world, and over time, it integrates into your outward behaviour.

Together, your Sun, Moon, and Ascendant form a powerful trio. Their interaction paints a fuller picture of who you are—how you act, how you feel, and how you process the world. The magic of this trinity lies in its dynamic nature. You are not fixed; you are capable of transforming, transcending, and aligning more closely with your Higher Self throughout life. — *"Always remember that astrology is not fatalistic. The stars incline; they do not compel."* – Linda Goodman.

If you are curious to explore your personal blueprint in depth, I highly recommend having your natal chart calculated by a skilled astrologer. This chart offers a snapshot of the cosmos at the precise moment of your birth, and includes the positions of all the planets. A well-interpreted natal chart reveals striking detail—and often, powerful truths.

The more you explore astrology, the more you will realise it is so much more than magazine horoscopes. A natal chart is deeply personal, and when calculated and read properly, it provides rich insight with startling accuracy.

A little thought… ★

I was particularly drawn to astrology and Sun signs as one of the first steps in my Self-discovery. They are responsible for the beginning of my Spiritual journey, and I forever find mySelf being drawn back to them. For me, I find a level of comfort, grounding, and reassurance from the knowledge they give. And challenge in finding the strengths in some of the less desirable characteristics they have presented me with! If you are looking for a source, my favourite is Linda Goodman. I have borrowed a few quotes from her in this book, and I highly recommend any of her works. Enjoy!

"*Alone among the sciences, astrology has spanned the centuries and has made the journey intact. We shouldn't be surprised it remains with us, unchanged in time – because astrology is truth – and truth is eternal.*" - Linda Goodman.

Have you looked into the characteristics of your own sun sign? Or have you gone further and had your full natal chart drawn before? How would you look to further this exploration?

Now that we have explored the distinctions, we are ready to dive into the last two points of the guiding star system, starting with your external – your *Out.*

Out

OUT is the reflection of our energy allocation and focus. The mirror of our consciousness. The physical canvas on which we paint our lives. It is the visible and physical expression of our relationship to Self and Soul. The embodiment of authenticity and integrity. This is the outside world, the physical.

As you move through this chapter, reflect on how your external reality reveals the energy you hold inside. Your body, your lifestyle, and your surroundings all offer insight into how you are allocating your energy. Some external reflections may align with your highest Self, while others may reveal areas in need of recalibration. Out is your visible frequency—where the internal meets the material.

Lifestyle

The physical world we live in—and the lifestyle we lead within it—are reflections of our inner selves and the energetic frequencies we carry. Every choice we make, every habit we adopt, every space we inhabit is an extension of the energy we hold within. Our lifestyle is not just how we spend our time; it is a living, breathing mirror of our consciousness. It tells the story of what we value, what we tolerate, what we believe we deserve, and how connected we are to our authentic Self.

Many people assess the quality of their lives based on how often they escape their day-to-day reality—through holidays, weekends, digital distractions, or fleeting pleasures. But a Soul-aligned life is not something you need to escape from. The true architect of a meaningful life understands that joy is not reserved for the occasional high point, but can be cultivated in the ordinary. There is profound beauty in the everyday—the smell of morning coffee, the stillness of a walk in nature, the way you speak to yourSelf in quiet moments, and the energy you bring into your home.

"A Soul-aligned life is not something you need to escape from."

Your lifestyle is the sum of countless micro-decisions you make each day. What time you wake up. How you nourish yourSelf. Whether you move your body. How you speak to others. Whether you scroll or sit in silence. These small actions compound into your entire lived experience. They become your frequency. And that frequency attracts more of the same—either keeping you locked in the same loops, or gently lifting you toward new levels of expansion.

An aligned lifestyle supports coherence between the mind, body, and Soul. It honours your energetic needs, prioritises emotional regulation, and makes space for joy and presence. It's not about perfection—it's about creating a container that reflects your truth and supports your evolution. This may mean simplifying. Slowing down. Saying no more often. Or making brave changes that feel uncomfortable but necessary.

Lifestyle, in this light, becomes sacred. It becomes a living, intentional framework for who you are becoming. It is where your values are embodied, your boundaries expressed, and your healing sustained. It is the frequency you live by—and the frequency that speaks for you long before you say a word.

"Most persons are so absorbed in the contemplation of the outside world that they are wholly oblivious to what is passing on within themselves." – Nikola Tesla

The Physical Body

The human body is our personal vessel, our own physical representation and reflection of our inner world. It is not separate from our consciousness, but rather an extension of it and how we show up in the external world. Through the body we are able to explore and experience the external world, to feel, to act, and to navigate the lessons our Soul came here to learn.

We often think of the body only in terms of biology—muscles, bones, organs, and systems—but it is so much more. The body is a translator, continually communicating the state of our inner world through sensation, health, vitality, and even appearance. Low energy may signal not only physical depletion, but also misalignment in how we are living.

We can eat the healthiest foods, move our bodies daily, sleep well, and follow every wellness trend—and yet, if our inner world is not cultivated with love, peace, and authenticity, it will still be reflected in our physical body and the life around us. Illness, fatigue, or imbalance are not punishments but invitations: signs from the body that something within us is calling for attention and healing.

Equally, when we nurture our inner world—through Self-awareness, emotional healing, authentic living, and Soul alignment—the body responds. Energy flows more freely, vitality increases, and the outer world begins to shift. The skin glows, the eyes brighten, the posture straightens. These are not simply aesthetic changes, but reflections of coherence between body, mind, and Soul.

The physical body therefore becomes both a guide and a teacher. By learning to listen to it with compassion, we begin to recognise its signals not as obstacles but as wisdom. In this way, caring for the body is not about striving for perfection or control, but about creating a harmonious vessel for the Soul to live, express, and evolve.

The 5 Senses of the Physical Body

The human body is equipped with five physical senses to help navigate and interpret the world: sight, hearing, smell, taste, and touch. These senses help us learn from our environment.

> "The 5 senses help our human bodies navigate and interpret the outside world."

All sensory information is electric in its nature. It travels to the brain, where it is interpreted through the filters of our personal memory bank—our perceptions, shaped by past experiences. This interpretation is energetic, and unique to each of us. Vision is our dominant sense, and we tend to trust what we see. But our perception fills in gaps all the time, without our conscious awareness. So even what we see is not always the whole picture.

These senses are our tools for this incarnation. They help us learn what the Soul came here to learn. Interestingly, in dreams, we often experience sensations just as vividly—sometimes even more so—despite no real sensory input. Dreams can feel physically real, even though our 3D body is not involved. Still, our dominant senses in waking life remain dominant in dreams—especially vision.

The Gut–Brain Connection

The gut is a hub of intelligence—home to over 200 million neurons and hundreds of millions of bacteria. Often referred to as our *second brain*, it plays a vital role in emotional and energetic regulation. When we experience strong emotions, we feel them in the gut. That "gut feeling" or punch-in-the-stomach sensation is not just metaphorical, it's real.

The gut can be regarded as an organ of its own, a vital organ, key to our vitality and longevity. The enteric nervous system. It is the vagus nerve that connects the brain and the gut, and they are on a continuous dialogue of communication. It is the neurotransmitters that are the language used to communicate within the nervous system, throughout the body. And serotonin is the well-being or "happy" neurotransmitter, and 95% of this is produced in the gut, and enters the blood stream.

Recent research shows that trauma can cause a hypersensitive gut, disrupting its communication with the brain and creating a loop of emotional and physical dysregulation. The gut is sending these frantic signals to the brain, affecting the communication between the gut and the brain via the vagus nerve. Sigmund Freud once referred to "psychic colitis," noting that unexpressed rage could physically manifest as expulsion through the bowels. Gastro-psychoanalysis is a developing area of scientific discovery, and may reveal interesting connections in future science.

The Heart–Brain Relationship

The heart is responsible for circulating life force—our blood—throughout the body. It is the first organ to form in the womb. Some believe it originates from a single cell of the *Flower of Life*, linking it with sacred geometry and divine creation. The heart emits its own electromagnetic field—a powerful frequency that radiates beyond the body and forms part of our aura. This frequency is shaped by the emotions held in the body, both current and stored.

The brain also emits a frequency, but while it often believes that it is in charge, it is really the magnetic nature of the heart that tends to lead the way energetically. The brain is electric; the heart is magnetic. When the heart and brain are in conflict, we often "just know" what feels right. That knowing resonates through the whole body.

LOVE
LOGIC

connection
FEAR
LOVE
grounding

A little thought... ★

I know I am not alone in finding mySelf in moments where my heart and my brain seem to be in disagreement — a tug-of-war within. The brain, wired for survival, often speaks in fear; the heart, attuned to truth and love, whispers with compassion. When we feel challenged or threatened, it is almost instinctive to react from the brain — to protect, defend, retreat, or lash out. Yet it is possible, with practice, to pause and respond from the heart instead. This shift is not always easy; it requires awareness, patience, and the courage to sit with discomfort rather than react to it. But over time, we can train ourselves to return to the heart's steadier wisdom.

Can you recall a time you felt triggered and acted from the fear-based brain? How did you feel after space and time softened the moment? And imagine now — how might that same situation have unfolded if you had responded from the heart's perspective?

Perspective and Our Viewing Lens

Children are born in their subconscious form. They are not even aware of their physical bodies—they do not know that they *have* a body. It is said that babies cry when they enter this world because they remember the Spirit realm they have come from, and the transition into physical form is a bump, quite literally. As they grow, babies develop awareness of their physicality and surroundings—their *Out*—along with their conscious state. Our bodies are our first identity: our physical Self.

In childhood, our environments, relationships, and early life experiences shape our foundational beliefs. Our subconscious minds are wide open during this time, and we absorb everything, forming core beliefs rapidly. This is a survival mechanism, rooted in the primal need to survive. Whether those beliefs are true, helpful, or healthy does not matter at that point—they are adopted as part of our unique programming. No two people will carry the same set of core beliefs, not even identical twins raised in the same home.

Awareness itself is your identity—as the observer—and you are always within your awareness. As you begin to raise your energetic frequency, you will inevitably begin to challenge your core beliefs. The more willing you are to question these internal programs, the more deeply you reconnect with your Soul and your truth. And some of us have a longer journey back than others.

As we have explored through the unlearning spiral, our perspectives are shaped by our past experiences. These perspectives become the lenses through which we view the world. And as your frequency elevates, your lens will change—what once seemed absolute may suddenly appear limiting or untrue. Awareness of this process is already a shift in perspective. From this new vantage point, you naturally begin to operate from Soul rather than ego. This is an entirely different frequency—one led by the heart, not the mind.

A little thought... ★

When you begin looking at the *out* of yourSelf, you are often examining the areas you wish to improve — the things in your external world that don't feel fully aligned with your highest Self. When I first started this work, I remember being confronted with a lot of negativity about where I was at that point. It's easy to slip into self-criticism when you start noticing what doesn't fit or what feels out of place.

But it's vital to bring Self-love and Self-acceptance into every stage of this journey — and to every part of yourSelf you encounter along the way. No human being is perfect. We are all here to learn, to grow, and to better understand who we are. Accepting the parts of yourSelf that you may not love right now doesn't mean you approve of every action or choice you've ever made. It means you're willing to look honestly, without shame, and hold space for the person you've been while moving towards the person you're becoming.

Simply having the courage and foresight to do this work — to examine your life, to ask hard questions, to take responsibility and seek growth — is already a huge achievement. Honour that. See that this willingness alone is evidence of strength and love for yourSelf, even if the process feels uncomfortable or confronting at times.

The Distraction of Pleasure from the *Out*side

When we decide to distract ourselves with pleasure, we are ultimately distracting ourselves from something within. These behaviours offer fleeting pleasure, but they are an output of energy rather than an input. There is a clear difference between enjoying a nourishing, healthy meal and over-indulging in something we know is not good for us. One is rooted in Self-love and purpose, the other in avoidance.

When we engage in these behaviours, we are temporarily numbing ourselves — distracting from discomfort, pain, or unprocessed emotion. Sometimes we are conscious of this, but often we are not. Either way, it diverts us from our path, our purpose, and the connection with our true Self. For many, the thought of facing what lies beneath is simply too overwhelming — and so distraction becomes a survival mechanism. We do what we can to get through, and sometimes that requires forgiveness and compassion for ourselves. These are the moments where pleasure and avoidance team up to keep us stuck.

But once we become aware of our behaviours, we gain the opportunity to trace them back to their root. What are they covering? What wound or unmet need are they soothing? With that awareness comes a powerful invitation to heal. And what we often realise is that no amount of the behaviour will ever be enough to fill the void. The moment we engage, we want more. One biscuit is never enough. One scroll becomes an hour. One drink leads to the next.

There is a balance to be found — between simple, healthy enjoyment and compulsive distraction. That balance is yours to define. And as you become more whole, the desire for fleeting pleasure begins to fall away. You no longer *need* it.

A little thought... ★

Have you ever looked at someone's life and thought, *"They have it so easy"*? As though everything arrives with less effort, less struggle, and more grace? It may be that, in this lifetime, their Soul is on a "resting phase" of its journey through the human experience.

Each Soul follows its own unique cycle of growth, healing, rest, and service. Sometimes a Soul chooses a lifetime of gentler lessons—to recover from the intensity of a previous life, or to prepare for the depth of a future one. A "gentler" life is not a lesser one; it serves a different but equally sacred purpose.

Understanding this can help us soften judgment — both of ourSelf and of others. Each Soul has its own timing and curriculum. We are all walking different, but perfect, paths.

Exercise

Where are you now? Here is your time now just to give an honest reflection of your current life in terms of your unique outside world, and how *you* see it. This is not anything other than an acknowledgement of what currently is. You do not need to include anything that you want to change, this is just an exercise to bring to your awareness these sections of your life as they are now, in a factual style. For example, how are these individual areas for you? What comes to mind as what you would like to change, or what you would like to keep? This is a current snapshot of what is…

	My current outside world:
Physical body and health	
Everyday lifestyle	
Home	
Financial income	
Family (including partner, if applicable)	

Friends and community	
Time	

Take a moment to reflect on your journey through life so far. These are deeply reflective questions, so take some time in your own silence, and answer them in all your truth and honesty. The more that you can put into these, the more you will get out of them.

What has brought you here, to reading this book?	
What have been your most defining moments in life?	
What lessons can you take from these?	
What patterns can you trace in your past that altered your direction, shaped your learning, or shifted your perspective?	

What parts of yourSelf did you abandon, deny, or discover? (Either as a result of the above answers/events, or if not, the result of something else entirely).	
If you could go back to one point in life and give yourSelf advice, when would that be and what advice would you give?	
Do you feel that advice is still your truth now?	
Has this exercise brought anything into your awareness that you want to work on? Is there anything that you feel you may be hiding from yourSelf? An issue you feel you need to address?	

In

> IN is the direction of our energy, the decision, control, and allocation of our creative Soul power energy. Self. Soul. Our truth, the only truth. Knowing. Being.

As you move through this chapter, reflect on how you connect with your inner energy, how you choose to direct it, and what that says about who you truly are. Some insights may feed the mind, some may stir the heart, and some may awaken the Soul. This is the centre of your being—the source of your power, your knowing, and your alignment with the universe.

The Energy Body

The energy body refers to the subtle, non-physical layer of our being. It exists alongside and within the physical body, interfacing with it in ways that science is only just beginning to understand—but that Spiritual traditions have honoured for millennia. Every human being possesses an energy body. It is not imagined, nor is it exclusive to those on a Spiritual path. Rather, it is an integral part of what it means to be alive. Just as our five physical senses help us navigate the material world, our energetic or *non-physical* senses help us interpret and interact with the unseen. These subtle senses—often dormant or undeveloped—are our access points to intuition, inner knowing, and direct connection with the Soul. The more we learn to tune in to these senses, the more we come into alignment with the totality of our being.

The Aura

The aura is the electromagnetic field that surrounds the body—a living reflection of our energetic state in any given moment. It mirrors the quality of our thoughts, emotions, and physical vitality. You can think of it as an energy signature that expresses how we are being, right now. It shifts and responds to internal states and external influences alike.

The aura is deeply personal, yet it also serves as a bridge between the inner world and the outer one. It contains subtle information—emotions, memories, intentions—and expresses this information as colour, shape, lightness, and density. A vibrant, balanced aura reflects harmony and clarity. A dull, fragmented, or heavy aura may suggest depletion, stored trauma, or energetic interference. Most importantly, the aura acts as a protective shield. It is our first layer of energetic defence, and when intact and strong, it acts as a filter, protecting us from absorbing energies that are not ours to carry.

Imagine the aura like a shimmering rainbow bubble surrounding your body. Everything you wish to create, manifest, or share in the world must pass through this energy field. Likewise, everything you encounter is first interpreted through the lens of your aura. This is why energetic maintenance is so beneficial for creative power and emotional clarity.

A little thought... ★

When you're going through a challenging time, you may feel your aura deflated and depleted — like the very field that once protected and held you has collapsed inwards. During my own healing, one of the most powerful practices I created was a meditation devoted to rebuilding my core values and aura.
I would ask mySelf: *What are my true core values? What does my Soul really stand for?* Then, with each intentional breath, I would breathe life back into those truths. As I repeated them, felt them, and believed them, I would visualise my aura expanding — growing stronger and larger with every inhale. I'd see it radiating outward into a vibrant, protective field of light, shimmering around

me like a living shield. I would invite colour into it and imagine this field protecting me.

Over time, I realised that my aura had only deflated because the beliefs it was built upon weren't strong enough to withstand life's storms. They were never truly *mine*; they had been borrowed, inherited, or shaped by fear. They were directing me to what I could change. To learn how to be rooted in my own truth. I decided to choose new values for mySelf—ones that were true to me… and you're invited to do the same! You can create a new energetic foundation — one that is strong enough to hold you, no matter the storms that come. ☺

Non-Physical Senses: The "Clairs"

Our energy body doesn't only protect and radiate—it also perceives. Just as our eyes see and our ears hear, the Soul perceives through its own intuitive channels. These are often referred to as the "Clair" senses, short for the French word *clair*, meaning "clear." These extrasensory abilities were once honoured and nurtured by ancient civilisations, but are often dismissed in modern culture. Nonetheless, they remain active and available to some. Some people are more naturally attuned to these intuitive senses, but they can be awakened, developed, and strengthened over time. It is through such strengthening that our perception of the *In* can be enhanced. Here are the primary Clair senses:

Clairaudience (Clear Hearing) - This is the ability to hear beyond the physical realm. Those with clairaudience may perceive words, phrases, tones, or guidance not spoken aloud. This communication may sound like it comes from the "inner ear"—a subtle voice that brings insight, reassurance, or direction. It may even sound like a familiar voice. This gift is often linked with musicians, poets, or those with a refined sense of rhythm and resonance.

Clairvoyance (Clear Seeing) - Clairvoyance is the ability to see with the mind's eye — beyond the limitations of physical vision. This may include seeing symbolic images, energy patterns, timelines, or beings from other realms. Clairvoyants often receive messages as vivid mental images, dreams, or visions.

This gift is closely linked with imagination and Spiritual sight, and it opens doorways to deeper dimensional awareness.

Clairsentience (Clear Feeling) - Clairsentients experience energetic information through feeling. This may include physical sensations such as tingling, pressure, temperature shifts — or emotional energy that doesn't originate from within. Empaths, highly sensitive people, and those with a deep connection to animals and nature often possess strong clairsentient abilities. This gift allows one to "read a room" instantly, sense unspoken truths, or physically feel another's pain or joy.

Claircognisance (Clear Knowing) - Perhaps the most elusive, claircognisance is the ability to just know. With no logical reasoning, no prior knowledge, you simply receive insight that is undeniably true. This inner knowing often arrives spontaneously, with certainty and precision. It may feel like déjà vu or like downloading information from a higher source. Claircognisance is deeply linked with Soul memory and may carry wisdom from past lives or higher dimensions.

Awakening the Energy Body

Tuning into the energy body is about remembering who you already are. These subtle layers of your being have always been present—they may simply have been quiet or suppressed beneath the noise of modern life. Awakening them is a gradual process of learning to listen again.

You are not limited to what your five senses perceive. You are a multidimensional being with access to infinite streams of guidance, protection, and wisdom. Your Soul has its own language, and the energy body is the translator.

"You are a multidimensional being; intuition is your native language."

By tending to your energy field, cleansing your aura, and honouring your inner senses, you begin to live with greater awareness, protection, and alignment. You begin to trust the invisible layers of life, and can live from intuition rather than fear. And in doing so, you begin to walk through the world not just as a human being—but as a Soul, in motion, remembering who you truly are.

As Nikola Tesla one said, *"[I]nstinct is something which transcends knowledge. We have, undoubtedly, certain finer fibres that enable us to perceive truths when logical deduction, or any other wilful effort of the brain, is futile."*

The Chakras of the Energy Body

The energy centres of the body are most commonly illustrated through the system of the seven chakras. Originating from ancient India and first mentioned between 1500 and 500 BCE in the Vedic texts, this system has stood the test of time in both Spiritual and energetic practices. The word *chakra* translates to "wheel," symbolising the turning, spinning, or movement of energy. These wheels of energy are located at specific points along the spine, from the base to the crown of the head, and they each correspond to different aspects of our physical, emotional, mental, and Spiritual experience.

When the chakras are in balance, energy flows freely throughout the body, mind, and Soul. This supports our overall well-being, clarity, and vitality. If they become blocked or imbalanced, however, it can manifest as physical symptoms, emotional disruption, or a sense of energetic disconnection.

The discipline of Kundalini Yoga focuses specifically on the awakening and flow of this subtle energy, known as *kundalini*, through the chakra system. By activating and aligning these energy centres, practitioners aim to elevate their consciousness and access deeper states of awareness, intuition, and unity with Self.

Chakra	Body The physical	Mind The emotions	Soul The individual Spirit
Crown	Top of the head, the halo, the hair. The pituitary gland, that controls the hormones. The brain.	Knowledge, the highest part of Self, and the overriding guidance and "control". The submitter of your frequency.	The antenna, the receiver of frequency and information. Psychic and medium abilities. Higher Self and source energy.
Third eye	The pineal gland, the regulation of cycles in the body and regulation of sleep. Vision, hearing, and smell.	Awareness and imagination. Calm, quiet, and stillness to access this.	Intuition, in all forms. Any of the Claire senses. Non-physical wisdom.
Throat	Thyroid, regulation of metabolism. Control of temperature. The space between brain and heart. Taste.	Communication and ability to express oneself. Emotional boundaries. Flow and freedom to express.	Expression and conversion of third eye / Spirit knowledge into life! Soul boundaries known and in force.
Heart	The heart area, extending down all of the arms, circulation and movement. Thymus, regulation of the immune system.	Love and compassion, empathy, strength. Love for Self and all. Awareness of a collective consciousness.	Energy and electromagnetic frequency in flow. Your "bubble" or aura largely dictated by heart energy.
Solar plexus	The core, the very centre. Upper abdomen, pancreas, metabolism. The kidneys and liver.	Wisdom, power, purpose. Action, achievement, identity. Core belief and strength.	Soul identity realised. A knowing, and inner strength of Self. True Self.
Sacral	The lower abdomen, the nervous system, adrenal glands and stress regulation. Digestive system. The gut. Female sex organs. Feeling/touch.	Emotion, feeling, creation and creativity. Problem solving. Stress, overwhelm.	Gut feeling, life, creation. Contentment. Peace.
Root	The base of the spine, the pelvis, running down the legs all the way to the sole of foot and toes. Lower colon.	Survival, trauma. Storage. Root system to Self and being. Strength of Self, development of true Self.	Grounding, safety. Roots to Self. Ability to ascend and grow. As above, so below. Unshakable Soul developed in roots.

A person's individual journey can be either up or down the chakra system, or just on a single chakra requiring some attention and energy. The knowledge and knowing of the chakra system within us, helps us develop our relationship with our IN.

The Encoding of Spirit

Have you ever wondered why you are drawn to certain things over others? Or why some people have a particular talent that seems to come so naturally? What is it that links us to these gifts, passions, or preferences? This is your *encoding*—a blueprint imprinted in Spirit before birth, brought into your physical being through your body and energetic memory.

Your encoding is the set of gifts, interests, and natural inclinations you're born with. These may not always align with what the ego wants or desires, but they are yours nonetheless. They are part of your Soul's design. An example of this comes from a beautiful human, Craig David. His debut album, aptly titled *Born to Do It*, came from his reflections on how kids at school naturally flourished in specific areas—whether in sports, academics, or creative pursuits. These abilities were not just learned; they were *remembered*. Encoded. And for Craig, it was music—in all its many evolving forms, and his incredible career has surpassed the test of time.

Encoding doesn't begin and end with our immediate parents—it draws from the entire ancestral field. The energy that informs who we are is not limited to one generation, but weaves itself through the tapestry of our lineage, sometimes re-emerging in a new and evolved form. We often inherit more than just eye colour or bone structure; we inherit patterns, sensitivities, gifts, and unfinished stories.

Our Soul's encoding draws from this broader energetic field—not only from our family of origin, but from the deeper reservoir of those who came before. Some of what lives in us may have no clear origin in this lifetime, and yet it pulses through us with undeniable familiarity. We are not just the continuation of our ancestors—we are also the evolution. And through us, something ancient is trying to be remembered, rewritten, or reborn.

It's also worth remembering the concept of a skipped generation. Sometimes, we carry traits, talents, or sensitivities that seem to have no direct link to our parents. This can feel confusing—like a mismatch in the mirror of our immediate family. But if you find parts of yourSelf that feel un-reflected in those who raised you, try looking further back. Somewhere in your lineage, those attributes may be waiting—dormant, forgotten, or unspoken, but present.

Perhaps your intuition echoes that of a great-grandmother who read tea leaves, but was never allowed to speak of it. Maybe your sense of justice mirrors an ancestor who defied convention in ways history never recorded. Gifts can skip generations, bypassing those unable or unwilling to express them, only to land in you—ready to be reawakened. And lineage doesn't always express itself in a straight line. Sometimes, we are here not only to carry forward the light of our ancestry but to rekindle what was lost along the way.

I've always loved the phrase, *"You can't help what you love."* That simple truth speaks volumes about our encoding. What gives you joy and lights you up inside, comes from somewhere and is a part of your encoding.

"You can't help what you love; its your encoding speaking"

A little thought... ★

For me, that connection came through my grandfather on my mother's side. I've always called mySelf a "geek", with affection! I have always loved books, learning, studying; and later in life this has expanded to include writing too. These traits never seemed to match my immediate family, but they aligned deeply with my grandad. He always encouraged my love of learning and made me feel seen in ways that only he could. I still remember how he'd show up for dinner with my favourite chocolate bar, and how I'd convince him to take me to the stationery shop so I could buy new pens for my homework. He never said no—he just asked to see what I created.

Later in life, he began writing a book about his story, though he sadly never finished it. And while this book of mine isn't a life story, it *is* a book. A beautiful one. I know he would be so proud—wherever he is.

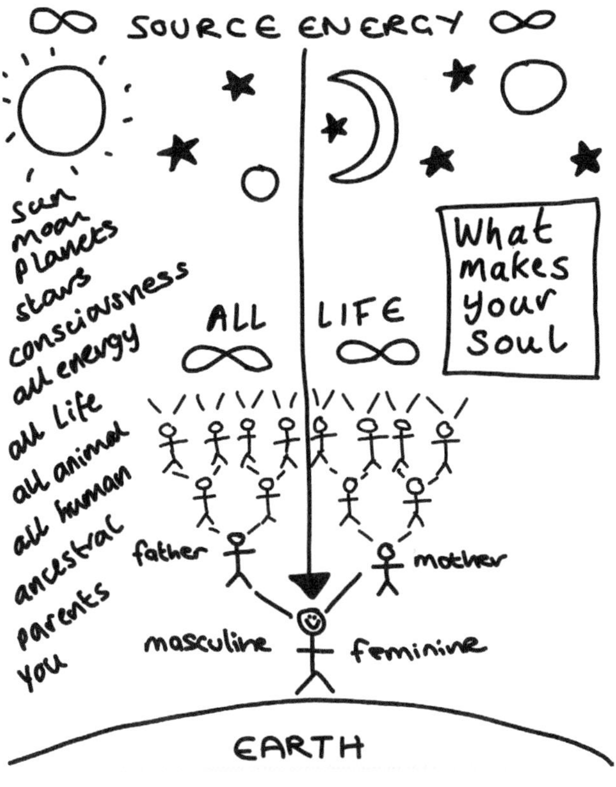

Exercise

If you're curious about your own encoding, a great place to start is by speaking with your parents or grandparents—if you're able to and if it feels right. What do they love? What are they gifted in? What have been their lifelong challenges? These clues can illuminate patterns and offer insight into your own Soul map. Then turn the lens inward. What do you love? What comes naturally to you?

What have you always been drawn to, even if no one else around you were at the time? Can you trace this back to anything you were actively taught—or is it something you have simply always *had* within you?

A little thought... ★

The topic of encoding naturally brings up the question: *Do we have a predetermined path in life?* Is our entire journey decided before we even arrive in our physical body? What do you believe?

I believe, yes—to an extent. The lessons we are here to learn are predetermined and personal, designed for our Soul's growth and evolution. Yet within that framework, we are powerful creators. We can alter the *experience* of our path, transform its challenges, and even change its outcomes through conscious choice. Life may hand us certain themes and opportunities, but how we respond, and the depth of our healing and joy — is ours to shape.

Now you are aware of this, what are you going to do? Is there anything that you feel you will change? How will this help you expand?

No matter what the original blueprint may be, the rate of progression is determined by you. Life will keep presenting the same lesson in different forms until it is learned. This mirrors the Buddhist and Hindu principle of karma: the cycle of cause, effect, and rebirth, which leads me on perfectly to the next section.

Karma

Karma is a concept rooted in ancient Eastern Spiritual traditions, particularly Hinduism, Buddhism, and Jainism. While interpretations may vary across cultures and philosophies, at its core, karma refers to the universal principle of cause and effect—the idea that every thought, word, action, or intention generates energy that ultimately returns to its source. In its purest sense, karma is not a system of punishment or reward, but one of energetic balance. It is the unfolding of consequences—seen or unseen—that align with the vibration we emit. When we act in alignment with love, compassion, and truth, we generate harmonious energy that tends to return to us in kind. When we act from fear, harm, or disconnection, that too creates a ripple that may eventually return—not as punishment, but as an opportunity to learn, grow, and recalibrate.

From a metaphysical standpoint, karma is electromagnetic energy in motion. Every interaction, emotion, and decision we make sends out a frequency—one that interacts with the field around us. According to the universal laws of resonance and reflection, this frequency will, in some form, find its way back to us. It may be in this lifetime, or another. It may be immediate, or decades later. But the energetic imprint remains, awaiting resolution or transformation.

Importantly, karma also transcends time and space. It can be carried through lifetimes, woven into the threads of our Soul's journey. This is why certain people, patterns, or experiences may feel inexplicably familiar or weighted—as though they hold meaning beyond this life. These may be karmic relationships, contracts, or lessons we have chosen at a Soul level in order to evolve.

It's also essential to understand that karma is not inherently "bad" or "good." These are human constructs. Karma is neutral. It simply mirrors the energy we put into the world—an energetic accounting system that ultimately brings us closer to awareness, Self-responsibility, and liberation.

When we begin to live consciously, we can work with karma rather than be bound by it. We can become aware of the cycles we are repeating, ask what they are trying to teach us, and consciously choose a different response. In doing so, we alchemise karma into dharma—our path of truth, service, and Spiritual purpose.

Karma reminds us that nothing exists in isolation. We are co-creators in a web of energy, and everything we do matters. Every intention, no matter how small, has an impact, as every IN-tention is our IN. And the more we align our actions with integrity and love, the more we shape a reality—and a future—that is aligned with the Soul. This is the expansion of our IN.

The Unshakable Soul

The *unshakable Soul* is a term I use to describe the profound state that occurs when you are deeply attuned to your Soul's frequency. You are listening to its guidance, trusting its nudges, and allowing it to lead you forward. This inner knowing always comes *before* the physical world catches up—or your *in* before your *out.*

Many people who have experienced remarkable success—Spiritually, creatively, or materially—often speak of this kind of deep knowing. A quiet certainty. A conviction that they were always on their way to where they were meant to be. Developing this unshakable knowing means reaching a point where nothing anyone says or does can pull you off your path. You are no longer swayed, because you are grounded in Soul—not ego. Referencing the *mind continuum,* this is when you are more strongly in the Soul frequency for your energy, beliefs, actions, and way of being. And this is the place we strive to live from.

The unshakable nature of this, is your natural preservation and protection of it above all else. This becomes your number one priority and commitment. You have a robustness towards this that forms your personal integrity.

Integrity is such a strong and beautiful word. Your personal integrity will always be one of your core values. Truly understanding the meaning of this word sits at the centre of your belief system. It's the perfect foundation to build from. This is the ultimate way of expanding and living your *in,* by just living in your being.

A little thought... ★

Being: Learning to be… is all we are here to "do". Beneath every goal, is a single invitation: to return to presence. We can spend so much of life striving to become, to improve, to achieve, yet the deepest transformation happens not through endless doing, but through allowing ourselves to simply *be.* To be aware. To be present. To be whole as we already are. In the stillness of being, the noise of comparison fades, the chase for worth dissolves, and the truth of our existence emerges — we are here to experience; to remember. Being is both the path and the destination.

"When you are anchored in Soul, nothing anyone says or does can pull you off your path."

Death

What happens when we die? Or more profoundly — what happens to *us* in Spiritual form, when we are no longer in physical form? The truth is, no single religion, Spiritual visionary, or scientific authority can give us a definitive answer. Death remains one of life's great mysteries, a threshold cloaked in the unknown. And perhaps it is meant to be that way. If we were meant to know for certain, we would. The mystery invites us to surrender and to live with the unanswered.

Most people fear death not for what it is, but for what they *think* it might be: pain, loss, the end of everything they have known. But if we dig deeper, it is often *loss* and the *fear of suffering*—not death itself—that disturbs us. Our culture has programmed us to associate death with darkness, grief, and fear, yet countless Spiritual traditions and philosophies view it not as an ending, but as a transformation.

Energetically, physics teaches us that energy cannot be destroyed, but only changed in form. The human body, once expired, decays and returns to the Earth. But our consciousness—the spark of awareness that animates us—has never been conclusively located within the physical body. What happens to *that*? Many believe it returns to a larger field of consciousness, to Source, Spirit, or the infinite whole. It becomes something that can be tuned into—an energetic frequency still accessible beyond the veil of physical form.

In tarot, the Death card is not a symbol of tragedy, but of transformation. It signifies rebirth, endings that lead to beginnings. This reflects the true nature of energetic evolution—death as a passageway, not a full stop.

Linda Goodman put it best: *"The only way to approach such a personal matter as life and death is by yourSelf."* That is perhaps the most sacred truth of all. Your relationship with death will be deeply personal, and if you choose to explore it consciously, it may shift how you experience life.

By contemplating death, you paradoxically become more connected to the miracle of your existence. For in exploring death, you meet life—honestly, fearlessly, and fully. And in doing so, you expand your *in*, and live more in tune with yourSelf.

Exercise

Here is where you create your ideal dream life, without any restriction. Whatever you would like, whatever makes your Soul happy in the world, in all the abundance that you wish. How big would you dream if you knew that you couldn't fail? If you could have anything, what would you ask for?

We start this exercise by asking you to describe your outside world, but based on the feelings of truth from your inner world. What do you *really* actually want? What is your *in* telling you? Let it guide you.

	My chosen outside world... (from the honesty of my *in*side world)
Physical body and health	
Everyday lifestyle	

Home	
Financial income	
Family (including partner, if applicable)	
Friends and community	
Time	

Now we are going to go deeper into this exercise, and further into our *in*side world. The more courage you apply here, the more you will get to the root of the truth, the more you will become aware of your true desires and your intention behind them. The book reiterates the teaching that your outside world is a reflection of your inside world, and here is where you get to tune into your *in*side world in all of its truth.

	Describe it in all the details you can...
How does this FEEL, for this (your above description) to be your life? Describe all of the lovely feelings for this to be now .	
Why do I want this? What is your intention behind these desires?	
Who will benefit from this? You, those closest to you, the world? How will they benefit?	

In order be able to live this dream life that you have described, and to get to experience these things, what qualities and values do you think you would have as this person? How do you think this person would be able to *hold this energy*? How are they *being*?

YOU	To be this person, what would it be like?
FUEL How would you fuel your life? Your body, your mind, your Soul? What will maximise your energy?	
MOVEMENT How do you want to move your body, your mind, your Soul? What will maximise your energy?	
REST How do you want to rest your body, mind, and Soul? What will maximise your energy?	
OUT How will you show up in your outside world? What will maximise your energy?	
IN What is your inner world like? Your true Self, your Soul? What maximises your energy?	

The Meeting Point of *Out* and *In*

The whole of The Guiding Star System brings you to this point here, the meeting point of the *out* and the *in*. The lesson that echoes through the teaching of this book is that your *in*ternal world is projected into your *out*side world, much like the projection of a movie onto a projector screen. But here we go much further, and you are invited to try the tools to turn this from *knowledge* into *knowing*, to really live a life that is lead from the internal.

In this section we look at belief systems, energy systems, the link; emotions, money/labour of love, the spoken word and creation, the darkness, and a guidance section. These all guide you to explore your own meeting point, and discover how to be all that you know you can be.

Belief Systems

The Trodden Path

Imagine how exhausting life would be if you had to consciously consider every tiny decision, every single day. Our minds are designed to create efficiency. That is why the thoughts and behaviours we repeat frequently become automatic. We shift into subconscious autopilot—habitual, efficient, and often unconscious.

These automatic routes of thought are like well-trodden paths in a forest. The more they are used, the clearer and easier they become to follow. They feel natural and require no conscious effort. This is helpful when the path leads somewhere good. But when those neural pathways are trauma-based or rooted in fear, they can create unhelpful, even harmful, patterns.

The good news is that the brain retains something called *neuroplasticity*, the ability to change and rewire itself. The more you fire new thoughts and behaviours, the more the brain wires them together. This is how new trodden paths are created. The more you walk the new path, the easier it becomes—and the more the old, outdated path fades and grows over.

Your belief systems are the internal architecture of your world. They shape your reality and define what you believe to be true about yourSelf, others, and life itself. These beliefs are formed mostly in childhood and are reinforced by your perceptions and experiences.

"Your belief systems are the internal architecture of your world."

We are all equipped with something called a *reticular activating system* (RAS), which is a network of neurons that filters incoming information to match what we already believe. This is known as *confirmation bias*—where you unconsciously seek out evidence that supports your existing beliefs. Whether those beliefs are empowering or limiting, your mind will find proof for them. This bias prevents us from reassessing what we believe to be true. It is not inherently negative—it exists for your survival. But left unchecked, it can keep you locked in patterns that no longer serve your growth. We tend to prioritise negative beliefs because they are linked to safety, and thus are more deeply embedded in our neurological wiring. When beliefs are unhelpful, they can significantly impact our lives—dimming our sense of Self, shrinking our possibilities, and lowering our frequency. Reprogramming them requires awareness and intention. And like every part of this journey, it starts with noticing.

Our beliefs also have ceilings—limits that define what we think is possible or acceptable. These ceilings are often most visible in what we think we deserve: our financial earning capacity, our career trajectory, our health, or our relationships. They tie directly to our sense of Self-worth and the Self-love that we hold internally. Thankfully, these ceilings are not fixed. They can be raised. And breaking through them—gently and intentionally—is one of the most empowering steps you can take. Sometimes the ego resists, because once the ceiling is gone, so too is the excuse. Success and expansion feel unfamiliar and unsafe, and you are entering new territory of the unknown.

Exercise

Reflect back to the exercise that you have just done where you were creating your dream life. Have a look back at your list, and when you consider living this life that you desire, what are the limiting beliefs that come up for you? These are the beliefs that may judge, restrict, contradict, or bring up guilt or shame – the internal blockages to all that you know you can be. It takes real courage and deep reflection to be able to go here, but here is where you really discover. Write these in the first column. An example may be; *"My illness keeps me safe"*, *"I don't deserve a life of freedom"*, *"I can't earn any more money"*.

The second column is for you to consider when and where is was that you first learned this limiting belief? This is likely to be a childhood memory, something that you experienced, something that you were repeatedly told? It is helpful to take some space to really consider this, as this is where the belief was originally formed.

	My limiting beliefs	**When did I first learn this?** (think back to your earliest childhood memory of when this belief was formed?)
Physical body and health		
Everyday lifestyle		
Home		
Financial income		
Family (including partner, if applicable)		
Friends and community		
Time		

In writing down the above, you are facing yourSelf and your limiting beliefs. You are shining light on the darkness. You have even been able to identify where they first came from, and can perhaps understand these beliefs as just something that you learned. A great way to help these leave your energy field is to write them all down on a piece of paper, and burn them. As you watch them burn, visualise and feel them leaving you and your energy system: As the flames transmute them into smoke and ash, you transmute into who you are in all your freedom and power, without what had been weighing you down. The more focus and energy that you give this, the more power it will have. *(Please burn these safely, and seek guidance on how to do this, if needed!)*

Next in the exercise is where you can create the desired or helpful new belief that you want to become. This is as if that limiting belief had never existed in you, and you chose what you want to believe. These represent the beliefs of your highest Self, and that which can create and hold all that you desire.

	The belief I choose to upgrade to as my highest Self
Physical body and health	
Everyday lifestyle	
Home	
Financial income	
Family (including partner, if applicable)	
Friends and community	
Time	

Identifying and acknowledging what needs to change, is followed with integration. The ego will always attempt to pull you back into its habitual patterns. Even once you understand something intellectually, it takes repetition and reinforcement to imprint it into your belief system. It is *now* that you retrain the mind, by creating new habits and wiring in new beliefs. We are going to go deeper into this process later in the chapter, so remain open, and carry on!

The Mind Continuum

In the earlier foundational concepts chapter, the mind continuum was introduced, in which the span of ego to Soul was explored. Here we look at ego in the concept of our belief systems, including how it interacts with our decision-making processes, and why it is important to challenge it.

The ego and its many layers can be complex—and often amusing—once you begin to observe them. The ego will do whatever it can to get its own way, and it will try to persuade you out of growth at all costs. It can be so incredibly convincing. One of my favourite examples of this is from Russell Brand, an intelligent and inspiring individual. Russell is a recovering addict, and has found support in his Spirituality. In discussing plant medicine and their Spiritually-enhancing potential, he shared how his ego—clever and relentless—tempted him with the idea that using plant medicine might be a valid Spiritual path, despite being in recovery. While others may have a different path, his truth meant recognising this as a trick of the ego, potentially opening up the path of addiction once again. You can just imagine the cartoon angel and devil, the ego and Soul, battling it out! The right path is deeply personal for everyone. What will work for one person will not necessarily work for another, and that is the beauty of being able to live in alignment with your own truth.

"The ego is a "crafty little bugger", and requires checking on a continual basis; checking from honest self reflection."

The ego will always try to deceive, and it is intelligent enough to do it very well. There is no escaping it — it's part of you. But you can work with it consciously. Every lesson in life involves the ego to some extent. And when you start looking at your *out*, and identify the external areas of life that no longer reflect your *in*ner alignment, you are destined for a powerful breakthrough.

The Mind Continuum, Expanded

Let's take this deeper. Here I invite you to consider both light and dark being able to exist within ego *and* soul. This means that the ego has a light side, and the Soul has a shadow or dark side. Though *ego* often carries a negative connotation, it is absolutely vital to human life. It helps us survive, assert our individuality, and protect ourselves. The challenge arises when the ego goes unchecked, hidden in the unconscious. That is when it acts as though it must fight the world to survive, competing rather than coexisting. The conscious ego recognises its own power and also acknowledges the Soul, the subconscious, and Spirit. It unites these powers in harmony, working with them instead of in opposition.

In fact, it is often the ego that initiates the journey of awakening. It senses that there is more to life. It wants to improve, to grow, to realise its potential. The ego, when in alignment with consciousness, becomes a servant of the Soul. It recognises the Self, the unique blueprint of each person, and works with the greater Spiritual whole.

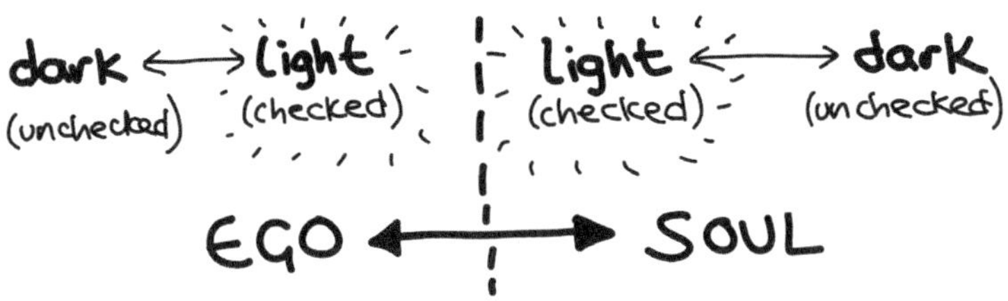

Equally, the Soul is not without shadow. The darker aspect of the Soul can come in a few forms. It can lead someone to prematurely believe that they have healed all wounds, reached enlightenment, or made it to the centre of *the unlearning spiral*. It can lead someone to believe that they have ascended above others, and are therefore different in some way, (or better). Or, it may lead to living a life that it out of balance; heavily based on the spiritual and 5D, and not the 4D and 3D. This can ignore the humanness of the human experience. These are all a trick of illusion. True mastery is knowing that you will never stop progressing, even if you are one of the few humans that reaches enlightenment. There is no finality to it here.

It would seem that we may only aim to maintain our internal balance and respond with grace to whatever arises, embracing our human experience. Mastery may be found in the ability to keep showing up, to meet each new challenge with open arms, and to surrender to the next lesson. We may never be able to see the full path ahead. The ego wants certainty—it wants to know in advance. But that is never how this journey works. We only ever comprehend what we are ready to at that moment, and the next lesson comes to expand our capacity. Mastering the art of *not knowing*, and becoming comfortable with that, will be one of the greatest tools for your journey.

"Mastering the art of not knowing, and becoming comfortable with that, will be one of the greatest tools for your journey."

A little thought... ★

An example of me challenging my ego can be seen in my early experience with yoga. I first came to yoga because of an injury that prevented me from doing what I loved most — gymnastics. Yoga wasn't a "proper sport", and it was too "easy" for me. I reluctantly began classes, as the only exercise I was permitted to do, and I began full of anger and frustration.

I was quickly humbled in assuming it was *easy*. I was approaching it only as a physical practice, and was struggling to find any joy in it. I just was not connecting with it, and I wasn't connecting with mySelf. At that point, I had no idea who I was, and as much as my love for gymnastics was a true love, I had latched onto it as a part of my identity. Having that stripped away left me empty, as a part of it had been masking my emptiness. It was not until I reflected and took a new approach to yoga that things changed. I aligned my breath, my intention, and my consciousness with the movement and began to unlock its deeper gifts. It remains a large part of my practices today and I have found a genuine love for it.

Where have you had to challenge your own ego? How did you feel after you had done this? How can you use that experience when the opportunity arises again?

Energy Systems

Our energy systems present us with an opportunity to explore ourselves further. They form a part of our *in*, and as we open to this awareness, we also open to the healing processes that will naturally follow. All energy systems are unique to the individual, but if you have been drawn to this book, the likelihood is that you will find the following section something that feels like your own truth.

The Throat Chakra

The throat chakra governs our ability to express ourselves and to communicate our truth with the world. Our voice—its tone, freedom, and strength—is a direct reflection of our connection to our true, authentic Self. When this energy centre is open, we are able to speak with integrity, take responsibility for our words, and feel safe and happy to be heard. A strong throat chakra empowers us to express what we truly feel and believe. However, the throat chakra is often the most blocked of all! Many people fear public speaking or expressing their inner world to others, which indicates suppression in this area. This blockage does not just affect communication—it impedes the flow of energy from all other chakras. When we are afraid to have difficult conversations, afraid to step beyond the confines of our conditioned small Self, or believe we are not worthy of having a voice, we compress this energy inward. Over time, this suppression can manifest as depression. Depression, in this energetic sense, is the collapse of expression—the Souls truth being silenced.

The throat chakra acts as a bridge between the feminine heart and the masculine mind. It thrives on balance. Those who have experienced trauma—especially narcissistic abuse or CPTSD—often struggle to express themselves through the spoken word. For many, trauma occurred precisely because they spoke their truth and were repeatedly criticised or shamed for it. Over time, the voice becomes suppressed in an attempt to avoid further harm.

Healing the throat chakra means unlocking the ability to express your true voice again—internally and externally. It means reclaiming your truth, your power, and your authentic Self. For people who have been unable to say "no" or to set healthy boundaries, finding their voice becomes one of the most powerful and transformative healing journeys. It requires courage, but it brings lasting freedom.

"The bottom chakras root us here in who we are, allowing us to be in our true authentic selves in the outside world."

The Underrated Importance of the Lower Chakras

For anyone who has suffered trauma, the physical body and the 3D world can feel profoundly unsafe. This disconnection often stems from the internalised belief that the Self was unable to protect them when the original trauma occurred. As a result, many are naturally drawn to Spiritual practices that provide the comfort and safety they no longer feel in the physical realm. These practices allow reconnection to the authentic Self and Soul, often through the upper chakras. They offer solace, insight, and a beautiful remembrance of who we truly are in essence.

This inner connection is sacred—it opens the door to Soul truth. But real healing requires more than connecting with Soul in the higher chakras; we must learn to embody that truth in the physical body and bring it into the 3D world. For those who have learned to avoid their bodies to survive, this is the ultimate challenge—and the true marker of deep healing. Its where inner creation meets outer action.

Experiencing Soul alignment in the higher chakras can feel addictive. It offers the nourishment and safety we have always longed for. But the ego can subtly hijack this experience, keeping us in the Spiritual realms and avoiding embodiment. This can become a trap—an avoidance disguised as awakening.

What is often under-acknowledged is the beauty of returning to the physical body after being disconnected from it. For those who have not been able to be present in their body, the experience of dropping back in—of feeling safe, grounded, and alive—can be utterly transformative. This is when the energy body harmonises with the physical body, aligning body, mind, and Soul. It is true wholeness.

A little thought... ★

Speaking from experience, I am more deeply connected to my upper chakras. My natural pull was upward. But when I finally began grounding into the lower chakras, for the first time I was introduced to the feeling of true safety, true Self, and full embodiment. Ironically, this descent into the body was the most profound Spiritual experience of all.

We often hear about climbing higher, striving for ascension and transcendence, reaching for the crown. Yet the journey downward is equally sacred. It is in the lower chakras that we reclaim safety, belonging, and the right to exist fully in our human form.

If you have ever felt unsafe in your body or disconnected from the 3D world, know that the return to presence within the body can feel nothing short of magical. It is a coming home, a merging of Spirit and matter.

How do you connect to your presence in this moment? Here and now? How does it feel for you? Do you feel safe? Whether yes or no, can you feel into why this is?

The Importance of Establishing Roots

Before we can expand upwards, we must establish strong and sturdy roots. These roots will be tested and challenged, making them stronger and furthering their growth. Anything less is ungrounded and ultimately unsustainable. The tree cannot flourish if its roots are weak. Without firm grounding, we will find ourselves returning to the same patterns and lessons, forced to rebuild over and over again.

These roots are anchored in truly knowing your Self, your Soul, and your essence. While your expression of this may evolve over time, your connection to it may remain steady. Without this foundation, the structures you build—your insights, your healing, your elevation—will lack the stability to grow.

At some point, you will find yourSelf at peace within your own being. When that happens, your roots stop digging and begin to feed the fruits of your life. Just like a tree, once stable and nurtured, you begin to bear your fruit. This fruit is your service, your purpose, your sacred offering to the world. It does not matter whether you are still growing your roots or already bearing fruit—what matters is that you are on the path.

Your roots can stem from ego or from Soul, or somewhere along the spectrum between the two. If more rooted in ego, they may be strong, but they are rooted in fear, identity, and illusion. When your roots are grounded in the truth of your Soul, your alignment and contentment become inevitable. Only then can you experience the full embodiment of *being*—the harmonisation of *out* and *in*.

A little thought...

Consider this: your roots may never have had the chance to form properly. This is true for many people and is rarely recognised for what it truly is — a profound disconnection from Self. Those with C-PTSD, for instance, often have no early memory or inner reference point of their authentic Self. Their identity was built for survival, not for freedom. Instead of exploring who they were, they learned who they needed to be to stay safe.

In a healthy childhood, there is space to experiment, to try and fail, to discover preferences and personality with relative safety. Society expects children to stumble and explore, and offers grace for mistakes and learning. But that same grace is rarely extended to adults. We are expected to know who we are — even if we were never given the conditions to find out.

If you didn't have the freedom to explore who you were as a child, it may well be part of your Soul's mission to discover it later in life. This is sacred work. The journey to Self is not bound by age or time. You are here to uncover your true being — no matter when you begin.

If this resonates with you, you may wish to journal on these questions: What is it that I know is true about mySelf? What do I like? What makes me feel joy?

The Link: Emotions

The Link of *Out* and *In*

Emotions are the bridge between *Out* and *In* — between our experience of the external world and our internal truth. Emotions are not just feelings; they are evolutionary tools. They help us navigate, protect ourselves, and discover meaning. When they work *for* us, they are powerful allies. Every emotion carries a frequency, and that frequency affects the body. Hormones shift. Neural pathways are activated. Thought patterns are altered. Extreme emotional reactions are often felt throughout the entire body.

"Emotions are the link between "out" and "in"... they give a charge and feeling to our thoughts, and are therefore responsible for our "out" world."

A little thought... ★

Emotions may be the key to truth — to discerning what is real and aligned with our Soul. The lessons they carry elevate our consciousness. Yet interestingly, when the emotional charge is removed, what remains is often a deeper truth. For example, a trigger that once evoked a strong emotional reaction may, over time, lose its charge. This might signal that the lesson has been integrated.

Perhaps one of the goals of emotional evolution is to reduce the intensity of these charges. The highest frequency emotions — peace, contentment, authenticity — often have a much softer, more subtle presence. They are not loud like anger or fear. They don't demand. They *reside*. And that may be the greatest lesson of all — that as we grow, the lessons become quieter. And we begin to listen more deeply.

When can you remember your emotions guiding you to a real truth of yours after you released the emotional charge? What is it that you learnt from the experience?

Positive thoughts resonate at a higher frequency — they vibrate at a faster, lighter level. Negative thoughts, by contrast, are lower in frequency, slower, and denser. But it is important to understand that while thoughts carry energy, *feelings* hold even more. Feelings are where true transformation lies. Thoughts trigger emotions, and those emotions move energy through the body. The ultimate frequency — the highest of all — is the frequency of pure love and authenticity. This is the divine frequency we all seek, the one that connects us most deeply to our Higher Self and source energy.

Your personal frequency is sacred. It must be protected — consciously and consistently. This becomes especially important when your frequency is higher than that of the environment or the people around you. Your awareness and energetic integrity have the power to uplift others simply by being. Living in alignment with your Soul and shining your unique light becomes not only your gift but your purpose. You change the world by being fully, radiantly *you.*

"Every emotion has a certain frequency, which can be either an input or output of energy for us."

We often experience our thoughts in layers — some surface-level, others deeply rooted in belief and emotion. The more deeply ingrained the thought, the more powerful its emotional charge. This charge directly influences our frequency, affecting how we move through the world and what we attract into our lives.

Emotional Frequency and Maslow's Hierarchy of Needs

Maslow's well-known *Hierarchy of Needs* offers a valuable framework for understanding how emotional frequency relates to our stages of human development. At the base of the pyramid are our basic physical needs — food, water, sleep, and shelter. These correlate with the lower, survival-based frequencies of the 3D human experience. These needs must be met first. Until they are, we cannot build anything stable above them. They are non-negotiable, and when they are not met, our systems default to addressing them above all else.

Once these foundations are secured, we move up to safety and security — the need to feel protected, both physically and emotionally. Then comes love and belonging. Human connection is an instinctual need, just as vital to our well-being as food or water. Numerous studies have shown that mammals, including human babies, fail to thrive — and may even die — without loving connection, even when all physical needs are met. We are wired for love and belonging. We are wired for connection.

Above connection lies Self-esteem — our relationship with ourselves, and the value we place on our identity. Self-esteem is essential for the final step: Self-actualisation. This is the realm of the Soul, of inner truth, of Spiritual alignment. To truly reach this stage, our esteem must be fluid, not fixed. The Self-actualised person understands that identity is not rigid — it evolves and flows with life. Self-esteem becomes rooted not in ego, but in *being*.

> "Learning to be aware of our emotional frequency allows us to utilise it to our advantage."

Negative emotions drain energy from your system. This is not to say that negative emotions are bad — they are simply part of the polarity of human experience. They have lessons to teach and truths to reveal. Where attention goes, energy flows. Your thoughts will control you unless you become conscious enough to control them. You have the power to choose which thoughts you feed and which ones you starve. This is the practice of conscious living — the ability to become the observer of your inner world and intentionally shift your energy toward truth, clarity, and light. Here being in connection to your IN.

Base Level Frequency

Your **base level frequency** is how you feel on a day-to-day basis without any external stimulation or interference. It is simply you, in stillness, with nothing but yourSelf. It does not require meditation or silence, but refers to your general, natural state of being. You can think of it as your internal *set point*, and we can imagine this on a scale from 0 to 10. A *0* would represent the lowest possible frequency — states such as despair or hopelessness — and a *10* would reflect the highest: love, joy, peace, and deep contentment.

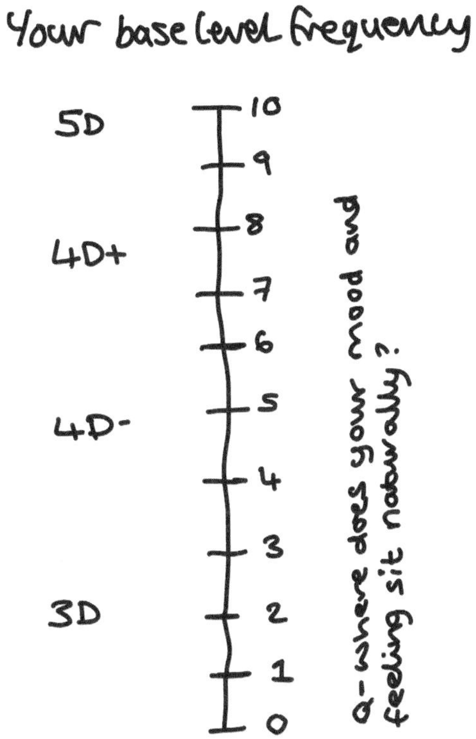

When you are operating in a lower frequency range (1 to 3), you are living in 3D survival mode. This is the realm where artificial stimulation is often sought to artificially elevate mood. These efforts — whether through substances, behaviours, or distractions — offer only temporary relief. They provide *borrowed energy*, raising your mood to around a 5 or 6 at best, but never to the deeply aligned and sustainable states of 7–10. High-frequency living cannot be faked or synthetically achieved. The 7–10 range comes only from natural, Soul-aligned living — mind, body, and Spirit working in harmony.

Our base frequency is constantly being influenced — both positively and negatively — by what we experience. A bad night's sleep, stress at work, an argument, or even a rude stranger can momentarily lower your frequency. On the other hand, laughter with a friend, time in nature, or the warmth of Sunlight can uplift you. People who are energetically sensitive or empathic are often more attuned to these fluctuations and can be more affected by external energies.

"When difficult emotions arise, its not a case of denying them as they are teaching us something. We have to tune in to the Lesson in order to release it."

The goal is not to reach and stay at a perfect 10 — that is unrealistic — but rather to *train* your baseline to consistently sit at a higher level. With time and practice, you will begin to notice that the old coping mechanisms or addictive patterns that once *lifted* you now actually pull you down. When your baseline is elevated, anything artificial feels off, and instead of being soothing, it becomes disruptive. This is a powerful turning point. It marks the moment you begin to *embody* higher consciousness. You will look back on where you once were and will recognise the profound shift. You will know how far you have come, not just because of how you think, but because of how you feel — consistently.

Reaching a 10 is possible, and many of us experience glimpses of this state — during moments of love, alignment, insight, or Spiritual connection. But these are usually fleeting, and they are not intended to be sustained constantly. Life is not designed to be lived entirely at a 10 — nor at a 0. The human experience is about learning to hold a higher baseline, even amidst the inevitable fluctuations of life. This is the true balance of the *out* and the *in* — experiencing and feeling the lessons that life presents you, whilst maintaining the growth and gift of every one, and enhancing your *in*.

A little thought... ★

I spent a significant period — perhaps 3 to 4 years — operating at a level 0 or 1 during my experience with M.E./Chronic Fatigue Syndrome. Low-frequency living can become so embedded that it feels like your normal. This is particularly relevant for anyone caught in the trauma loop. If trauma goes unaddressed for too long, it may anchor your base level frequency in the lower ranges indefinitely. But always hold true that healing *is* possible. As we begin to consciously raise our frequency — gently and compassionately — we start to shift our baseline. With time, we move beyond survival and begin to experience life through a lens of wholeness. While we cannot change what has happened in our past, we *can* shift the frequency through which we carry it, and take any of the lessons that it gave to us forward with us in our life.

Have you had a time in your life where you feel like your baseline frequency was lowered? How did you elevate this? What was your key lesson from this experience?

Money/Labour of Love

This is one of my favourite ways to illustrate the meeting point of *out* and *in*! This is because money is always viewed as such a part of the outside 3D world, but your relationship to money is a reflection of your internal world and belief systems. This is also the same for how you *earn* money – or as we get to understand in this section – what we exchange for money and the value that we provide. Here we look deeply into the energy behind our financial income.

Labour of Love

Daydreams, wishes, and desires are messages from your Higher Self. These quiet wonderings, repeated nudges, and subconscious visions rise to the surface to bring your conscious attention to something important. They carry insight into your deeper path and the direction of your evolution. Healing clears space for your true desires to rise again—untwisted by fear—and for those whispers to be heard once more.

If you feel pulled in a certain direction, take a step, just one. Then another. You may not be able to see the whole path, only the next one or two steps. The path unfolds with your every movement. Even when you're unsure, even when you feel blind—take the step. Blind is brave; brave holds intention; intention fuels belief; belief creates reality. Take the step.

We are each destined to discover our unique labour of love—something that brings us alive, that we can offer to the world in truth and joy. When you align your life, success becomes a natural by-product. Your energy flows effortlessly, and what you give out magnetises others. You become your own fuel source of energy. As Kahlil Gibran once said, *"Bread baked without love is a bitter bread that feeds but half a man's hunger."* When your work is infused with love, it nourishes the whole being—yours and others.

When we create only from ego, we burn out. When we force a path that isn't ours, we become drained, dissatisfied, and detached from joy. But when we align with what we love—what lights us up from the inside—we move with momentum and grace. Your individuality becomes your gift. Your Soul's signature becomes the power behind your service.

Challenges still arise, but the energy with which you face them is transformed. Those who aren't aligned with their true path will often hear ego-based excuses: *it's too late, you're too far gone, nobody really loves what they do*. But these are lies of limitation. It's never too late to realign. Even if you've wandered far, there is always a way back—and often, the path home is lit by the very discomfort and dissatisfaction that triggered your questioning in the first place.

"It's never too late to realign– the path unfolds as you walk it."

If you feel lost, trust that something greater is guiding you. Your sense of misalignment is not a flaw—it is a signal-the elastic band of the Soul at a point of pressure, gently guiding you. There is something waiting within you, something that only you can bring to life. And you don't need to know exactly what it is before taking the first step.

"I am credited with being one of the hardest workers and perhaps I am—if thought is the equivalent of labour, for I have devoted to it almost all of my waking hours. But if work is interpreted to be a definite performance in a specified time according to a rigid rule, then I may be the worst of idlers."—Nikola Tesla

Money

Money is simply a physical representation of energetic exchange. It is governed by the same universal laws of energy that govern everything in life. There is a mystique to money that most people never realise. What we use as money—or "currency"—has changed many times over human history. From jewels and gold coins to paper notes, and now to tapping a phone or watch to reveal a digital balance. We are seeing less and less tangible money in the world, with new forms emerging, such as cryptocurrency and digital assets. It's not hard to imagine a near future where global digital currency exists. And yet, regardless of how money looks or is stored, the energetic rules behind it remain unchanged.

The work we offer to the world—whether through a profession, business, or creative pursuit—is usually the method through which we receive money. This is why money and the concept of a *labour of love* are so deeply interconnected. The energy you bring to your work shapes what you receive in return. When your work is infused with genuine love, passion, and purpose, it will resonate differently. It will attract more, and it will serve more powerfully. Conversely, when work is done from a place of fear, obligation, or disconnection, it often feels heavy and sterile—both for the giver and the receiver.

This is where we see how the outer reflects the inner. People who love what they do naturally offer a higher vibration of service, often without even realising it. That frequency is attractive, abundant, and magnetic. They offer value and not time. Many professions today have lost this connection, becoming mechanical and disconnected from the heart. The truth is: it's not what you do, it's the energy and intention with which it is done.

There are four energetic categories through which people typically receive money. Each one is governed by a different set of beliefs, intentions, and vibrational frequencies:

1. **The Hamster Wheel of Survival** – Living day-to-day, exchanging time and energy for the ability to meet basic needs. Work here is purely functional and often exhausting, creating a cycle that's hard to break.
2. **The Ego of Wealth or Fame** – Seeking large sums of money or public recognition as a substitute for internal fulfilment. There may be financial gain, but often without peace.
3. **Soul Purpose** – Doing the thing you couldn't *not* do. The passion, the obsession, the calling. Even if you weren't paid, you'd still do it. You love it, and that love infuses your work with magnetic energy. Combine this with commitment and focus, and abundance will follow.
4. **Inheritance** – Receiving money passed down through generations. In many cases, if you trace the origin of this wealth, it can be linked back to someone in category three—someone who created a legacy by following their Soul.

Naturally, category three is the ideal. It is the place where fulfilment and abundance meet. It is alignment in action—where the inner frequency of purpose and passion is reflected in the outer currency of money. Categories one and two are often sustained by unconscious programming. Many in group one are simply exhausted—caught in cycles of survival without the space or Self-belief to imagine a different way. For those in group two, the lesson often comes only after achieving external success and realising that happiness still eludes them.

Those in group four may face their own challenges. They may carry wealth without a sense of purpose, and feel guilt or emptiness as a result. Society may not validate their discomfort, but wealth without direction can feel deeply hollow.

The powerful truth is: **abundance follows alignment**. Those who are aligned with their true Soul path naturally radiate the kind of energy that draws opportunities, ideas, people, and income toward them. They are magnetic, because they are in truth. That doesn't mean life becomes challenge-free, but it does mean the path becomes clear—and their energy remains in flow. Money, like all energy, must move. It is meant to circulate. It is meant to serve. And it is meant to reflect the love behind the work.

Purpose doesn't have to be flashy or dramatic. It doesn't have to match anyone else's idea of success. Your labour of love might be quiet, simple, or deeply personal. It might not look impressive from the outside, but it fulfils you on the inside. It is your gift, and it is sacred. Purpose can also evolve over time. What felt aligned five years ago might no longer be right, and that's ok. The path will refine itself as you walk it.

"Purpose doesn't have to be loud or dramatic; it only has to be true."

Some of the most financially successful people in the world achieved abundance not by chasing it, but by doing what they loved—and doing it with their whole heart. In contrast, those who pursue money for its own sake often end up dissatisfied, even if they succeed financially. The old truth remains: *money cannot buy happiness*. It was never meant to.

Wanting abundance is not wrong. In fact, it is natural. But it must be rooted in the right intention—an energy of contribution, alignment, and service. Money, when earned and used in alignment with Soul purpose, becomes a powerful tool for expansion. But it is not the goal. It is the by-product of a life well-lived, and a purpose fully embraced.

The Rules for an Abundance of Money

1. Locate your Soul purpose and work within it.
2. Give 50% of your excess money away—through circulation or gifting.

I know! This may sound radical at first, especially as it goes against most of what we've been conditioned to believe. But when you are working in alignment with your Soul purpose, money flows naturally. And it doesn't just trickle in to cover your basic needs—it arrives in abundance. This abundance supports your life, your well-being, your rest, your creativity, your fulfilment. It funds the experiences, hobbies, and adventures that allow you to grow and recharge, so that you can give even more of yourSelf to your Soul purpose. This is the energetic circulation of life, and money is simply one part of that living exchange.

Like all forms of energy, money must flow. Stagnation disrupts harmony; flow invites expansion. Circulating money can be as simple as spending it with joy and freedom.

Giving must be done freely. True giving comes with no expectation of return. It is pure intention that allows energy to come back to you in unexpected, often magical ways. In moments of true giving, you're not just meeting a need—you're becoming the answer to someone's prayer. You're allowing Spirit to work through you.

A little thought... ★

One of my favourite ways to circulate money is by supporting small, independent businesses—knowing that my contribution is not just a transaction, but a direct investment in someone else's vision, creativity, and path. In doing so, I am helping to fuel their purpose, their livelihood, and the unique gifts they bring into the world. These businesses are often built with authenticity at their core, rooted in passion rather than mass-market conformity, and the energy of that authenticity carries its own frequency. When you choose to support them, you are consciously choosing to increase the flow of energy, abundance, and possibility—not just for them, but for the collective. And because energy is cyclical, this generosity and alignment inevitably return to you in some form, at some time—perhaps as an unexpected opportunity, a deepened connection, or a gift of your own that is supported in turn. In this way, spending becomes a conscious act of co-creation, one that keeps abundance moving and growing for all.

Where do you most circulate your money? Are you conscious of where your money flows out, and to whom and what you are consciously or unconsciously supporting? Is this something that you would like to reconsider for yourSelf?

Balance of Ego and Soul

Why do you do what you do? Where does your drive originate—from ego, Soul, or a blend of both? As with all polarities, neither end of the spectrum is ideal in isolation. While the ego-driven path is often obvious in its imbalance, the Soul-driven path can also become distorted if it's disconnected from the human experience. True alignment lies in integration.

Soul purpose often intersects with elements of the ego. Your calling will likely involve things you are naturally gifted at, things you enjoy, and things that support you financially. And that's not only ok—it's beautiful. When you serve from the Soul, you are also serving the Self. There is joy, fulfilment, and personal reward in helping others. That's the mirror of love in action.

Living your Soul purpose means your actions are fuelled by the desire to share your unique light. And when you do, something magical happens: the act of giving becomes the act of receiving. You pour so much of yourSelf into your purpose that it naturally spills over, nourishing others. Their transformation from this fuels you in return. It is another example of energy in transference and transformation.

A little thought...

Writing this book is one such example. This is not a Selfless act—I write because I love to write. I write because this process has helped me heal, clarify, and align with my own truth. I wanted answers, and I wrote my way to them! In the act of sharing my knowledge, I deepen my *knowing*. I revisit old lessons, see them in new ways, and integrate them more fully. And then, I pass them on—not just for the benefit of others, but also for the gift of giving. This book is a tool, a legacy, and a vibration I leave behind. Yes, I absolutely hope it helps others. I hope it raises frequencies, opens hearts, and shifts awareness. But first and foremost—it is for my Self. And that is the most Soul-aligned reason of all.

What do you think about this statement? Can you see why the energy shifts when you do something for yourSelf because you love to, and how this then overflows to others? What is it that you love to do? And would you like to develop this further?

"When you serve from the Soul, the act of giving becomes the act of receiving."

Spoken Word and Creation

The Power of the Spoken Word

Every word we speak emits a frequency. It can either raise or lower your overall energetic vibration. The beauty of the spoken word lies in just how personal it is to each individual—it is the purest expression of your unique energetic makeup. You could say the exact same words as someone else, but the sound, tone, and energy will differ depending on your mood, intention, and emotional state.

Words carry the power to create. This has long been understood by ancient traditions, particularly in forms of magic and witchcraft, where words are used in spells—intentional declarations to bring a desire into physical form through focused energy. The term *"spelling"* literally originates from this. Witchcraft has gained a negative reputation over time, largely due to fear and misunderstanding. But perhaps the true fear should be reserved for those who persecuted the women and men practising it, rather than the practitioners themselves. At its core, a spell is simply the act of speaking an intention into being.

A little thought... ★

The words we speak are entirely within our control. Becoming conscious of this is one of the most profound shifts you can make. I had always believed I was a positive person—until my researched revealed information to me about the frequency emitted by different words. I decided to become aware of my speech, just to observe. What I noticed surprised me: I was often using negative language as a way to bond with others. It seemed more socially acceptable to complain than to celebrate. From that moment on, I made a conscious decision to change my speech—to speak about the good things, to notice beauty, and to share that. It was difficult at first, but the change in this made positive changes in my life. A helpful way to track your speech is to record yourSelf for a day. At first, you're aware you're being recorded, but before long, you fall back into natural patterns. Listening back can be confronting, but also enlightening. This is how others experience your frequency. Ask yourSelf: Is this the version of mySelf that I want to be? Is this who I truly am?

You are so powerful that the words you speak quite literally shape your world. This truth is not widely shared, and only reaches those who are ready to receive it. That in itself speaks to its sacred nature.

Exercise

Affirmations are a powerful tool to direct the spoken word toward conscious creation. Starting with the words "*I am...*" sets a vibration in motion. Here is your opportunity to write your key affirmations that you are bringing into your being. Look back at the earlier exercise in the chapter on your limiting beliefs, and look at the new belief of your highest-Self column to help you. To turn your upgraded belief into an affirmation, put "*I am...*" at the start of the sentence, and adjust the wording of the new belief to naturally follow. Always remember affirmations are about new, and what you want to start, and not what you want to stop. Keep your affirmations simple and clear. These are not just phrases: These are your truths. By writing them down, you already take a powerful step in bringing them into the physical world. An example may be, *"I am in perfect health, and I am safe", "I live a life of freedom, and I love it", "I am financially abundant, and I receive... (give details)".*

	My affirmations. I am…	Why do I want this?
1		
2		
3		
4		
5		
6		
7		

Speak them with emotion, belief, and gratitude, as though they already exist. This gives them life. The most powerful way to practice this is in the morning, while looking into a mirror. Speak to yourSelf, to your reflection.

Here is how to turn these affirmations into lasting beliefs:

- **Speak them out loud** every day—especially in the morning, and looking at yourSelf in the mirror. Speak them with conviction, as if they are already true (because they are).
- **Record yourSelf** reading each new belief out loud. You can use the voice notes app on your phone or any simple recording tool. **Play it back as often as** possible. Let the sound of your own voice reinforce these truths.
- **Do this consistently for at least 28 days.** Science suggests it takes 21 days to form a habit—but lasting change is about *embodiment*, not just repetition. Over time, you will begin to notice shifts—not just in

how you think, but in how you feel, how you behave, and what you attract.

- And here is the beauty of it: as you continue spiralling deeper into your unlearning and learning journey, you will be able to **refine, update, and upgrade these beliefs** anytime. You are learning a process that will serve you for life.

A little thought… ★

Honestly, I know this sounds so simple, and probably like something you don't want to do! I understand… that was exactly how I felt; *"It feels weird and awkward"*, *"What if someone can see me?"*, *"That sounds pointless!"* If this is how you're feeling right now, that is absolutely fine. Just sit with it, take a breath, and maybe just consider a possibility that these feelings could be your very intelligent ego just trying to keep you in its protective comfort zone, where it knows you have managed to survive so far. If you don't want to make the changes to your life, then I'm guessing that you wouldn't be here reading this book?! So here is your opportunity to actually begin making changes in your life, however odd this may feel to start with. This is where you begin to become the magic that you were seeking.

Have a little check in with yourSelf… How does this feel? Does it feel awkward? If so, why? And if not, are you really connecting with what you are doing, or are you just going through the motions? Only you can ever know the truth of this, but what is the real truth?

Does this mean we can never speak negative words? Of course not! The goal is not to repress or deny human experience. The spoken word can be a powerful tool in healing and release. In therapy, for example, you may need to revisit and articulate past pain in order to release it. You may also need to express boundaries or confront challenges with others. The key is intention. Speak with the aim of releasing and healing. If the expression is part of your movement toward growth, truth, or resolution, it holds value—even when it explores pain. What matters is your awareness. Speak with consciousness and know the power of your words. Don't let them control you—own them. Use them to align with who you are, and more importantly, who you are becoming. That is where the spoken word helps you to bridge the *out* and the *in* of your world.

Fate to Destiny, and the Magic of Creation

Fate is the path that happens *to* us—without intervention. It is unconscious, reactive, and shaped by external circumstances. Destiny, on the other hand, is something we awaken to when we understand our innate power to intervene. Our *in*ner world becomes the architect of the outer world.

True creation is clear in its intention but never controlling of the how. The root of creative power must come from the *in*—the Soul—not the *out*—the ego. When we create from ego, the results are misaligned with our Souls truth and are unlikely to bring lasting fulfilment. We are living in a time of collective awakening and rediscovery—a powerful moment in which many are reclaiming their creative power and consciously shaping their lives.

We have already explored the encoding of Spirit—how our unique Soul signatures and qualities are programmed within us. This is the *true Self*, the authentic Soul essence: the *in*. Alongside this, we experience programming from the external world—life experiences that shape the *out*. The *out* often distracts from the *in*, creating disharmony. Our Souls lesson is to learn how to bring these two into balance, to work in harmony with the energetic laws of the universe. Understanding is the first step; the next is practice. The journey from knowledge to knowing is the true work of a lifetime.

Creation is about bringing our existence into physical form through experience. But ultimately, we are not seeking the thing itself—we are seeking the *feeling* we believe the thing will bring. Dr Joe Dispenza teaches this beautifully, showing how our greatest creative power comes from fully feeling the emotional frequency of what we desire—*before* it physically exists. If you can tune out the *out*, and deeply tune in to the *in*—to that feeling—then the outer world must eventually shift to match. This is the law.

"By using free will, or the power of the Soul, anyone can dominate his mood, change his character, control his environment and the attitudes of those close to him. When we do this, we become movers in the chess game, instead of pawns. There's enough magnetic power in you to make you immune to the strongest planetary pull, now or in the future. What a pity to submit so easily and let your potential remain unrealised."— Linda Goodman

"In taking responsibility for our lives and ourselves, we take back our power. In owning our power we understand that we are the creators of our "out" world."

The Creation Rules

How do we create? The process of creation begins with desire and is powered by intention. True creation starts in the 5D—the realm of imagination—then moves into the 4D through the mind and emotions, before being brought into the 3D through action. These dimensional stages bridge the non-physical and physical realms, turning energy into form. The steps below outline how to consciously create:

1. **Imagine your future** — What do you truly desire? Be free and uninhibited in allowing yourSelf to dream. You need a vivid, detailed vision of what you want. Be clear, decisive, and concise.

2. **Ask and you shall receive** — Ask in as many ways as you can for your desire to manifest. Ask for it to move from the *in* to the *out*. Ask for guidance. Ask to be shown the next steps. Ask to be aligned.
3. **Bring it into the physical** — Write about it. Speak about it. Draw it. Plan it. Express it. This pulls your creation from 5D into 3D. Get it down on paper. Make a plan, even if the plan later evolves. Starting something is what creates momentum for the energy to flow.
4. **Tune in** — Align your energy with the feeling of already having what you want. Like tuning into a radio station, select the frequency that matches your desire. Feel it. Imagine all that would result from having it. Infuse this vision with love.
5. **Be the person who has it** — Who are you as the version of you who already lives this creation? Every version of you already exists. You must align with the one who holds your desire. *Act as if it is already here.* Use affirmations, meditations, journaling, "spelling" aloud, or hypnotherapy—whatever resonates. Your 3D world will catch up with the energy you're living in now.
6. **Give** — Giving and receiving are one and the same in energetic law. So, ask yourSelf:
7. a. How can I give up and release the older version of me?
8. b. What space can I make in my life to allow it in?
9. c. Can I offer something—perhaps to nature or Spirit—as a gesture of gratitude?
10. **Settle the nervous system** — This is one of the most overlooked yet crucial steps. Your nervous system must feel safe to receive. If it's activated in fear, doubt, or disbelief, you'll unconsciously repel your creation. Soothing your system anchors belief and allows reception.
11. **What action can I take?** — You will be guided to take action of some kind, in order to bring the creation into physical form. What action can you take?
12. **Trust** — Let go and trust. Like placing an online order, you trust it's on its way. Don't cling to the energy of *wanting*—this reinforces lack. Let your creation come in its own time and way, which is usually not how you expect!

13. **Thank** — Gratitude is one of the highest frequencies. Dwell in it. Be thankful for all that you are, all that you have, and all that is. Feel the gratitude as if you've already received your desire. Ask for the discipline to keep what you create, and the wisdom to help it grow.
14. **And so, it is** — Seal it with belief. Trust the unfolding. You have asked, aligned, and acted—now allow.

"I do not think there is any thrill that can go through the human heart like that felt by an inventor as he sees some creation of the brain unfolding to success. Such emotions make a man forget food, sleep, friends, love, everything." — *Nikola Tesla*

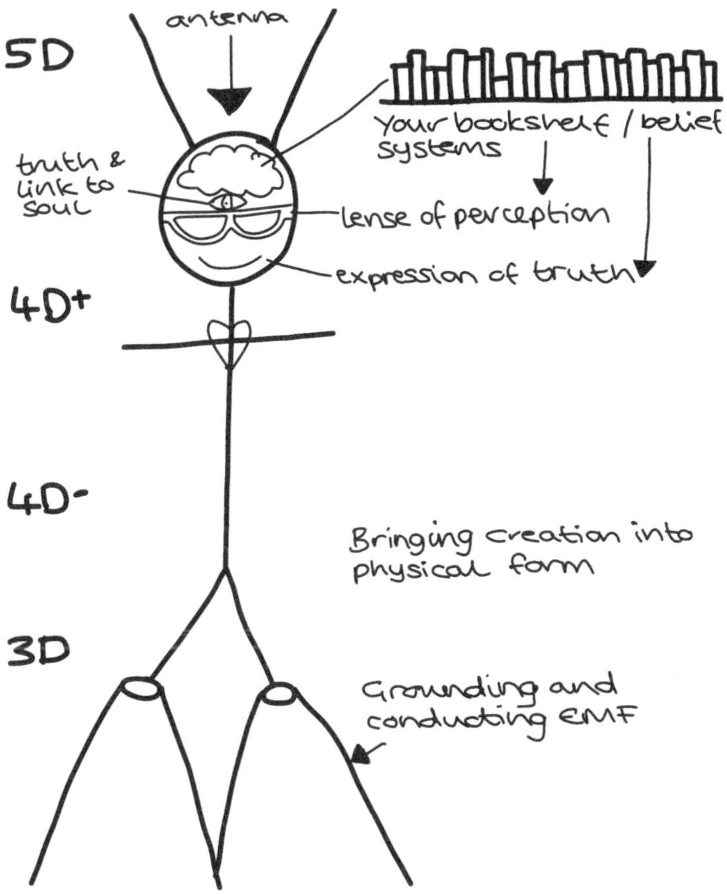

Evolving Karmic Ties

It is easy to assume that karma predetermines your entire life and that you are powerless under its influence. In reality, karma is a foundation, not a prison. It determines what you *start* with—but how you work through it, rise through it, and transform it is up to you. If you do nothing—if you stay asleep—you'll drift along the river of karmic flow. But once you awaken to your power to choose, to learn, and to create, your path becomes a matter of destiny. You move from *fate* to *freedom*.

To break a karmic cycle with someone, you must *respond* rather than *react*. Accept what has happened. Recognise that retaliation only prolongs the karmic bond. Release. Forgive. This does *not* mean condoning—but it does mean you no longer allow it to control your energetic field.

To truly break a karmic tie, you must accept full responsibility—not in a way that invites blame, but in a way that honours the deeper truth. Even if you do not understand the cause in this lifetime, trust that something from a previous life is being brought into balance. You do not need to remember the details. All you need is the willingness to break the cycle. Importantly, karma can be cleared by *either* party—the giver or the receiver. The one who chooses forgiveness, acceptance, and growth becomes the alchemist. And that transformation brings its own reward.

A little thought... ★

When I first began reading about karma, I was at a point in my journey where the idea of karma made me feel worse, not better. It led me to believe that I had to passively accept what was happening to me — that every painful experience was some kind of cosmic debt I had no choice but to repay. To be clear: this is not the truth of karma. This misunderstanding can be especially heavy if the Self is weakened or fragmented. But it is not your job to passively endure suffering. Soul contracts are never valid when abuse is present. Abuse violates spiritual law. If you've endured trauma, your karmic task is not submission — it is self-healing, self-rescue, and self-liberation. Karma exists to help you evolve, to guide you back into your power. You can explore with compassion and curiosity: why did this energy enter my life? What patterns am I here to break? Where can I reclaim my power and end this cycle? It takes courage to unlearn abuse. But when you do, you return to yourSelf in a way that is whole.

"The ancients taught that the evolved Soul must reach the point of seeking the truth of karma to end the cycles of rebirth. Therefore, faith in reincarnation is a gift—a reward for the Soul advanced enough to search for the meaning of its existence in the universe, and its karmic obligations in the present life. Proof would remove the individual free will of discovery, so perhaps man must always look for the answers to reincarnation in his own heart." — Linda Goodman

Delayed Gratification and Action

Delayed gratification is the act of resisting an immediate reward or temptation in favour of a greater reward at a later point. A simple example of this is budgeting and saving money to invest in something more meaningful or substantial further down the line. While often discussed in the context of finances, delayed gratification applies to every area of life. It is underpinned by discipline and the conscious control of ego, which ultimately allows Soul to be the recipient of the reward.

From an energetic perspective, delayed gratification illustrates that you have the frequency and discipline not only to create something, but also to maintain and sustain it once it has manifested. It is not enough to know how to create—you must also be capable of holding and honouring it. This requires a steady, consistent frequency. If your actions today mirror the habits you will need once your creation manifests, you are proving energetically that you are prepared to receive and retain it.

During periods of intense delayed gratification, there is usually heightened focus. This focused energy is directed toward the desired creation, and during these phases, life can often feel unbalanced. We each have a supply of energy, and where it is allocated can shift dramatically. Whilst balance is always the goal, these seasons of imbalance can be necessary in order to bring about transformation and birth a new reality. Often this intense focus will be directed toward the *out* area of your life. Understanding that this imbalance is temporary—and a necessary part of the surrender process—can help you accept the journey of receiving what you have been working to create.

Manifestation requires energy—your energy—given in exchange for what you seek. When this energy flows from a place of alignment, it replenishes itself. What once felt like output begins to generate input because you are so aligned with what you are doing that the process itself becomes fulfilling. Effort and focus links this. It grounds your intention, raises your vibration, and draws your creation closer. Drive and ambition are sacred when they come from Soul. The energy is different when it is ego-driven. The awareness, the journey, and the results—everything changes when your intention is driven from Soul.

Pressure often carries a negative connotation, but when it is present in manageable amounts, pressure can be a powerful ally. It focuses and propels. Your perception of pressure determines whether it becomes an energetic input or output—whether it inspires or drains you. The feeling of achieving a goal after a period of intentional waiting and work is unlike anything else. It becomes a frequency of its own—one that fuels further movement, expansion, and growth, for both the OUT and the IN.

While practising delayed gratification, it is positive to also find a way to enjoy the present moment. You cannot wait to feel whole until the outcome arrives—you must embody it now. Focusing on what you are creating while also surrendering to the idea that it is already yours is a powerful state. It not only magnetises your creation, but accelerates its arrival.

A little thought...

If delayed gratification starts to feel like a permanent state, or if it becomes draining rather than energising, this can be a sign of misalignment or Self-sabotage. It may indicate a belief that you don't deserve what you're asking for, or that you must sacrifice endlessly in order to receive it. Overdoing deprivation can lead to a false sense of security. It can become a comfort zone that mirrors your nervous system, especially if you've lived in survival mode.

This was true for me. For many years, while building my business, I restricted mySelf so completely that I couldn't even allow a small treat—a coffee, a meal out—because I was always saving every penny for the next project. And then the next. I was living in a cycle of lack. I had normalised the deprivation. It wasn't until I became aware of this pattern that I could begin to shift it. It took healing wounds of Self-worth, it took softness, and it took conscious rebalancing. That shift has been one of the most magical and necessary transformations for me so far.

What is your relationship with delayed gratification? Is this balanced discipline that you are happy with in your life, or something that you wish to change? How does it influence your *out* and your *in*?

Health

The Energetic Origins of Physical Health

There is no better representation of the meeting of *out* and *in* than that of our incredible human body. Our physical body is the final, most tangible expression of our inner world – our *in*. It is where energy crystallises into matter. Long before symptoms show up in the physical body, they are often present in the subtle bodies—the energetic, emotional, and mental layers that surround and inform the physical Self. In this way, the body is not simply a biological organism, but a messenger and mirror of the unseen.

Every ache, imbalance, or illness is not just a random malfunction—it is communication. It is the body's attempt to draw our attention to an area of our life, an emotion we have ignored, a truth we have avoided, or a frequency we have long outgrown. As Louise Hay beautifully illustrated in her pioneering work, there is often a direct energetic or emotional cause underlying each physical issue. Anger can lodge in the liver. Grief can weaken the lungs. A sense of burden may show up in the shoulders. Fear often resides in the kidneys. Stubbornness can manifest in joint stiffness. Even something as *everyday* as poor digestion may be linked to our ability—or inability—to emotionally process the experiences of life.

Our bodies do not lie. They are constantly processing not just food, but emotion, energy, thought, environment, relationship, and purpose. When one of these aspects is blocked or out of alignment, the body often absorbs the imbalance as a means of survival. But over time, that imbalance asks to be seen, healed, and integrated—and this is when we start to notice symptoms or dis-ease.

What if, instead of reacting to symptoms as something to suppress or fear, we welcomed them as an invitation to listen deeper? To decode the body's language and to explore the root cause with loving curiosity. This doesn't mean ignoring medical treatment, but it does mean expanding our lens. We are not just healing a body—we are healing the energy field behind the body.

When we learn to read the signals of the body energetically, we begin to take responsibility for our own healing. We stop outsourcing our power. We become attuned to what our body needs, and equally, what our Soul is trying to express through it.

Physical healing, then, is not simply about addressing the symptom—it is a process of energetic alignment. True healing works from the inside out. And when we address the root energetic cause—whether it be a long-held belief, an unprocessed trauma, or a way of living that is no longer in resonance—the body responds. Healing may not always be instant or linear, but it will always be sacred. The body is not your enemy. It is your ally. It is the compass guiding you back to wholeness.

"Your body is a translator, speaking the language of your inner world."

Where OUT Meets IN: The Physical Manifestation of Dis-ease

We are living in an exciting time when the connection between emotional trauma and the physical manifestation of disease is becoming more widely understood. Experts such as Gabor Maté and Bessel van der Kolk have extensively explored this connection, illustrating the profound impact of trauma on both mental and physical health.

Gabor Maté discusses the intricate relationship between trauma and physical disease—particularly how the repression of emotions and unaddressed trauma or chronic stress can lead to illness. He highlights conditions such as autoimmune disorders, cancer, and neurological diseases, noting that societal conditioning—especially around the suppression of emotions like anger—is a contributing factor, particularly in women. The body's prolonged stress response compromises the immune system and other vital functions, leading to disease.

Bessel van der Kolk explores how trauma becomes embedded in the body, creating a physiological imprint. When trauma is unresolved, the body continues to circulate stress hormones, trapping the individual in a replay loop of past defensive responses. This state of hyperarousal places ongoing strain on the body, reducing its ability to function optimally—and, over time, this contributes to the development of physical illness. In this way, persistent emotional stress and trauma—when left unresolved—create a continual output of energy, reflected not only in the outside world but also in the physical form. As I've shared earlier in the trauma section, being in a state of trauma often reflects a disconnection from Self and Soul. This internal disconnection manifests externally: in lifestyle, behaviour, relationships, and eventually, the body.

Bessel van der Kolk, in his powerful book; *The Body Keeps the Score*, identifies how trauma can be genetically passed down, siting studies on WWI veterans and their descendants. It is now accepted that the *fight-or-flight* response—often considered hard-wired—is passed down epigenetically. And whilst it can be changed within our lifetimes, it is likely that many of us are carrying the burdens of generational trauma without even realising it.

This knowledge, when turned into knowing, becomes empowering. It gives us the ability to change our outside world by addressing the trauma, stress, and unhelpful programming that exists within. Linda takes this further by linking health vulnerability to a person's astrological make-up: "*Astrology has always known that disease is triggered by the mind and emotions, and can be controlled or eliminated the same way; also, that people born under certain planetary influences are either susceptible or immune to particular diseases and accidents.*" To me, this also points to a person's unique energetic blueprint, or what I have described in the *encoding of Spirit* section.

The short-term and long-term effects of trauma on the body are immense. Trauma can become a new *normal* for someone—keeping them in a constant state of hyperarousal: fight, flight, freeze, or fawn. While fight and flight involve movement, freeze and fawn are often misunderstood; they too involve heightened arousal, but without that physical discharge, which can make them even more damaging to the system over time.

A little thought... ★

Left untreated, trauma can become debilitating and even life-threatening. This is a subject very close to my heart. I feel deeply called to share this information in the hope that it plants seeds of awareness, transformation, and healing. Whether this helps someone directly, or helps them support another, it is a powerful knowing that can save lives—not just physically, but emotionally and Spiritually. Once you recognise your own power—the power to look inward and restore alignment—you reclaim your ability to heal. And from that place, you raise your frequency, expand your life, and ripple this healing energy out to the world.

How do you feel about your personal experiences? Is there anything that you feel you want to address and release? How do you think you would feel when you are free from this?

"True healing works from the inside out."

The Darkness

Dark Night/Knight of the Soul

The Dark Night of the Soul refers to a phase of life in which a person is forced into deep inner change due to something intervening in their outer world, something profound — an experience powerful enough to shatter the illusion that the ego has built. As explored earlier in the chapter on trauma, once this illusion breaks, a person can no longer continue on the same path. Their inner beliefs are revealed to be misaligned with their Soul's truth. This breaking point initiates the Dark Night of the Soul. This often involves a significant loss — the death of a loved one, the end of a meaningful relationship, the loss of identity, purpose, or career. But trauma is subjective; what breaks one person may not affect another in the same way. The experience is uniquely personal.

What follows is often depression, despair, or a sense of hopelessness. But it is also the beginning of a profound inward journey. The Soul has orchestrated a moment where the only way out is in. It is through this inner inquiry that the person begins to see just how far they've strayed from their true Self. Even if they cannot name what feels wrong, they know something is fundamentally off. From this point, they begin asking the questions.

This internal breakdown occurs because the outer world no longer matches the truth within. The dissonance becomes unbearable, and something must change. The path forward is not external — it is internal. And as soon as the reconnection with the true Self begins, the outer world responds. Life begins to reflect this new internal state. As painful as this process is, it also births something sacred: the courage of the Soul. And once summoned, that inner strength is never lost. It can be called upon time and time again.

This period is marked by isolation and deep introspection — a time of disorientation, transformation, and the rediscovery of Self. Through this inner journey, the individual begins to integrate the ego and the Soul, learning how these forces interact and how they are meant to coexist. This integration realigns their energy, and the transformation within begins to reflect in the outer world. What emerges is a new version of the Self — one born from truth, and anchored in authenticity.

"Out of darkness and destruction, comes creation and light." – Me.

A little thought... ★

If you are in the dark night, know that you are not broken—you are breaking through. While it can feel isolating, heavy, and disorienting, it is also a sign that you are awakening. And though this descent into the unknown can be painful, it is also powerful. It is the invitation to rebuild not from fear, but from truth. What is out of alignment in your life? What do you want your life to be like? Here is your invitation to begin creating. If you allow it, it can be used as a reset button for your life, allowing you to reboot and create new in however many areas that you wish.

"If you are in the dark night, know that you are not broken - you are breaking through."

Exercise

Can you think back to some of your most challenging moments in life? What were they? Can you think about what lessons these have taught you in a positive way? I understand, this can be so challenging. And for now, the only thing that you may think of is that you experienced something that you know you never want to experience again. But, look as deep as you can and feel comfortable to…

Describe in detail, 1 or 2 of your most challenging moments that you have experienced in your life so far. Include any feelings the moments sparked in you; if you can't recall the feelings at the time, consider how recalling those memories/moments/events now makes you feel?	Name at least one positive thing that this experience has given you or taught you?
1.	
2.	

Accepting Ego and Our Human Nature

When we first begin the journey of uncovering our true selves, we often look to the light—the passions, talents, and inner sparks that light us up. These are the beautiful, Soul-based aspects of who we are. But there is another layer to true Self-acceptance: embracing the parts of us that are not so shiny or likeable. True acceptance includes the shadows.

The shadow Self is composed of the unconscious parts of the ego—repressed desires, unmet needs, and buried trauma. When we dare to turn toward these shadow aspects with compassion and curiosity, we unlock the truth of who we really are. This is where the power lies. In shining light on our conditioning, wounds, fears, and inner conflicts, we allow ourselves to become whole. Embracing the shadow is not about perfection; it is about authenticity. And this authenticity brings emotional resilience, creativity, and peace.

Growth arises from the integration of all parts of Self. We were never meant to be perfect. We were born into a human experience, full of messiness and contradiction. True peace comes not from erasing our imperfections, but from embracing them. In accepting that we are unfinished, raw, and layered, we reclaim the fullness of our humanity.

The ego's shadow side is not inherently bad—it holds potential. But when denied or suppressed, it can show up in harmful ways. It can lead to disproportionate reactions, unconscious projections, and inner conflict. Our triggers are mirrors, often reflecting back something we have yet to accept in ourselves. And just as we project our pain, we also project our healing: everything we admire in others is a reflection of something beautiful within us too.

Integrating the shadow means acknowledging the uncomfortable, making peace with it, and allowing it into the light. It means realising you are not only what you hope to be—you are also what you fear, what you avoid, and what you resist. But in acknowledging that, you free yourSelf. Acceptance dissolves shame. Without shame, difficult emotions are easier to move through. They are witnessed, understood, and released.

In this process, you begin to honour the role even your lowest moments played in shaping who you've become. Your survival strategies, your patterns, your defence mechanisms—they were part of your journey. These will likely bring into our awareness some parts of us that feel "true" but not necessarily "good." These are often aspects we've denied, rejected, or hidden. With awareness of polarity, we begin to see that we *need* these parts. They've helped you survive. They kept you safe. They gave you what you needed at the time. Now, you get to choose something new. But not in rejection of the past—in reverence for it.

Carl Jung was once praised by Alan Watts for being so deeply loved by his patients because he accepted all of himself—including the parts he called his "rascality." What a word! Jung embodied radical Self-acceptance. He was both brilliant and deeply human, and in this integration, he became whole.

Many people achieve greatness in some external form. But when that greatness is not met with humility and Self-awareness, it feeds an inflated ego that creates separation, not connection. When we place ourselves above others, we deny the very truth that makes us all equal: our shared humaneness.

Even when you have accepted yourSelf, lower emotions will still arise. But the difference is: they are no longer accompanied by shame. Without shame, you are free to feel what you feel. Your emotions are processed, not suppressed. And in this, your true Self is liberated.

Ultimately, ego is not the enemy. It is part of you. It can drive your growth, fuel your purpose, and support your evolution—if it is mastered. Left unchecked, it rules from the shadows. But brought into conscious awareness, it becomes a valuable ally. You are not here to destroy the ego. You are here to understand it, integrate it, and rise above it—with love. And in doing so, you bridge your OUT and IN, and achieve the life you truly want.

A little thought... ★

Have you ever considered that acknowledging the ego can lead to a paradox? In attempting to tame or transcend it, we can ironically fuel it further — especially if we're driven by the desire to become a "better" or "more evolved" person. That desire itself is rooted in ego. So, is there ever a desire for growth that isn't touched by ego? Is the desire to dissolve the ego an illusion of Spiritual progress? Is everything we do to overcome the ego, another act of the ego? Is this the final riddle of truth?
True unity with the collective consciousness — true surrender — may be incompatible with the drive to evolve the individual Self. The ultimate irony may be that only through the complete dissolution of ego can we see the truth... and by then, we may no longer need to. Could it all be a divine play — a cosmic game of consciousness experiencing itself?

Guidance

We All Need Guidance

We all need guidance on our journeys of Self-discovery. No one walks this path entirely alone—not truly. While the inner work is deeply personal, it is also part of a greater interconnected unfolding. We are meant to be guided—by signs, by synchronicities, by guides and mentors, by our inner knowing, and by each other.

When you decide to make changes and enter the unknown, you can be unsure which way to go. This is where guidance becomes essential. True guidance offers light. It mirrors back what is already within you.

Guidance can come from many places: a trusted mentor, a sacred text, a stranger's words at just the right moment, or even a breakdown that turns into a breakthrough. Sometimes it comes in silence—in a deep breath, a dream, or a sudden moment of stillness that connects you to something greater.

"True guidence offers light – it mirrors what is already within you."

You are wise for seeking guidance—it is a sign of readiness. Readiness to receive, to grow, and to remember the path you came here to walk. There is no shame in not knowing. There is only grace in being open to the learning. All of the most successful people in the world—whether in business, creativity, healing, or leadership—have guidance. They work with mentors, coaches, and teachers, as they are committed to expanding. True evolution requires reflection, accountability, perspective, and support. Those who thrive at the highest levels are not those who know everything, but those who are humble enough to keep learning and wise enough to seek insight beyond their own perspective.

A little thought...

My own growth accelerated exponentially when I finally called in the guidance of a wonderful Spiritually-led therapist. I had already read all the books, listened to the talks, and intellectually understood the work. But something was missing. It was not fully integrating into my body—into my cells. Having someone there to witness, guide, and hold me accountable, made all the difference. I had spent years internalising the belief that sharing my inner world was a burden to others, so I had learned to keep it all inside. Therapy was a space to unlearn that.

I deeply believe in integrative approaches. There is no one-size-fits-all model. What works for one may not work for another. Being open to this allows your path to unfold in its own way. Establishing and enshrining your own truth, built on Soul-aligned values, creates the unshakable Soul—strong, yet fluid. It is the kind of strength that remains open to growth and movement.

Is personal therapy something that you have, or have considered? How do you best receive guidance and support? What do you consider guidance could help you with?

Others Can Echo Your Truth

When we do not yet have a stable and established sense of true Self, we can feel lost. This is often because we are in the early stages of connecting with our Self—painting on a blank canvas and beginning to rediscover our truth. These formative moments lay the foundation for our mindset.

During such transitional times, especially if we are going through inner or outer transformation, it can be incredibly helpful to tune in to those with a strong sense of Self—individuals who reflect values and truths that resonate with our own. There are so many incredible motivational speakers and Spiritual teachers sharing empowering messages. When you find voices that align with your inner knowing, it becomes easier to find your own. You begin to establish your inner voice, your inner message, and your unique truth. This does not mean you must agree with everything someone says, or follow any one individual as your sole source of wisdom. Rather, it is about absorbing encouragement, clarity, and direction from those who mirror the values that feel true to you.

The information you choose to bring into your awareness becomes part of you. It shapes your belief systems, alters your perceptions, and directly impacts your energy field. What you focus on becomes a part of you. Choosing high-frequency and uplifting input is a support to your beliefs, thoughts, and energetic being. You will know what is true because it will feel different—it will resonate. Even if it is a new idea, it may feel like something you have always known.

A little thought... ★

I was at a point in my journey, where I was finding mySelf. I was aware that this was something to be done by me, and me only. I did not want the influence of others during this process, as I wanted this to be all my truth. That became a time of solitude, and what I later learned, some call the *hermit phase* of Spiritual awakening. Within this quiet space, I was able to connect to my truth, and build from there. And reading was my greatest guide – a soft presence that would guide but not overwhelm, ready whenever I was.

This is why The Guiding Star System exists—to guide you from your darkest moments into your brightest, and beyond. To invite you step into your potential and become all that you know you can be. And to do so from the safety of wherever you are now.
Have you found yourself at a point of solitude or a "hermit phase"? Or are you in one now? What lessons have you gained from your experiences?

Creating Change

The further we have travelled down the path rooted in ego, the more difficult it is to reach this moment of questioning and realisation. That path can be deeply ingrained—full of defence mechanisms, conditioned beliefs, and unconscious behaviours that have gone unexamined for years, sometimes decades.

But your Higher Self and your Souls encoded wisdom, will intervene. It will initiate a redirection. It will create circumstances that challenge your current identity and belief system, all with the intention of waking you up. The more deeply embedded you are in ego, the more radical this awakening may feel. You are called to turn around and look at everything: every mistake, every flaw, every choice that once felt justified but now rings hollow.

This process demands radical honesty. To admit what you have denied. To confront what you have avoided. In doing so, your subconscious narrative begins to shift. The ego-driven programming is now questioned by the Soul. Nothing is off-limits. Everything is up for reflection, reframing, and renewal. And this is where real transformation begins.

"The only thing to fear is the person that believes he knows everything" – Me.

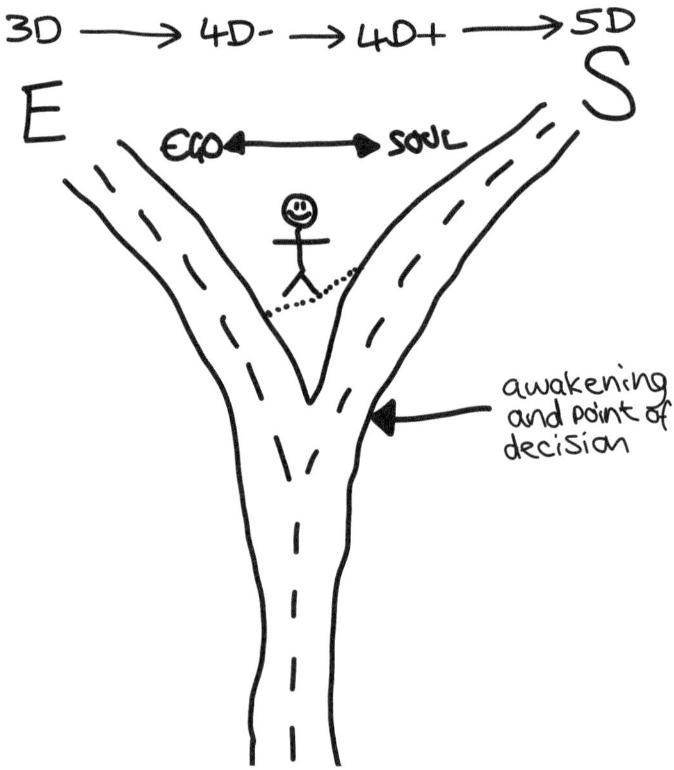

"Radical honesty is the doorway where ego yields to soul."

An example of this can be seen in the diagram of the two diverging paths: one representing the current ego-based direction, and the other the path aligned with Soul. The space between them illustrates the gap—the transitional void between who you have been and who you truly are. In order to cross that gap, you must be willing to *let go* of the previous path, including the beliefs, identities, and comforts attached to it.

Letting go initiates a new phase—one that invites unfamiliar emotions, reveals hidden fears, and demands the confrontation of parts of the ego that have gone unchallenged until now. This is the territory of transformation, where growth is both required and inevitable.

This awakening is not determined by age or stage of life. It can occur at any moment, to anyone. What varies is the severity and scope of the shift required. The further someone is from their true Soul-aligned path, the more significant the redirection and the more intense the resistance they may encounter. Yet no matter the distance, the Soul always knows the way home.

A little thought...

The Happy Trail. — This is a conversation I will always remember. It came out of the blue, as the most magical ones often do. I met a wise and kind new friend on an adventure in Scotland. We happened to share lunch in a little restaurant, and everything unfolded from there. A few weeks later, I surprised him and his wife with a visit to their healing shop and bakery in Lamington. During a short healing session, we had a beautiful conversation about happiness and how to tune into what truly makes you happy. His question caught me off guard: *What really makes you happy?* It was surprisingly difficult to answer. It hit something deep, and I became unexpectedly emotional. Yes, I do so many lovely things in my life, and I'm deeply grateful for them—but could I say I actually felt happiness in any of them?

If I was totally honest, while I enjoyed them all, each was tinged with pressure. The pressure to perform. The pressure to please. The pressure to succeed. I had been so consumed with making others happy that I had forgotten how to be happy mySelf. My happiness had become conditional—only felt when someone else was pleased or content. And in doing so, I lost my own.

My friend gently pointed to my belly—my sacral chakra—and said, *"It's in there. Follow it."* He told me to go back to a time when I truly felt free, innocent happiness. Not the kind created by achievements or doing things for others, but the kind that simply *is*. The happiness that is yours alone. I began to recall a few moments from childhood that lit me up: cycling through sunlit fields, spending time with horses on a warm summer day, playing endlessly with friends, laughing with no concept of time… or just being left alone, completely free to be mySelf.

This is the "Happy Trail." These moments are clues—fragments of truth—pointing to what happiness really feels like for *you*. It's not about what should make you happy. It's about what actually *does*. That feeling is your home frequency. When you find it, hold it. Revisit it often. Let it grow. You can make

happiness familiar again. It can be exercised like a muscle; the more you do, the more it becomes a natural state. Keep walking your happy trail.
Can you reflect on what truly makes you happy? Have you ever realized that you feel joy only when others are happy? Can you dig deeper, and discover what really makes YOU happy?

The Path to Awakening: How Do You Get There?

How do we travel along the path from *out* to *in*? What is the journey like? This is a different path for everyone, but it falls into one of two categories: I call these *Spiritual awakening*, or *gentle ascension*. The destination is the same, but the way in which we arrive will be our own unique route. A *Spiritual awakening* is often a single, profound event that triggers deep knowing and permanent transformation. This does not mean the person is done with their growth, but it signifies a complete understanding of truth, knowing, and life energy. These awakenings can come through near-death experiences, moments of divine clarity, encounters with nature, or powerful energetic experiences. The *knowing* from these moments becomes part of the person indefinitely. (NB – this is much like how trauma is a permanent imprint that we never forget, or an un-experience. It is a part of us and who we are, and how we choose to utilise it is up to us. The Spiritual awakening however, is just a wonderful!)

Gentle ascension, on the other hand, is the term I use to describe the gradual process of awakening. It is how most people experience Spiritual growth—step by step, layer by layer. It might be a moment of clarity, an "aha" moment, or an internal shift where something just *clicks*. These milestones are signs that you are progressing along your personal unlearning spiral of healing and transformation. Ascension is not linear, and it never really ends.

Most of us begin this journey through a triggering event that disrupts our "normal", leading us to deeper questions and answers. These moments of awareness can feel magical. They often appear unexpectedly, in moments of stillness or distraction, where the insight simply *lands*. Being open to receive, and learning to recognise these moments, can accelerate your growth in powerful ways.

A little thought... ★

During the gradual ascension, these "*moments of ascension*" or realisation, are quite magic! Some call them "*downloads*". I always find these come to me at very unexpected times. I am always in a situation where I am by mySelf, and it is usually quiet. Often, I am thinking about something totally different. And then it just drops in. Almost like an interruption. Being open to receiving this information, and recognising it, is key to helping you on your learning journey. If you can, keep track of them, write them down. These moments are powerful. You may like to keep a journal of these insights. Record your ascension markers—those moments when you know you have expanded. In intense periods of healing, these can become more frequent and often mark significant energetic shifts.
Can you think of one of your moments of ascension when this happened to you? Did you acknowledge it? Do you think you can allow yourSelf to be more open to receiving these more frequently?

You can have a Spiritual awakening in journeys using psychedelic plant medicines. If you feel called to these, they can be a helping hand from nature in attaining a connection with Spirit, or Soul. The insights gained can be permanent, even though the experience is temporary. They do leave you more open to receiving more insights and reconnecting with this energy. These journeys are not controlled by the mind; they bring forward whatever is stored in your energetic field—light or shadow. For those with trauma, plant medicine journeys may be helpful in breaking free from long-standing trauma loops. Research is expanding into these realms, and greater accessibility is on the horizon.

This connection can also be achieved organically through meditation, breathwork, or spontaneous insight. Dr. Joe Dispenza is a pioneer in this area. His work empowers people to achieve these states through deep meditation, backed by neurological measurement and brainwave mapping. His findings show real, lasting changes in brain patterns, emotional regulation, and life perspective after entering this altered state of being.

The path that you take from your *out* to your *in* may be in the form of gentle ascension or Spiritual awakening. They both end up in an awakening and awareness that will travel with you always. This is your connection to your *in*, something that once you are aware of, you cannot become unaware of. This deep knowing may not always be with you in your conscious 3D mind, but this 5D connection can be tuned in at your wish.

Boundaries

Boundaries are the ultimate preservation of your *in*. Boundaries are sacred. They are the energetic and practical expression of Self-respect and Self-love. They protect your integrity and your authentic Self. At their core, boundaries are the ability to say "no" — to uphold what is true for you and to honour the space you need to thrive. They are deeply personal, unique to each individual, and deserve the utmost respect — both from yourSelf and others. To learn how to set and maintain boundaries is to learn how to honour your power. It is a declaration of commitment to Self. And when you do this, you begin to experience true freedom.

Those who have experienced trauma, people-pleasing, or abuse often struggle to establish healthy boundaries. They may have been conditioned to believe that saying "no" is unkind, Selfish, or wrong. Or, even shamed for attempting to have them. But poor boundaries reflect a lack of Self-trust and a disconnection. Healing this is essential for growth, stability, and empowerment. First you find your *in*, and then you learn to enshrine it with boundaries.

Setting boundaries is rarely easy. You may encounter resistance — especially from those who benefited from your lack of them. You might feel guilt, shame, or fear. But remember: you are not responsible for how others react to your boundaries. You are responsible only for honouring yourSelf. Sometimes the most powerful thing you can do is walk away. By doing so, you give others space to reflect — whether or not they choose to do the inner reflection is not your burden to carry.

Boundaries are not about punishment or rejection. They are grace in action. They do not always need to be verbal or loud — sometimes your very presence, your silence, or your decisions, are boundaries in and of themselves.

"Boundaries are sacred: grace in action, the preservation of your IN."

The less we know ourselves, the fewer boundaries we have. And if boundaries are designed to protect our true essence, then we must first *know* and *accept* that essence in order to protect it. The more connected we are with who we truly are — the light, the dark, the good, the shadow — the more naturally boundaries will emerge. Setting boundaries is not a final destination. You will wobble. You will re-evaluate. You will outgrow some, and strengthen others. But through it all, hold this truth: boundaries are the ultimate expression of Self-trust and Self-worth and Self-love, they reflect where your *out* meets your *in.*

A little thought...

We often hear the phrase *Self-love*, and it has become almost cliché — a term we are all expected to understand and live by. But for many, it is a foreign concept. Many of us have learned that love is not safe. If you have never truly experienced Self-love, how do you begin?

The answer lies in cultivating trust — in your body, in your mind, and in your Soul. This triad is the foundation of true Self-love. You don't have to master it all at once. When you take moments of Self-reflection, simply notice where your trust wavers, and begin there. True trust begins with the physical body. When you trust yourSelf to care for your body — to nourish it, protect it, and honour its needs — you build a foundation of safety and survival. Next is the trust of the mind: trusting your perceptions, interpretations, and judgements. It is about trusting how you see the world and how you respond to it. And, most powerful of all, is the trust in your Soul, your intuition. This is where real Self-trust is born, and out of that, grows the love of the Self, and all that makes you, you. Where does your Self-trust falter? Is there a pattern of this? How can you look to improve this and show yourSelf the trust required to uphold it?

Forgiveness

Throughout this book, we have explored the lenses through which we each experience life, shaped by countless personal variables. Perspective is deeply unique. With this understanding, it becomes easier to see why misunderstandings and conflicts are such a common part of the human journey. People will hurt you, and you will hurt others—whether intentionally or not. This is a perfect example of *out* in action! One of the greatest gifts we can give ourselves is the ability to step into the role of the observer and approach these experiences through the lens of inner forgiveness.

Forgiveness, in its truest sense, is about liberation—it's about releasing yourSelf. When you forgive inwardly, you free your energy from the grip of an unresolved emotion, experience, or wound. Whether or not you have been consciously aware of it, these unresolved energies act as drains, quietly affecting your frequency and well-being. Forgiveness allows you to take your power back.

Importantly, this act of release is not directed outward to another person or circumstance. Forgiveness, most importantly, is extended inward—to your Self. You get to forgive yourSelf for not protecting yourSelf, from allowing others to take from you, for not knowing sooner, for not walking away earlier. Whatever it may be, you get to forgive yourSelf for not being perfect. This is the energetic truth of forgiveness: it restores your wholeness. It dissolves the energetic cords of guilt, shame, resentment, or regret, and returns you to alignment with your authentic Self. It frees you to connect with your *in* at a deeper level, and nourishes this interaction.

Forgiveness does not mean condoning harmful behaviour. And it does not mean re-opening doors to people who are not safe. That is a vital distinction. Forgiveness is not an excuse. It is not forgetting, or giving someone permission to re-enter your life. Rather, it is the conscious decision to accept that the past cannot be changed, and to release the hold it has over you. You can understand that someone acted from their own pain and trauma, without excusing their actions or allowing them access to your energy again.

Ultimately, forgiveness is a deeply personal process. You get to decide when, how, and if it happens. Whether extended or withheld, the energy of that choice must come from alignment with your highest Self—not from pressure, guilt, or fear. Let it be a sacred act of Self-honouring.

The Misconception of Perfection

Perfection does not exist — at least not in human form. The belief that perfection can be attained in ourselves, others, or life itself is a false benchmark that keeps us frozen. It feeds the fear of failure, the fear of not measuring up, and the fear of being seen. In aiming for perfection, we set ourselves up to fail — and that failure becomes a reason not to try, to not move forward. This illusion of perfection is a trick of the ego, whereas Soul understands that true love is found in the imperfection.

You will not be a completed project while you are here. Your journey is ongoing, and there will always be more to learn, more to experience, more to grow into. That doesn't make you less worthy. In fact, your *enough-ness* is found in your willingness to keep moving forward — one layer at a time. Yes, the journey can feel endless. Sometimes the growth feels exhausting. And when it does, allow yourSelf to pause and rest. Take a breath and look at how far you have come. There is no race, and no rush. Trust that you are exactly where you need to be, and that everything you're meant to know will reveal itself in perfect timing. Let the journey be joyful. Let it be yours.

"Let the journey be joyful. Let it be yours."

How to Further Explore and Advance your *Out – In:*

Self-awareness is the foundation of personal transformation. Once you've developed a deeper awareness of your patterns, programming, and emotional landscape, you can now work with that information constructively. You can unlock the ability to make conscious changes that elevate your frequency. These tools and practices offer powerful ways to release the unwanted, reprogram the mind, and align with your true Self:

- **Attachment Styles** – Understanding your attachment style (secure, anxious, avoidant, or disorganised) reveals how you connect in relationships, and where unmet emotional needs may be influencing your behaviour.
- **The 5 Personality Patterns** (Steven Kessler) – This framework helps you identify the unconscious survival patterns you developed in early life, and how these shape your personality and reactions.
- **The 16 Personality Types** (Myers-Briggs Type Indicator) – A widely used tool for exploring how you perceive the world, make decisions, and interact with others.
- **Human Design** – A Spiritual-meets-scientific blueprint for understanding your energetic design, life purpose, and decision-making strategy.
- **Internal Family Systems (IFS)** – A profound parts-based therapeutic model that helps you recognise and work with the many "parts" within your psyche, particularly those developed through trauma.
- **Therapy / Counselling** – One-on-one support with a trained practitioner to help you explore, process, and integrate your emotional and psychological experiences.
- **Breathwork** – Conscious breathing techniques that regulate the nervous system and access subconscious emotional layers.
- **EMDR (Eye Movement Desensitisation and Reprocessing)** – A highly effective therapy for trauma resolution and emotional processing.

- **NLP (Neuro-Linguistic Programming)** – A method for changing thought patterns, beliefs, and behaviours through language and visualisation techniques.
- **Hypnotherapy** – Bypasses the conscious mind to plant supportive beliefs directly into the subconscious.
- **Meditation** – A practice of stillness and inward attention that enhances presence, awareness, and emotional regulation.
- **Journaling** – Writing to access inner wisdom, clarify thoughts, release emotion, and track growth.
- **CBT (Cognitive Behavioural Therapy)** – Helps reframe limiting thoughts and beliefs through structured, evidence-based exercises.
- **Emotional Freedom Technique (EFT or "Tapping")** – Combines acupressure with affirmations to release stuck emotional energy.
- **Inner Child Work** – Addresses unmet emotional needs from childhood and offers them the safety and love they lacked.
- **Counselling or Therapy** – Ongoing support to process life experiences, develop coping strategies, and promote emotional healing.
- **Inner Critic Work** – Identifying and reframing the voice of Self-judgment and internalised shame.
- **Ego Defence Work** – Becoming aware of and disarming ego-based defences that block healing and connection.
- **Psychotherapy** – A broader approach to exploring the mind and unconscious, often used long-term for deep transformation.
- **Neurofeedback (NeurOptimal)** – A non-invasive technology that trains the brain to Self-regulate and return to optimal function.
- **Alexander Technique** – A somatic method that focuses on posture, movement, and tension release to support mental and physical integration.
- **Polyvagal Theory / Vagal Tone Work** – Understanding how your nervous system responds to stress and safety can deeply support trauma healing and emotional regulation.

- **Somatic Experiencing (Peter Levine)** – A body-based therapy for trauma that focuses on releasing stored tension and restoring safety in the nervous system.
- **Shadow Work** – A form of introspective work to uncover and integrate repressed or unconscious parts of the Self, enhancing wholeness and Self-compassion.
- **Parts Integration (NLP & IFS hybrid)** – A method for reconciling conflicting parts within the psyche and creating inner unity.
- **Voice Dialogue / The Psychology of Selves** – A practice of dialoguing with inner parts (similar to IFS) to bring awareness and integration.
- **Energy Psychology / Reiki / Energy Healing** – Addresses emotional and energetic imbalances directly through subtle energy fields.
- **Astrological Birth Chart Reading** – Offers symbolic insight into patterns, archetypes, and Soul lessons (especially helpful when used consciously, not as prediction).
- **Sound Healing / Binaural Beats / Frequency Therapy** – Uses sound frequencies to entrain the brain and body into healing states.
- **Creative Arts Therapies (Art, Dance, Drama)** – Helps access and process emotions through non-verbal, expressive mediums.
- **Systemic Constellations / Family Constellations** – A powerful method for resolving intergenerational trauma and hidden family dynamics.
- **Psychedelic-Assisted Journey (with legal and professional support)** – For those called to deeper states of consciousness and healing under careful guidance.
- **Past life regression** – Offers insight into karmic themes, Soul memories, and energetic imprints that influence your present experience.
- **True commitment to Self and learning** – The most essential tool of all. When you commit to knowing yourSelf, the path will continue to reveal itself.

"Until you make the unconscious conscious, it will direct your life and you will call it fate." - Carl Jung.

Summary

1. **The *out* reflects the *in*** – Everything in our external environment, from relationships to health, reflects the state of our internal emotional and energetic landscape.
2. **Your frequency dictates your reality** – Thoughts and emotions carry frequencies that shape our experiences. Learning to raise and stabilise your base frequency creates lasting transformation.
3. **Trauma manifests outwardly** – Unresolved trauma and emotional repression not only affect our mindset, but also lead to physical dis-ease and chronic conditions if left unaddressed.
4. **The ego and Soul must integrate** – Rather than eliminating the ego, we learn to work with it consciously, using it as a tool in service of the Soul, rather than being governed by it.
5. **Reprogramming limiting beliefs is the key** – Identifying and replacing subconscious beliefs rooted in fear allows us to move from survival to expansion, from ego to Soul.
6. **Reality is subjective.** It is individual, unique, and always a reflection—an exact mirror—of your own consciousness.
7. **Radical responsibility is the doorway to power.** When you're brave enough to own your consciousness fully, you begin to use it to your advantage. Reflect honestly, and give yourSelf credit for the good you've created too.
8. **Train your system to feel as if it's already true.** Embody the belief as knowing. This is how you recode your outer world—from within.
9. **Become the observer.** Witness your thoughts without attachment. Let them come and go like clouds in the sky. The more space you create, the more freedom you unlock.
10. **Embrace non-judgment and radical acceptance.** Drop the need to label your experiences as right or wrong. Accept everything with honesty, without guilt or shame. Acceptance is freedom.
11. **Listen to your inner voice.** At first it whispers. But the more you honour it, the louder and clearer it becomes. Build trust in your

intuition like any relationship—through presence, consistency, and action.

12. **Your nervous system is your foundation.** True embodiment of your power and presence requires safety within the body. Grounding, breath, and regulation are keys to sustaining your frequency.
13. **Question everything.** Stay curious and non-attached. Even your strongest beliefs are worthy of re-examination. Truth is found in openness.
14. **Your Soul purpose is not something you chase—it's something you remember, something you are.** The more you tune into your inner world, the more your purpose becomes clear. Let it emerge rather than be forced.
15. **Anchor yourSelf in the now.** The present moment is the only place you can create from. It is your point of power, and the place where your true Self lives.
16. **You are eternal.** Energy cannot be destroyed, and your consciousness is energy. You exist beyond the limits of this body, this lifetime, and this moment.
17. **Be you. Live you. Love you.** Your most powerful expression is your most authentic Self.

Exercise

THE 10 COMMANDMENTS OF SELF – this is the most transformational exercise. Here is where you get to decide. To declare. That from this moment forward, you uphold the following 10 commandments to yourSelf. And your "why" for having put these in place. An example may be, *"I will always be honest with mySelf, no matter how difficult.* Why? *Because I know that avoiding my truth not change it, and the sooner I face it, the better for me. I deserve the best life."* You have been through so much of the book now, and your commandments to yourSelf can include anything you wish – they may be based on your earlier affirmations, things that you have been invited to consider throughout the book, or something that you are integral to in your life anyway. If someone didn't know you, and they got to read these, they should give a snapshot of the most important things to you, that you stand by from this point onwards.

	Commandment	Why?
1		
2		
3		
4		
5		
6		
7		
8		
9		
10		

Relationships

Why Include a Chapter on Relationships?

The final and continual part of the healing journey is to understand and utilise the energetic dynamics of relationships. Relationships are a fundamental part of the human experience. They form our ultimate teachers in this lifetime—nothing makes us learn a lesson quite like the reflection of a relationship. The people we attract into our lives act as mirrors, showing us the parts of ourselves we most need to see. Sometimes this reflection is beautiful—love, patience, kindness—reminding us of our own light. At other times, it is uncomfortable, stirring old wounds, hidden fears, or forgotten truths. This goes for all of the relationships in our life, but particularly the romantic ones – they offer a deeper level of vulnerability and openness, and ability to wound us. All relationships are, therefore, reflections of your inner world projected into your external world. And they tap into each area of The Guiding Star System. This is what we explore in this chapter.

Relationship Energy

Every person has their own individual frequency, and this frequency is continually changing and evolving. Those around you—whether friends, family, or romantic partners—also carry their own frequencies. These energies interact with yours, and this interaction can either serve as an input (a positive increase in energy) or an output (a draining or decrease in energy).

Everyone has challenging days, and it is a beautiful act of love to be there for someone during those times. But it is equally important to recognise the people who *consistently* leave you feeling depleted. This is particularly relevant with those who are persistently negative, addicted to drama, emotionally toxic, or who embody the archetype of the energy vampire. These individuals are often unaware of the impact they have—they simply aren't at a stage of Self-awareness to see or acknowledge it.

As you move through your healing journey—and especially during any periods of ascension, where you are raising your frequency—you must be prepared to let go of relationships that hold you back. These are the connections that drain your energy and weigh down your evolution. This letting go often precedes a period of solitude, introspection, and personal growth. Yet it is this very space that you create that allows new, aligned relationships to enter. Without space, there is nowhere for new energy to come in.

You will experience a range of emotions—grief, relief, confusion, clarity—as you navigate these changes and losses. This too is part of the restructuring process as your new frequency becomes established. One thing to always remember: everyone is on their own path. They are responsible for their own healing and growth. Losing access to your energy may actually be a critical moment in *their* journey, just as it is in yours. Put yourSelf, your feelings, and your well-being first. That is your responsibility—no one else's.

If you have been surrounded by draining relationships, this may feel unfamiliar or uncomfortable. Saying "no" may feel like rejection and guilt. But these are the life skills that your previous experience has gifted you. Implementing boundaries and choosing yourSelf will have the most powerful impact on your frequency and your energy. Focus on what inspires you, where you want to go, and how you want to use your energy—because it is yours to choose.

The Mirror of Romantic Relationships

Romantic relationships can be beautiful and deeply fulfilling, but they are not simply for happiness and comfort. They are also designed to bring awareness to the areas of our being that are still calling for growth and healing. Until you are able to have an honest, loving, and accountable relationship with yourSelf, you cannot offer or request the same from another. *Self-awareness* and a genuine commitment to personal development are prerequisites for a healthy partnership.

Both individuals in a conscious relationship will be open to feedback, willing to hear each other's concerns, and committed to doing the inner and relational work required to grow. If one partner refuses to take responsibility for their patterns, it can be incredibly painful—and ultimately unsustainable. No one party can take this on for the both. Attracting a partner who is unwilling to evolve can be a reflection of your own inner work. Frequently, this relates to your capacity to set and uphold standards for yourSelf—standards of Self-worth, Self-belief, and what you are willing to tolerate. These painful moments of misalignment often serve as catalysts. Sometimes, the pain of leaving is what is needed to spark transformation. And that, in itself, becomes part of your ascension.

A little thought... ★

Ok, this is an odd one to write! Relationship experiences are the things that have cut the deepest and caused the most amount of pain. I can now see that they have cut me open in a way that has allowed me to discover that which I would not have discovered in mySelf. There was a point where I would never have been able to even consider this as a possibility!

In looking at the origins and roots of the wounds, you discover what they really are. When you feel through this pain that you've held within you, you can release it, and it remains something that no longer holds an emotional charge over you. I can now say that I can see how every relationship has been a lesson; a catalyst for growth, that have shaped me into now. I would not have been writing this book, or doing the work that I do, without each and every single one of them. And in a realisation like that, you find yourSelf paradoxically in gratitude, for what was once the deepest pain.

Have you ever experienced a shift in perspective like this? Where at different points in your life, you can view something in a different perspective? What experiences have now released their emotional charge for you?

"Relationships are mirrors – to reflect what you most need to see."

Exercise

Have a think about what you look for in another person? What are the things that you are attracted to? What is it that you look for with the different areas of The Guiding Start System? Have a think, and write these qualities and characteristics down. Include how you feel about these things?

	Qualities that I look for in a partner?
FUEL	
MOVEMENT	
REST	
OUT	
IN	

Now that you have brought awareness to what it is that you look for in a partner (the *out*), let's bring this back to the mirror, to us (the *in*). If the partner is the reflection, then what is it within us? It may be that what you are looking for in someone else, is what you feel you are lacking within yourSelf? Or these may be qualities that you already have and wish to share together? Look deeper now into truly why you want these things, and how you embody them in yourSelf, and to what extent?

An example may be, "IN: *I want a partner that makes me feel safe and loved, I long for this feeling"*. Why: *"I do not feel safe by mySelf, I am looking for a partner to fulfil this need". "I can become this mySelf by finding safety within me, confronting my fears, and connecting with a knowing that whatever happens, I've got me."*

	Why do I want this? Do I have this mySelf?	**How can I become this mySelf?**
FUEL		
MOVEMENT		
REST		
OUT		
IN		

"Until you can hold an honest, loving relationship with yourSelf, you cannot offer - or ask - the same of another."

The Partner: The Ultimate Mirror

When we enter into a romantic relationship, we encounter one of the most profound mirrors of Self. We are all unhealed in some way—but the degree of our healing will determine the type of partner we attract and the depth of the relationship we sustain. The more we have healed, the more we naturally attract partners based in the Soul level of the spectrum. All qualities are on a spectrum! An example is the spectrum of empathy and narcissism:

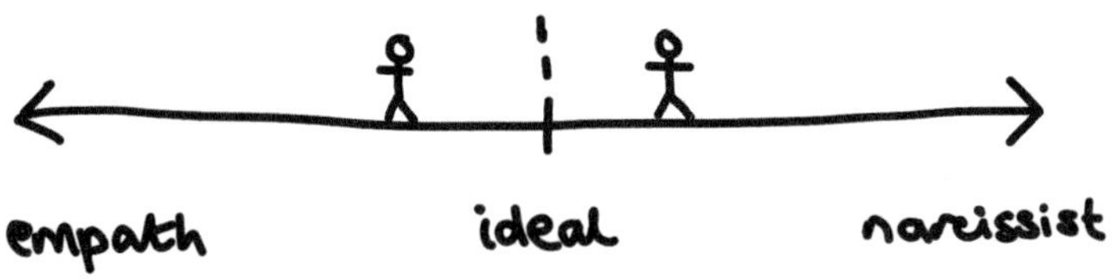

The extremes are the co-dependent empath to a narcissist. These represent the two ends of a polarity, with the ideal state—healed and balanced—resting at the centre. Think for a moment: where might you fall on this spectrum? Wherever that is, you are likely displaying traits that attract someone at the opposite but energetically equivalent end. This perfectly illustrates how Self-healing and ascension ripple outwards to transform every aspect of our lives. As your frequency rises, you attract on that same frequency.

That is why healing is your responsibility. It is only when you have done enough inner work to reflect, grow, and take true accountability for Self that you begin to attract different types of partners—those who are aligned with your values, needs, and Soul truth. If you find yourSelf repeatedly attracting the same kind of partner—someone who does not value you, honour you, or meet your needs—it is time to look inward. Your evolution and your standards are linked. When you heal, you raise the bar. You stop attracting relationships that reflect your wounds and start attracting those that reflect your wholeness.

When you meet a potential partner, you may see some beautiful traits that draw you in—but if you also see traits that are out of alignment with what your Higher Self knows you deserve, it's ok to walk away. Thank them for the clarity and insight, and release them with love. By doing this, you are setting an energetic boundary. You are saying to the universe: *I know what I want, so present me with the lessons I need in order to attract and hold this.* Each time you choose alignment over instant gratification, you signal your readiness to receive the kind of love that matches your Soul.

Soul-Based Love

When you enter into a relationship from a healed place, love becomes something sacred. It is not about filling voids or fulfilling unmet needs. Instead, each partner is already fulfilled, Self-loving, and operating from a high base frequency. These are people who can Self-soothe, regulate their emotions, and walk their healing path independently—even as they support and walk beside each other.

Love from this place is a choice and forms healthy interdependency. Both people come to the relationship from overflow. Your happiness is no longer placed in someone else's hands—it resides with you. In this way, your partner becomes a beautiful addition to an already fulfilled life. You give and receive from abundance.

This is not to say that you will not experience challenges or pain—of course you will. But in these relationships, both parties are committed to healing, to growing, and to learning the lessons together. You take the knowledge and turn it into knowing. This is conscious love.

Together, you hold space for each other's evolution, with compassion, safety, and care. The relationship becomes a sacred container—a catalyst for growth, anchored in kindness, curiosity, and truth. Importantly, neither of you loses your individuality in the process. You honour your own Self fully, while simultaneously honouring each other.

Soulmates, Twin Flames, and Karmic Partners

Many religions and mythologies speak of Soulmates and twin flames, though their true meanings are often diluted in modern interpretations. When approached from an esoteric and energetic perspective, these concepts become powerful tools of awareness that can help us understand the nature of our most significant connections.

Soulmates are kindred Spirits—gentle, loving, and deeply familiar unions based on mutual respect and unconditional love. These connections can span lifetimes.

While many imagine Soulmates only in romantic terms, they can exist in any form of relationship: a friend, a mentor, a family member. Their presence evokes a sense of deep recognition. Your Soul has vibrated with theirs before, and it is this resonance you feel. These connections transcend race, class, culture, or background. They are rooted in energy, not identity. However, both people must be grounded and present in order for this Soul recognition to occur. Without that readiness, such meetings can be bypassed or misunderstood.

Soulmate connections do not require a high level of Spiritual awakening to occur. The union may exist largely within 3D or early 4D frequencies and may still lack a wider awareness of collective consciousness. However, the relationship will carry a quiet strength, a deep knowing, and an energy of homecoming.

Karmic partners are also Soul connections or a form of Soul mate, but ones formed for the sole purpose of teaching a lesson. These relationships are often intense, difficult, and temporary. They frequently trigger trauma and shadow work, asking each partner to face themselves more honestly. Karmic partners often operate within lower 3D and 4D– frequencies and persist only as long as it takes for the necessary Soul lessons to be learned. They may feel like love, but they often bring patterns of chaos, co-dependency, or emotional pain. Still, their gift is awareness—and the realisation that only we can change our own patterns, not another person.

Twin flames are altogether different. This is a rare energetic phenomenon where one Soul has been split into two distinct energetic polarities. Spirit has no gender, but Soul essence is encoded with energetic polarity, and it is this encoding that causes the magnetic pull between twin flames. The connection is one of mirroring and unification in the truest sense—each partner reflecting the strengths and flaws of the other. At its highest frequency, the twin flame union is one of powerful alignment, shared mission, and Spiritual evolution. But it can also be the most triggering and difficult relationship a Soul will ever experience. When twin flames are not ready, or are living through the distortion of ego rather than Soul, the union can become volatile. If there is enough healing, awareness, and individual accountability, however, they can transcend into a sacred union and create extraordinary work in the world.

There is often a romanticised fantasy around twin flames and Soulmates that skips over the shadow and the polarity inherent in such relationships. These unions are not simply magical; they are magnetic mirrors of growth and transformation. They require groundedness, humility, and a deep willingness to do the work—individually and together.

To attract a Soulmate or twin flame, you must be vibrating at the same frequency. This does not mean that you are *done* with your journey; it means you are at the matching point for what your Souls require to grow together. The same is true of karmic partners—they meet you where you are. Your frequency draws in the perfect match for your next step, whether it is growth through challenge, or expansion through union.

A little thought...

In a moment, something made me question what I was really looking for. The answer? *Love.* A feeling of wholeness, happiness, and completeness. And then I got it— I was still looking for someone else to give me that feeling. I thought I understood this lesson intellectually, but in that moment, I realised I hadn't *experienced* it and *become* it mySelf. I saw the qualities that I was once attracted to, were the very parts of mySelf I had rejected or neglected. In looking for safety, where was I not providing that for mySelf? In looking for sharing, where was I not sharing with mySelf? The attractions had come from a desire to be completed by another, rather than from a state of inner wholeness. And here was where a lot of the inner work began for me – and what a journey! I can honestly say that I now welcome a loving relationship, but am also good if it doesn't happen. And those are words that I did not ever thought I would be able to say, let alone mean! But how can you truly love another person, if you cannot love yourSelf first?

Are you at a point where you can have this honest Self-reflection? If so, what are your key moments of realisation? What is it that you fear? How can you go further into this discovery and liberation?

"We are not a reflection of what we want, but of what we believe we are." — *Me*

Masculine and Feminine Energy

Masculine and feminine energies exist within all dynamics and polarities and extend far beyond the basic understanding of man and woman. They are fundamental forces—one of the seven Hermetic principles that govern existence—and they exist across the body, mind, and Soul.

Masculine energy embodies:
Purpose, drive, protection, stability, strength, structure, power, respect, grounding, clarity, direction, assertiveness, and physical world mastery.

Feminine energy embodies:
Sensitivity, peace, empathy, nurturing, compassion, kindness, intuitive knowing, receptivity, grace, emotional strength, surrender, and Spiritual world wisdom.

This sacred dance between masculine and feminine energies is present throughout the physical and energetic worlds. In fact, many Spiritual and business leaders now base entire methodologies on the balance and interplay of these two forces. Each of us carries both within, and when these are in harmony, they become powerful assets—inputs of energy rather than drains. In their wounded forms, however, they often signal energetic outputs and wounds that still require healing.

The Dance of Masculine Male & Feminine Female

When masculine energy is fully healed, rooted in Self-worth, and open to both giving and receiving, it begins to magnetise its complement—feminine energy. If both energies are individually grounded and loving within their own spheres, their meeting becomes natural, balanced, and energetically aligned.

A healed masculine does not seek aimlessly. He knows what he wants and is confident enough to lead with clarity and intention. He acts with purpose, not from ego, but from Soul-led desire. He is no longer dating for distraction or validation—he is seeking resonance, readiness, and depth. When a man is truly searching for a queen, he treats every potential interaction as sacred, approaching it with respect, discernment, and care. No games, no half-heartedness. If the answer is yes, he leads; if not, he steps away with grace.

Equally, the feminine energy naturally opens and submits—not in a weakened sense, but in surrender to the safety and structure offered by a conscious masculine. This submission is an act of sacred trust. Within this dynamic, she flourishes. And in return, the masculine receives more than he could have ever hoped for: radiance, support, intuitive guidance, and unconditional love. The feminine amplifies whatever she is given.

This dynamic is not about perfection—it is about intention. Both people will face challenges and make mistakes. But when each is committed to growth, mutual healing, and loving awareness, those challenges become opportunities. Effective, safe communication becomes the foundation for conflict resolution. Love languages are learned, vulnerability is honoured, and mutual expansion is inevitable.

When the feminine is in full bloom, her energy becomes a beacon. She leads the masculine home to his Soul, opening the door to a higher path he may not have seen without her influence. If they are Soulmates, she amplifies his individual purpose. If they are twin flames, she helps align their shared mission. When two people come together—in king and queen energy—with shared values and a unified direction, their union becomes a magnified energetic force. When multiple energies flow in the same direction, they amplify. The result is a relationship that uplifts the individuals, the couple, and those around them.

A little thought... ★

There is a period of solitude that arises once you are elevating your frequency and completing a cycle of inner work. It is not loneliness—it's preparation. It is a space where you learn to find peace, joy, and contentment within yourSelf, free from attachment to partnership. It is the perfect space to be learning about yourSelf and developing this ever-paramount relationship. You may be presented with potential partners, old or new, that no longer match who you have become.

Have you experienced an example of this? The ex gets back in contact? Or a new version of a past relationship dynamic introduces itself? What do you feel this could be teaching you? Could it be a test to see if you ARE your new energy vibration? Here may be your opportunity to *walk the walk*, and not just *talk the talk*? (Or should I say, *be the be*!)

Settling: A New Perspective

The term "settling" often carries negative connotations—suggesting we have chosen something less than what we deserve. But what if we reframe it? To settle on something is to *choose it fully*. It is a sacred commitment—not from lack, but from alignment. To settle is not to accept less; it is to choose deeply. It is an act of intention and devotion. When we settle, we quiet the ego and focus the Soul. We allow the nervous system to ground, the heart to open to love, the body to relax into abundance. We settle into our truth, our direction, and the challenges that come with it. And in doing so, we are free—not trapped.

This applies to relationships, careers, purpose, and lifestyle. When we settle *on*, rather than settle *for*, we access depth, mastery, and presence. We no longer skim the surface of life, forever waiting for something *better*. We are in it, fully. Fear of commitment or fear of missing out can keep us from ever settling, and in doing so, we miss the richness that only depth can bring. Settling means *choosing something*—and then growing with it. Knowing that the destination is aligned with the Soul, even if the path toward it is ever-changing. To settle is to say: *"I choose this. I commit to this. I will honour it. I will evolve with it. And I will meet mySelf fully within it."*

A little thought... ★

As a woman who once found feminine energy a foreign concept, I have lived through the dissonance of survival mode. I stayed predominantly in my masculine energy—driven, Self-sufficient, and wounded. I attracted similar energies in relationships and unconsciously rejected the very thing I longed for:

softness, safety, and surrender. To feel safe enough to receive, I first had to heal. The feminine needs protection and presence to bloom, and this is offered by healthy masculine energy. That is not true for every woman, but it is the polarity of my own Soul's path. I know the time will come, and the space within me is there. To meet your Soulmate or twin flame, you must feel at home with your own Soul first. Know yourSelf. Love yourSelf. Honour the time you have single. And when that sacred union arrives, you will recognise it—not as something new, but as something deeply familiar.

Sexual Energy

Sexual energy is one of the most potent and profound forms of energy we can access in human form. It is the foundation of all life, the most primal expression of creativity, and a deeply generative force. While commonly associated with sex itself, sexual energy is not limited to physical intimacy—it extends far beyond, encompassing vitality, passion, magnetism, and the capacity to heal, manifest, and awaken higher consciousness.

The ancients understood the power of sexual energy. Many Spiritual and philosophical traditions recognised its sacred nature and viewed the management of this energy as essential to a person's overall frequency and Spiritual advancement. Perhaps this is why many religions and societal systems sought to regulate, suppress, or control it—because anything this powerful, when ungoverned, can be feared or misused. To retain sexual energy is to contain an incredible reservoir of life force. This practice—often known as celibacy or energetic retention—can be used not as a rejection of sexuality, but as a redirection. Retaining and consciously channelling sexual energy allows it to be transmuted into creativity, vitality, wealth, and healing. This is the principle of energetic transformation, a law we have already explored in this book.

Napoleon Hill, in *Think and Grow Rich*, wrote of this same concept. He referred to it as sexual transmutation—redirecting sexual energy from physical gratification into creative and intellectual output, particularly for the purpose of manifesting success and abundance. This level of transmutation requires Self-discipline, awareness, and a deep connection to purpose. The better you know yourSelf, the more powerfully you can redirect this energy in alignment with your truth. In doing so, sexual energy becomes a tool for elevation, not just pleasure.

The sexual partner you choose holds great energetic significance. Sexual union is an exchange of energy, and this transference can elevate or diminish your frequency. Your auric fields merge, your bodies become one, and your Souls temporarily intertwine. This is particularly profound for women; whose bodies naturally receive more deeply during sex and whose hormonal responses create stronger emotional bonding. This energetic exchange happens whether you are conscious of it or not. Casual sex may be normalised in society (at the moment), but it does not prevent the reality of energy transfer. You are always impacted by those you share physical intimacy with—body, mind, and Soul. The more conscious and connected both parties are, the more powerful and healing the union becomes.

Orgasm is one of the highest natural frequencies a human can experience. In that moment, you touch an altered state of consciousness—ecstatic, transcendent, expansive. If both partners are aligned in intention, the energy of orgasm can be directed toward manifestation. The obvious creation is a child, but the intention can be shifted toward any form of manifestation. Love, healing, abundance, gratitude—anything can be created from this space when directed consciously. Use it wisely.

Summary

1. **Relationships are mirrors** — Every relationship reflects your internal world, showing both your light and your unhealed wounds.
2. **Energetic interaction** — Each person carries a frequency; relationships either energise and uplift you or drain and deplete you.
3. **Boundaries and self-worth** — Learning to say no, protect your energy, and choose yourself first is a core life skill and frequency upgrade.

4. **Romantic partners are catalysts** — Intimate relationships expose wounds and unconscious patterns; they call for honesty, accountability, and healing.
5. **Healing changes attraction** — As you heal and raise your frequency, you stop attracting partners who reflect your wounds and draw those who reflect your wholeness.
6. **Choosing alignment over instant gratification** — Walking away from misaligned relationships signals to the universe your readiness for true Soul-level partnership.
7. **Soul-based love** — Healthy love comes when two whole individuals meet, each self-loving and self-regulating, creating a sacred, abundant partnership.
8. **Masculine and feminine energy** — Both energies exist in everyone; when balanced and healed, they magnetise each other and create powerful unions.
9. **Preparation through self-love** — To meet an aligned partner, you must first know and love yourself, feel safe in your body, and embrace your own Soul.
10. **Sexual energy as creation** — Sexual union is a potent energetic exchange; conscious intimacy can elevate frequency, healing, and even manifestation.
11. **Energetic responsibility in intimacy** — Sexual partners exchange auric and emotional energy; consider the unseen impact.
12. **Manifestation through orgasm** — Orgasm is a peak frequency state; with intention, it can be channelled for love, healing, or creation.

Conclusion

The Guiding Star System (TGSS) began as a way to map the foundational elements of our human experience through five key areas: Fuel, Movement, Rest, Out, and In. On the surface, these concepts may seem distinct and separate—fuel is food and drink, movement is exercise and location, rest is sleep and stopping, out is the reflection of the physical world, and in is our inner Self. But as we journey deeper into each pillar, we uncover the truth: they are all interconnected, anchored by a unified centre, and guided by energetic laws that govern our internal and external realities.

When you view your life through the lens of energy—when you begin to *feel* rather than just *know*—you tap into the power to truly transform. Knowing is when those words take root in your heart and cells, becoming the lens through which you live. Many of us begin our journeys in 3D with knowledge, but it is through experience, reflection, and healing that we ascend into 4D and 5D—into deep knowing.

The transition from 3D to 5D is not linear. 4D is a spacc of fluctuation, a bridge where we acquire understanding, confront challenges, and begin to shift. It is both our training ground and testing space. 5D, the frequency of Soul, love, and Spirit, reveals the interwoven magic that underpins all of life. But no one stays in 5D indefinitely. We are here, in human form, to integrate the divine and the Earthly. The goal is not to escape the 3D, but to bring our highest frequency *into* the 3D—to bring heaven to Earth, through ourselves.

Authenticity, not perfection, is the highest frequency. The aim is not to become flawless, angelic beings who float above the messiness of life. The aim is to live as our whole selves—messy, raw, evolving, real. Living in integrity with our Soul creates what I have called the "unshakeable Soul": a state of grounded power, where your truth cannot be shaken by external forces. You trust your inner compass. You live from the inside out.

And that is what TGSS is truly about. It is not about becoming someone else; it's about remembering who you are. It's about reclaiming your energy, your voice, your wholeness. You are already encoded with everything you need. When you follow it—through the unlearning spiral, through the wounds and the wisdom—you find clarity. You find your path. You find peace.

And if you haven't realised it already, here is the truth: Your Self and your Soul are your internal Guiding Star. And it is this that integrates all together; fuel, movement, rest, out, and in. Soul is present in all.

When you take responsibility for the only thing you can control, yourSelf, you put yourSelf in the ultimate position of power, the creative divinity within. We take responsibility for our choices, our energy, our healing, and the way we show up in the world. Our purpose is to become the most aligned, conscious, and loving version of who we truly are. And when we do, that radiates, touching everyone around us. We choose relationships that honour us—spaces where we are seen, safe, and supported. And from this place of truth, we truly live. Fully. Freely. Soulfully.

Healing is not about erasing the past. It's about integrating it. Alchemising it. There are no bad parts—only parts that separated from your core to keep you safe. By identifying them, hearing them, and reintegrating them, you reclaim your power. This is the essence of the work pioneered by modern parts therapy and echoed throughout ancient traditions: wholeness comes from inclusion, not exclusion.

This is also where we understand that Spiritual bypassing—denying our humanity in favour of only light and love—is not healing. True elevation requires roots. Expand your energetic antenna upward, yes, but deepen your roots just as far down. We must live in the body, in the world, with grounded practices and real-world actions that bring Soul into form.

The energetic laws of the universe exist for philosophical understanding, but most importantly for practical application. Why study them if we do not use them to elevate our 3D reality? You are here to create. You are here to bring your unique frequency to life. This means accessing and maintaining your energy in real ways: knowing how to Self-regulate, reprogram limiting beliefs, protect your frequency, and live in accordance with your inner truth. TGSS is not about one fixed method. It is a framework that brings together diverse modalities and guides you back to your Self—your wholeness.

The journey may not be linear. It may not be easy. You may be tested. You may fall down. You may pretend to be healed before you really are. I did too. But every challenge has brought me closer to truth—closer to healing, to clarity, to my Soul.

My own path has led me through chronic illness, adrenal exhaustion, autoimmune conditions, endometriosis, trauma-based CPTSD, narcissistic abuse, grief, and the deep valleys of shame and Self-doubt. These weren't just obstacles—they were teachers. They brought me to this path, and to this work. And if your path has led you here, I hope that TGSS brings you a sense of direction, empowerment, and reconnection. You are the alchemist.

Live from the *in*side-*out*.

And follow your Guiding Star.

From the girl who had lost touch with her own soul, in silence, who was given a voice by the written word... ♡

"You are endless galaxies - and you have seen but one star." – Linda Goodman

Integration

We have gone through the individual sections of the guiding star system, and there is a lot! The integration of the individual points of the star come together, and all form the center point. Here is where all becomes clear together, and all becomes a part of you.

Summary of How This May Present in Your Life

	FUEL	MOVEMENT	REST	OUT	IN
3D	Craving drinks and foods, being controlled by what you consume and when you consume it. More output of energy in processing this, than what you are inputting, leaving an energy deficit. Lacking nutrients. Survival mode. Addictions. Convenience. No awareness of this situation	Movement in the form of exercise at a minimal. Usually only to carry out minimal but required tasks in order to stay in maximum comfort zone. Survival mode. Cannot be bothered. Any attempts are minimal. Blaming and unmotivated. Lack of awareness. Couch potato syndrome. Lack of	Never feeling rested or revitalised from your sleep. Sleeping problems, whether getting to sleep or staying asleep. Trying to compensate from bad sleep with not doping much, but then a constant feeling of being unable to relax and rest. Lack of awareness. Survival mode. Not looking to improve.	An ego run life. Automatic survival mode and comfort zone. Default mode. No emotional awareness. Living in a state of blame and no personal responsibility. Consumed by money and success making you happy. Unhappy and a feeling of being lost. No Self-confidence, even if the	No awareness whatsoever to the fact that this even exists! Unheard. Guarded. Naturally defensive. Living in low frequency feelings. The complete hiding from your true Self. A reluctance to look for something more. Stuck in unhappiness and the lack of the fulfilment.

	and its effects. Numbness.	personal responsibility.		outwardly projection would suggest otherwise.	
4D- I believe this is the hardest stage, as you are aware that you are not happy where you are, and you need to improve, but the results are very minimal and the effort is big. Being kind to yourSelf whilst staying on track is the key. Don't give up! All addictions will be kicking in, and the brain will be trying to get you back to habit and comfort.	Food and drink awareness that the 3D state above is not right. You are not doing the best for yourSelf and your body. General research of something better. Less than 50% energy intake. There is an increase in energy, but not enough to tip the scales. Many are impatient or lack the discipline to continue, so fall back to the later stage.	Awareness that movement in the body is beneficial and will increase energy levels. The beginning of some discipline and regime in place. An understanding that whilst increasing your exercise may temporarily make you feel more tired, that this is only temporary, and the energy systems of the body adapt so that you feel much better overall. Making an attraction to exercises that can display a level of Self-destruction, by doing too much too soon and failing to listen to the body, or in your attitude towards it. Overly high levels of expectation.	An awareness that something is not right, you are not getting what you need in terms of physical or mental rest, and a desire to understand and begin to improve this situation. Investing in your rest, and understanding the effects that this has on you. Understanding sleep and rest are different, and physical and mental rest are also different. Some falling back into old patterns as the balance of the scales has not been tipped to over 50% yet.	An awareness that You are not feeling content and complete. This is generally bought on by achieving something that you thought would give you a feeling of happiness and contentment, and that feeling not being there. Starting to look for reasons as to why this is, and gaining a sense of Self responsibility and the requirement to look inwards as opposed to looking to automatically blame something or someone else. New neurological pathways are being discovered and walked.	An awakening of and tuning into your state of feeling. How do you feel? An understanding that there is more, that there are high frequency feelings, that it is a possibility that you can achieve them. A brief brush the belief that you deserve to achieve them. Using feeling as a guide to working through the layers if you think you are, to get to who you actually are. Starting to recognise the concept of intuition, I'm looking into how this can be furthered.
THE TIPPING POINT – over 50% positive energy **(sources of energy giving more to you than taking away)** You are going form absorbing other energy and living in a state of reaction, to emitting your own energy and frequency.					

4D+	Awareness that there are other sources of fuel and these are explored. Over 50% of the time, food and drink consumption are of that which actually inputs cellular energy to the body. The tipping of the scales begins! There is an introduction of the conscious awakening of other points of the star, and how all is interlinked.	An understanding developing that movement of the physical body affects movement in other areas of your life such as your thoughts and your feelings. It also has an effect on taking movement in your life, like a movement of motivation and taking that next step in front of you. Over 50% of your movement energy is positive. The results cause you to further your journey with movement.	And awareness of physical and mental rest on the body, and your energy cycles. An openness to play by these rules. The understanding of the altered/alternative state of consciousness that is sleep and dreams. And meditative states. Understanding of sleep cycles and hormones, and how to use the knowledge to maximise energy.	You are managing to balance your ego, and keep it in check. Achieving this at over 50% in practice. The understanding that your physical world is something that you are unable to control, and you are only able to control yourSelf and your reactions to the outside world. This is what you are here to learn and master. Prepared to put in the work and do the work on yourSelf. Setting in to the new pathways, and using them over 50% of the time.	For more than 50% of the time you are living in high-level frequency feelings. You are tipping the scales of your life in the right direction and enjoying the effects in all areas. Making positive feeling than normal, the comfort zone. Lack of fear. Understanding the feeling of intuition compared with any other feelings. Walking new pathways throughout. Understanding that control is all within and not outwardly.
	Cellular fuelling	**Cellular movement**	**Cellular rejuvenation**	**Cellular mirror**	**Cellular control**
5D	The understanding that this is a collective of sources to input energy, to maximise the output of energy. Food, drink and other sources are used merely to feed the cells	The understanding that there is unity between the movement of your body, The movement of your life, the movement of every cell in your body. And help all of this is linked to the	Resting physically and mentally in practice. Altered states of consciousness in relation to energy and the universe as a whole. The effect of these altered states on physical life. Connection of this energy to the	A complete death of the ego. The blending of oneself into the concept of one whole collective universal energy. The outside world is a mirror of you	You are in tune with your true sense of life purpose. A continued feeling of gratitude and love. Top levels motivation and wholeness. A true feeling of

	and body, and are not simply for pleasure or for an immediate fix. Vibrational frequency in practice. Listening to the intuition of what you need. Fluidity in your fuel sources. Interlinked frequency understood and in practice. Natural elevation of the other star points.	universe as a whole. Collectively, movement raises energy and vibration. Awareness of the importance of Self-love.	universe as a whole.	inside world that you have control over and that you understand you have created. And understanding that in order to change the outside world you have to change your inside world.	synchronicity and that you are exactly where you're meant to be. Belonging. At one. A desire to better humanity and the universe as a whole. Ability to maintain this in the 3D world. **Most powerful.**
THE ULTIMATE OF HUMAN CONSCIOUSNESS IN PRACTICE					

The Quickest Route to Healing and Ascension

The most direct path to healing and ascension is to recognise your innate power of creation—and to step boldly into the driver's seat of that power. When you choose to elevate the frequency of your inner world, your external reality will naturally shift to match it. As within, so without. This universal truth forms the foundation of all transformation, and it is always the most powerful and efficient route.

That said, The Guiding Star System offers multiple pathways for healing. Each arm of the star provides its own supportive or alternative access point. Whether you begin with inner alignment or physical adjustments, your route is your own—and as long as your choices are grounded in truth, they will lead you to where you need to go.

The Most Effective Way to Use The Guiding Star System

We're often first drawn to the physical practices. Fuel, movement, and rest feel more tangible, more immediately accessible. And rightly so—they are essential aspects of our human experience and can bring powerful shifts in energy and well-being. However, if the deeper inner work is not done, these physical practices can become surface-level efforts—nourishing the body but not fully transforming the Soul.

The physical arms of the system are most effective when used in support of the inner work. They are bridges—grounding you, preparing you, and aligning your body so that it can hold the frequency of your Soul. When paired with truth, intention, and internal coherence, these tools become sacred. They amplify the shifts occurring within and help you sustain a new vibrational baseline.

Let the inner guide the outer. And let the outer support the inner.

Frequency Hacks

Here are a variety of ways to raise your energetic frequency, combining physical, emotional, and Spiritual practices into your daily life. Each is designed to support you holistically—body, mind, and Soul—while reconnecting you to nature, rhythm, and your own intuitive intelligence. Think of them not as rigid prescriptions, but as invitations: small rituals you can weave into your life, building your own personal frequency practice over time.

Magic Water

Create energised water by using distilled or ionised water, stored in glass and charged outdoors for 24 hours in both Sunlight and moonlight. Use coloured glass if desired to solarise the water with specific frequencies. Add fresh lime juice and drink it first thing in the morning on an empty stomach. This helps to alkalise the body, reduce inflammation, and gently detoxify. For a deeper ritual, place the water in front of you during your morning meditation. Visualise it absorbing the energy and intentions you want to embody that day. Drink it with reverence—nourishing not only your physical body, but also your energetic field.

Morning Mind Activation

The frequency you begin your morning with sets the tone for the entire day. Start by reconnecting to your parasympathetic nervous system and grounding into your body:

- 30 seconds of rebound jumping
- 30 seconds of shaking
- 30 seconds of body drumming
- 10 rounds of breathwork (box breathing or slow extended exhale)
- Visualise your energy sphere and connect to your intention for the day

These practices wake the body, regulate the nervous system, and prime your field for clarity and alignment.

I Speak and I Create

The first words you speak each day carry power. Begin with tongue scraping—a simple Ayurvedic detox practice to remove toxins released overnight. Follow with natural, fluoride-free toothpaste (such as coconut oil with tea tree oil). Then, use your voice intentionally: speak affirmations, smile, sing, or pray. Words shape reality, and your vocal frequency is a direct declaration of creation. All whilst looking in the mirror.

Super Baths

Water is medicine. Take regular detox baths using filtered water, Epsom salts, essential oils, coloured lighting, candles, or incense. Meditate or play healing music. Bathe for 35–40 minutes to allow for both detoxification and absorption of minerals. Add crystals to the water, then recharge them afterwards in moonlight or Sunlight. These baths clear stagnation, restore balance, and reset your frequency.

Sea Dips and Cold Immersion

Cold water therapy is profoundly grounding and energising. Sea dipping returns you to the Earth's frequency, supports cardiovascular health, and strengthens resilience. It sharpens presence, draws your awareness fully into your body, and builds discipline. Immersing yourSelf in the cold is a training ground for energetic mastery: meeting discomfort with calm, and turning shock into vitality.

Food Rainbow

Food is frequency in physical form. Eat a vibrant range of raw fruits and vegetables, especially those rich in colour. Consume fruit immediately after cutting to preserve nutrients. Include seeds and pips for their potent nutritional density—apple pips, for instance, contain vitamin B17, a rare and powerful compound. Each colour carries a different vibration; the more colours on your plate, the more frequencies you bring into your body.

Herb Garden

Growing herbs reconnects you to the living intelligence of nature. Even a small windowsill garden offers culinary and energetic nourishment. Harvesting, tending, and using your own herbs brings you into relationship with the Earth's rhythms, strengthening the bond between you and the food-medicine you consume.

Juic-ie's

Make a fresh alkaline juice weekly—cucumber, green leaves, apple, and ginger are ideal. Soak produce beforehand in filtered water with bicarbonate of soda. Freeze juice in ice cube trays for easy use in smoothies throughout the week. For a powerful nutritional hit, blend with raw nuts, fruit, and magic moon-charged water. This is a simple ritual that delivers living energy to your cells.

Alkaline Smoothie Day

Give your digestive system a reset with a smoothie-only day. Blend avocado, cucumber, apple, lime juice, Celtic salt, raw honey, and charged water. Drinking only these throughout the day allows your body to redirect energy from digestion into healing, clarity, and higher frequency states.

Plant Family

Plants are living frequency keepers. Surround yourSelf with greenery, especially in your bedroom. They oxygenate your space, cleanse the air, and bring soothing, restorative energy into your home. Caring for them also anchors you in presence and nurtures a reciprocal relationship with the living world.

Beach Fire

If possible, light a fire at the beach and sit close to the Earth, watching the flames and listening to the waves. This simple ritual combines firelight, grounding, sound healing, and elemental connection. The rhythm of fire and water together creates coherence, returning your field to balance.

Plan Out of Comfort

Frequency rises when we expand. Regularly schedule something unfamiliar or outside your comfort zone. Whether it's cold water therapy, a solo trip, or trying a new activity, purposeful discomfort keeps your energy fresh, your mind adaptable, and your Spirit courageous.

Reflective Relationship Assessment

Relationships are mirrors. Continually observe your connections: Who uplifts you? Who drains you? Every relationship reveals something about your Self-worth and boundaries. Raising frequency often requires releasing relationships that no longer resonate, and deepening those that do.

Monthly Discovery

Make exploration a non-negotiable. Schedule one new adventure every month—whether big or small. Newness keeps your energy fresh, opens perspective, and invites joy. Stagnation lowers frequency; curiosity raises it.

The Superfood Circuit

Rotate high-frequency superfoods to nourish the body in a variety of ways. Your intuition will let you know which ones at which times:

- Irish sea moss
- Shilajit
- Barley grass powder
- Black seed oil
- Fermented garlic and honey
- Wild blueberry powder
- Medicinal mushrooms
- CBD oil
- Raw honey and red onion syrup
- Full spectrum trace minerals

Each superfood carries a unique energetic and nutritional code that supports higher states of vitality.

The Colour of Life

Your aura is naturally drawn to colours it needs. Notice what shades you are attracted to, and bring them into your wardrobe, environment, and art. Colours are frequency—they communicate with your energy body and influence your state of being.

Day-Off Pass

Sometimes the most powerful reset is rest. Give yourSelf full permission to do nothing—guilt-free. One day off can recalibrate your entire system, replenish your energy, and remind you that worth is not tied to productivity.

Exotic Fruit Exploration

Subscribe to a seasonal fruit box from organic suppliers offering Sun-ripened, alkaline-rich fruit varieties. Tasting new fruits expands both your palate and your frequency, offering minerals and nutrients your body may be craving.

Local Farm Produce

Buy meat, dairy, and produce directly from organic farms whenever possible. This reduces waste, increases nutrient density, and brings you closer to the origin of your food. Food sourced with integrity carries a different energetic resonance.

Grounding meals

Create a beautiful meal full based in grounding ingredients – those that have been grown underground. Have your meal outside somewhere, ideally say under a tree, or in direct contact with the Earth. For an even deeper grounding, include some calming breathwork beforehand.

Personal Meditation

Record your own meditation. Use your voice to speak directly to your subconscious. Begin with full-body relaxation, then guide yourSelf through affirmations, Soul-aligned desires, and visualisations of your ideal future. Practiced daily for at least 30 days, this becomes a powerful tool for reprogramming.

Energy and Aura Cleanse

Your energy field is porous and picks up debris from environments and interactions. Cleanse it regularly with:

- Palo Santo or sage
- Essential oils (e.g., frankincense, lavender)

- Salt baths
- Wind, rain, Sunlight, and moonlight

Cleansing restores vitality, protects your boundaries, and keeps your field radiant.

EMF Detox

Electromagnetic frequencies affect your system more than you may realise. Support your field with simple practices:

- Switch off electronics at night
- Use timer plugs to cut Wi-Fi automatically
- Avoid sleeping near charging phones or plugged devices
- Replace Bluetooth earbuds with wired headphones
- Limit screen time
- Ground barefoot outdoors
- Use protective crystals (e.g., shungite, hematite)
- Drink plenty of charged water

These practices are not about doing everything at once. They are about weaving small, intentional shifts into your daily rhythm—each one raising your baseline frequency. Over time, the body, mind, and Soul become more coherent, aligned, and radiant. The higher your frequency, the more clearly you hear the guidance of your Soul, and the more effortlessly you co-create your reality.

Places of Writing

Some of the places I have been when writing this book…

The Hut, Alumhurst Road, Westbourne
Ounce coffee shop, Westbourne
Branksome Beach
Limewood, Lyndhurst
Macdonald Leeming House, Lake District
The Ivy, Glasgow
The Z Hotel, Glasgow
Oban Ferry
Isle of Mull Hotel and Spa
Iona Chapel
Glengorm Castle, Isle of Mull
Unorthodox Coffee Shop, Stirling
Broomhall Castle, Stirling
Stirling Central Library
My beautiful home – under construction
Lou and Mitch's House, Perth, Australia
Pelican sands, 203 and 602, Tugun, Australia
Niche & Co, Tugun, Australia
Cripple Creek Hospitality House, Colorado
Gold Crush Cafe, Cripple Creek, Colorado
The Warwick, Denver, Colorado
Boulder Reservoir, Colorado

Thrive Cafe, Boulder, Colorado
SuStudio, Canford Cliffs, England
My beautiful home – finished and lovely
Ferdinand, Geneva, Switzerland
La Clemence, Old Town, Geneva, Switzerland
Durley Chine beach bench in the woods
Safe and Sounds Studio, secret location, Dorset
Camden coffee roastery, Camden, London
Vernon House, St Mark's Square, Camden
Mildred's, Camden high street, Camden
Greenberry's, Primrose Hill, Camden
Le Tea Cosy, Primrose Hill, Camden
Oka, Primrose Hill, Camden
Maples Place, Tower Hamlet, London
St John's Boutique Hotel, St John's Wood, London
The Little One cafe, Primrose Hill, London
The Hilton, Wembley Stadium, London
Heathrow airport, terminal 2, London
Singapore airport arrivals
U-tube hotel, Uluwatu, Bali
Kude cafe, Uluwatu, Bali
Saundara Sunset Cafe, Uluwatu, Bali
Nourish, Uluwatu, Bali
Salty coffee, Bingin Beach, Bali
Pink Coco, Gili Air
Mowie, Gili Air
Boho Bingin, Bingin Beach
Alchemy yoga, Uluwatu, Bali
Villa Sunshine, Ubud, Bali
Sala, Ubud, Bali
Bournemouth airport, Bournemouth
Nobu hotel, Ibiza Bay
Ibiza bay, Ibiza
Ibiza airport

Durley Chine beach bench in the woods
The Museum, Farnham
Compton Abbas Airfield, Shaftesbury
Blend on The Hill, Bournemouth
Deus Ex Machina, Boscombe
Isle of Arran ferry
The Lagg, Isle of Arran, Scotland
Hunters Coffee Shop, Isle of Arran, Scotland
Malaga Airport, Malaga
Old Town Square, Malaga
Byoko Merced, Malaga
C. Juan de Herrera, Malaga
Pestana Chelsea Bridge Hotel, London
Battersea Park, London
S'ardeviu, Soller, Mallorca
Mallorca Airport
Kempinski Hotel, Andalucia, Spain
Morocco Ferry, Morocco
Heathrow Virgin Airport Lounge
The Hilton, Anaheim, USA
Laguna Beach, California, USA
Chateau Marmont, LA, USA
City of the Gods, Mexico City
Puerto Vallarta Airport, Mexico
Susurros del Corazon, Mexico
Pastuzo's Local, Poole, UK

Dedicated to my Charlie Brown, a true Soul love.

With special thanks to:
Jenni Powell
Linda Goodman
Ella McCrystal
Carol Mason
My wonderful supportive friends

Dear reader, ★

Wow - what a book journey! Thankyou for all that it has taken you to get to this point, here and now. I see you. I appreciate you. From my heart, I hope that this has resonated with you and your truth in some way. :) And remember, your journey is ever changing. You can revisit this book as many times as you wish on the way to becoming all that you know you can be.

Sending you so much love, ♡

Hayley xxx

End Note

I have sections of writing that didn't make the book, and if you would like these shared with you free of charge, please visit the website.

If you feel like you are seeking more guidance, I have made a step-by-step online course to take you deeper into your journey. I do also work one-on-one with a handful of clients, so if this is something that appeals to you, it could happen! I have a waiting list and can get in contact when there is availability.

I would always love to hear from you with your personal feedback and experience with the book. Feel free to reach out on socials or my email is hi@theguidingstarsystem.com.

If this book has guided you in anyway, it would be such a great help if you share this with others… posting a photo of you with the book on Instagram, passing on videos on YouTube to those that you think may benefit, or interacting with any of the platforms out there. And thankyou in advance for your contribution.

Hx

The second book… yes it will be here! I am going to be starting this very soon. If you would like to keep up to date with this, please join the mailing list.

Website: **www.theguidingstarsystem.com**
Instagram: @theguidingstarsystem
Facebook: @theguidingstarsystem
YouTube: @theguidingstarsystem
TikTok: @theguidingstarsystem

Bibliography

Allen, R.P. (2002) Scripts and strategies in hypnotherapy, volume one. Crown House Publishing Limited, Wales.

Aron, E.N. (1997) The highly sensitive person. Broadway Books, USA.

Aron, E.N. (2000) The highly sensitive person in love. Broadway Books, USA.

Battino, M. (2000) Guided imagery and other approaches to healing. Crown House Publishing Limited, Wales.

Battino, M. & South, T.L. (2000) Ericksonian approaches: a comprehensive manual. Crown House Publishing Limited, Wales.

Benson, H. & Klipper, M.Z. (1975) The relaxation response. Morrow, New York.

Bowlby, J. (1969) Attachment and loss. Basic Books, New York.

Bradshaw, J. (1988) Healing the shame that binds you. Health Communications, USA.

Bradshaw, J. (1996) Bradshaw On: The Family: A new way of creating solid self-esteem. HCI, USA.

Branden, N. (1985) Honoring the self. Bantam, USA.

Brown, B. (1999) Soul without shame: A guide to liberating yourself from the judge within. Shambhala, USA.

Brown, D. (2016) Happy: Why more or less everything is absolutely fine. Bantam Press, UK.

Chopra, D. (1994) The seven spiritual laws of success. Harmony Books, USA.

Clear, J. (2018) Atomic habits: An easy & proven way to build good habits & break bad ones. Avery, USA.

Cloninger, C.R. (2004) Feeling good: The science of well-being. Oxford University Press, USA.

Craig, D. (2022) What's your vibe? Penguin Life, UK.

Damasio, A. (1999) The feeling of what happens. Harcourt, New York.

Dispenza, J. (2014) You are the placebo. Hay House, USA.

Dziemidko, H.E. (1999) The complete book of energy medicine: The ground-breaking guide to complementary healing techniques. Healing Arts Press, USA.

Epictetus. (1995) The art of living. HarperOne, USA.

Faulkner, R.O. (1990) The Ancient Egyptian Book of the Dead. University of Texas Press, USA.

Frankl, V.E. (2006) Man's search for meaning. Beacon Press, USA.

Freud, A. (1936) The ego and the mechanisms of defence. Institute of Psychoanalysis, USA.

Goddard, N. (1944) Feeling is the secret. Martino Fine Books, USA.
Goodman, L. (1968) Sun signs. Taplinger Publishing, USA.
Goodman, L. (1978) Love signs: A new approach to the human heart. Harper & Row, USA.
Goodman, L. (1987) Star signs: The secret codes of the universe. St. Martin's Press, USA.
Goodman, L. (1998) Relationship signs. Bantam, USA.
Gunnison, H. (2003) Hypnocounselling: An eclectic bridge between Milton Erickson and Carl Rogers. PCCS Books Ltd, Monmouth.
Hadley, J. & Staudacher, C. (1996) Hypnosis for change (3rd edn). New Harbinger Publications Inc., USA.
Hall, J. (2003) The Crystal Bible. Godsfield Press, UK.
Hartmann, E. (1991) Boundaries in the mind: A new psychology of personality. Basic Books, New York.
Hay, L. (1984) You can heal your life. Hay House, USA.
Hof, W. (2020) The Wim Hof Method. Sounds True, USA.
Hoyle, F. (1983) The intelligent universe. Holt, USA.
Hunter, R. (2014) The art of hypnosis: Mastering basic techniques. Crown House Publishing Limited, Wales.
Jacobs, M. (1999) Psychodynamic counselling in action. Sage Publications, UK.
Jacobs, M. (2010) Psychodynamic counselling in action. Sage Publications, London.
Jampolsky, G.G. (1979) Love is letting go of fear. Celestial Arts, USA.
Johnson, R.A. (1991) Owning your own shadow. Harper San Francisco, USA.
Jung, C. (1983) Memories, dreams, reflections. Flamingo, UK.
Karle, H. & Boys, J. (2010) Hypnotherapy: A practical handbook (2nd edn). Free Association Books, London.
Kennerley, H., Kirk, J. & Westbrook, D. (2017) An introduction to cognitive behaviour therapy. Sage, London.
Lepera, N. (2021) How to do the work. Harper Wave, USA.
Lerner, H. (1985) The dance of anger. Harper & Row, USA.
Levine, P.A. (2008) Healing trauma: A pioneering program for restoring the wisdom of your body. Sounds True, USA.
Levine, A. & Heller, R. (2010) Attached: The new science of adult attachment. TarcherPerigee, USA.
Lipton, B.H. (2005) The biology of belief. Hay House, USA.
Malkin, C. (2015) Rethinking narcissism. Harper Perennial, USA.
Maslow, A.H. (1954) Motivation and personality. Harper & Row, USA
Masters, R.A. (2013) Emotional intimacy: A comprehensive guide for connecting with the power of your emotions. Sounds True, USA.
Masters, R.A. (2018) Bringing your shadow out of the dark: Breaking free from the hidden forces that drive you. Sounds True, USA.
Maté, G. (2018) In the realm of hungry ghosts: Close encounters with addiction. Vermilion, UK.

Maté, G. (2019) When the body says no: The cost of hidden stress. Vermilion, UK.
Maté, G. (2022) The myth of normal: Trauma, illness and healing in a toxic culture. Vermilion, UK.
McCrystal, E. (2022) Wounded warrior wisdom: From childhood abuse to self-love and healing… how you can do it too! Independently published.
McLeod, J. (2019) An introduction to counselling and psychotherapy: Theory, research and practice (6th edn). McGraw-Hill Education, Maidenhead, UK.
Mellody, P. (2003) Facing love addiction: Giving yourself the power to change the way you love. HarperOne, USA.
Miller, A. (1997) The drama of the gifted child: The search for the true self. Basic Books, USA.
Murphy, J. (2007) The power of your subconscious mind: Unlock your master key to success. Wilder Publications, Radford, VA.
Myss, C. (1996) Anatomy of the spirit. Three Rivers Press, USA.
Myss, C. (2009) Defy gravity. Hay House, USA.
Naparstek, B. (1994) Staying well with guided imagery. Warner Books, USA.
Ogden, P., Minton, K. & Pain, C. (2006) Trauma and the body: A sensorimotor approach to psychotherapy. W. W. Norton & Company, USA.
Paar, N. (2022) Serpent rising: The Kundalini compendium. Winged Shoes Publishing.
Parker-Hall, S. (2009) Anger, rage and relationship. Routledge, UK.
Porges, S.W. (2017) The pocket guide to the polyvagal theory: The transformative power of feeling safe. W. W. Norton & Company, USA.
Rogers, C. (1979) On becoming a person: A therapist's view of psychotherapy. Constable, UK.
Rogers, C. (1980) A way of being. Houghton Mifflin, USA.
Rosen, S. (1982) My voice will go with you – The teaching tales of Milton H. Erickson. W. W. Norton & Company, USA.
Sanders, P. (2011) First steps in counselling: A student's companion for introductory courses (4th edn). PCCS Books Ltd, Monmouth.
Schwartz, R.C. (1995) Internal family systems therapy. Guilford Press, USA.
Schwartz, R.C. (2021) No bad parts: Healing trauma and restoring wholeness with the Internal Family Systems model. Sounds True, USA.
Siegel, B. (1986) Love, medicine, and miracles. Harper & Row, USA.
Siegel, D.J. (2012) The developing mind: How relationships and the brain interact to shape who we are. Guilford Press, USA.
Singleton-Ward, R. (1957) My two hands talk. Christopher Johnson, London.
Somé, M.P. (1994) Of water and the spirit. Penguin, USA.
Stafford-Clark, D. (1975) What Freud really said. Penguin Books, UK.
Stahl, S. (2020) The child in you: The breakthrough method for bringing out your authentic self. Penguin Life, UK.
Stein, M. (2010) Jung's map of the soul. Open Court, USA.
Steiner, R. (2005) The fifth gospel from the Akashic record. Anthroposophic Press, USA.

Subby, R. (1984) Healing the family within. Health Communications, USA.
Todeschi, K.J. (1998) Edgar Cayce on the Akashic Records: The book of life. A.R.E. Press, USA.
Tolle, E. (1997) The power of now: A guide to spiritual enlightenment. New World Library, USA.
Tolle, E. (2005) A new earth: Awakening to your life's purpose. Penguin, UK.
Trower, P., Casey, A. & Dryden, W. (2011) Cognitive behavioural counselling in action. Sage, UK.
Van der Kolk, B. (2014) The body keeps the score: Mind, brain and body in the transformation of trauma. Penguin, UK.
Walker, P. (2013) Complex PTSD: From surviving to thriving. Azure Coyote Book, USA.
Walker, P. (2024) Holistically treating complex PTSD: A six-dimensional approach. Azure Coyote Book, USA.
Whitfield, C. (1991) Co-dependence: Healing the human condition. HCI, USA.
Wilber, K. (2000) A theory of everything: An integral vision for business, politics, science and spirituality. Shambhala, USA.
William, A. (2015) Medical Medium: Secrets behind chronic and mystery illness and how to finally heal. Hay House, USA.
Wilson, B. (2019) The way we eat now. Fourth Estate, UK.
Zaccaro, A., Piarulli, A., Laurino, M., et al. (2018) How breath-control can change your life: A systematic review on psycho-physiological correlates of slow breathing. Frontiers in Human Neuroscience, 12:353.
Zweig, C. & Abrams, J. (1991) Meeting the shadow: The hidden power of the dark side of human nature. Tarcher-Penguin, USA.

Audiobooks:

Arabi, A. Becoming the Narcissist's Nightmare. Audible, 2024.
Byrne, R. The Power. Simon & Schuster Audio, 2010.
Cure, E.J. Empath and Narcissist. Apple Books, 2024.
Dass, R. Polishing the Mirror. Sounds True, 2013.
Dispenza, J. Becoming Supernatural. Hay House Audio, 2017.
Gallagher, K. The Goddess Path. Audible, 2022.
Gawdat, M. Solve for Happy. Apple Books, 2024.
Jung, C.G. Modern Man in Search of a Soul. University Press Audiobooks, 2024.
Kessler, S. The Five Personality Patterns. Audible, 2015.
Louise, R. The Dysfunctional Dance of the Empath and the Narcissist. Amazon Audio, 2020.
Masters, R.A. Emotional Intimacy. Sounds True, 2024.
Maté, G. Scattered Minds. Penguin Audio, 2023.
Orloff, J. Becoming an Intuitive Healer. Sounds True, 2001.

Peters, S. The Chimp Paradox. Penguin Audiobooks, 2023.
Peterson, J.B. 12 Rules for Life: An Antidote for Chaos. Penguin Audio, 2018.
Purkiss, J. The Power of Letting Go. Apple Books, 2024.
Singer, M.A. The Surrender Experiment. Sounds True, 2015.
Smith, M.J. When I Say No, I Feel Guilty. Apple Books, 2023.
Swan, T. The Completion Process. Apple Books, 2024.
Thomas, C.W. Calling In 'The One'. Sounds True, 2018.
Wattles, W.D. The Science of Getting Rich. Gildan Media, 2015.
Watts, A. You're It! Sounds True, 2019.

Author Bio

Hayley Gabriella Miller is the creator and founder of *The Guiding Star System*, a healing framework born from her own transformational journey. With a diverse background spanning law, property development, gymnastics coaching, and more recently hypnotherapy and psychotherapeutic counselling, she brings a unique blend of insight and creativity to her work. Hayley shares her message with the world so others can access the guidance she once longed for herself. *The Guiding Star System* is not only her life's work—it is the path that saved her life. This is her first book.